THE CHURCH IS A COMMUNION

THE CHURCH IS A COMMUNION

Jerome Hamer O.P.

Sheed and Ward - New York

This book first appeared in 1962, under the title *L'Eglise est une communion*, published by Les Editions du Cerf, Paris. The English translation is by Ronald Matthews.

The text used for biblical quotations is in general taken from the translation of the Bible by Ronald Knox, copyright, 1944, Sheed and Ward Inc., New York. On occasion, however, the Revised Standard Version is used, where that translation better makes the point of the author's French version. Where this is the case, the words 'R.S.V. text' occur after the quotation.

Library of Congress Catolog Card Number/64-20436
Nihil Obstat: R. D. Dermitius Fogarty, D.D., L.C.L., Censor deputatus.
Imprimatur: H. Gibney, Vicarius Generalis.
Datum Southwarci die 6a Octobris, 1964

Made and printed in Great Britain.

CONTENTS

PART TWO

THE MISSION OF THE CHURCH

THE GENERATIVE CAUSES OF COMMUNION

PART THREE

COMMUNION IN ITSELF AND IN ITS VARIOUS MODES OF EXPRESSION

Appendices

INTRODUCTION

WHAT is the principle of the Church's unity? This book is an attempt to answer that question. Social groups are characterized not only by their membership; the various ways in which the members may combine among themselves is an even more relevant factor. So to arrive at an understanding of what the Church is, it is not enough to study the people who belong to it: we must look for its principle of cohesion and its over-all structure.

The Church, mystery of God made visible to man, has its own special type of social organization. Its solidarity is a spiritual and visible fact, whose inner nature eludes the eye of the observer. Only faith can adequately realize the unbreakable union of the part with the whole and hence with the other parts of the same whole. 'You are Christ's body, organs of it depending on each other' (I Cor. 12:27).

It is therefore at the heart of a theological definition of the Church that we shall find the specific form of its solidarity, or of its social nature. Our method will be a simple one. In the first part, we shall deal with this definition. Should the word 'communion' really prove capable of expressing this inner cohesion of the Church, the rest of our study will follow naturally. The second section will consider what engenders this communion; the third will be devoted to its nature and to certain of its more important manifestations.

The reader must not expect a treatise on the Church. We will tackle various aspects of the nature of the Church, but only in relation to a single question. This book originated in a course of lectures in the faculty of theology at Le Saulchoir. I added to this first group of studies gradually, as the outlines of the plan slowly emerged. A number of these chapters, in their final form, are to be given as a special course at the University of Montreal.

I should like to thank all those who have so unselfishly helped me to shape this work, which deals with a theme very dear to me. In revising the manuscript, I have tried as far as possible to avoid over-technical terminology in order to make the book accessible to a wider readership. The demands of the subject and its treatment have not always made this possible; occasionally it has been essential to employ a technical vocabulary; but such cases are rare and the context and notes should enable the reader to overcome the difficulty.

J.H.

Le Saulchoir, (Etiolles, Seine-et-Oise),
4 January 1962

PART I

DEFINING THE CHURCH

The Word 'Communion'

I

MEANING AND IMPLICATIONS OF THE ENCYCLICAL *MYSTICI CORPORIS*

THE principal effect of *Mystici Corporis,* Pius XII's encyclical of 1943, was to give a new and decisive orientation to ecclesiology. With the weight of authority, it revived the great traditional idea of communion: the unity of Christians with Christ and with each other, within a Church which is at once both mystery and society, linking the means of grace entrusted to the Apostles' successors indissolubly with the inner realities of faith, hope and charity. A study of this encyclical will enable us to arrive at the definition of the Church and, within this definition, at the nature of its social structure.[1]

1. A FORERUNNER OF THE ENCYCLICAL: THE SCHEMA *DE ECCLESIA* AT THE FIRST VATICAN COUNCIL (1870)

On 21 January 1870, in the thirteenth general congregation of the First Vatican Council a *Schema constitutionis dogmaticae de Ecclesia Christi* was presented to the Fathers. Its first chapter was as follows:

> 'The Church is the mystical body of Christ.
> 'The only Son of God, who enlightens every man born into this world, and whose help has never in any age failed the luckless sons of Adam, when time had arrived at the fullness fixed in advance by eternal wisdom, having been made like to men, appeared visibly in the form of our body which he had assumed, so that earthly, carnal men, putting on the new man who was created

1. The summary of Part I (p. 94) will show how the study we are beginning here paves the way for the development of thought in the remainder of the book.

by God in justice and the holiness of truth, might form a mystical body of which he should be the head or chief.

'In order thus to bring about the union of this mystical body, the Lord Christ instituted the holy bath of baptismal regeneration and renovation, through which the sons of men, divided among themselves by so many different appellations and above all fallen from grace through sin might, when cleansed from all the stains of their errors, become members of one and the same body and, united to their divine master through faith, hope and charity, might all be animated by his sole Spirit and receive in abundance the gifts of the heavenly graces and the charisms.

'Such is the admirable representation of the Church which should be set before the minds of the faithful so that it may be firmly anchored there, and which cannot be over-stressed; the head of the Church is Christ; it is from him that the whole body, firmly held together and united by an operation proportionate to each member, derives its growth in order to be built up in charity.'[1]

Why was the term 'mystical body' chosen in the first place to describe the nature of the Church? The annotations which accompany the schema give the reasons. Firstly, it is the image most frequent in the Bible. Secondly, it expresses the most inward and most important element in the nature of the Church, its divine form and quality; any description of the Church should begin with this point. Thirdly, it makes it possible to answer the objections of Protestants (Baur and Jurieu are quoted) who accuse Catholics of considering only the external and perceptible elements in the Church. Fourthly, any proper assessment of the external aspect of the Church demands consideration of its inner form (*interna Ecclesiae species*). Fifthly, in a carnal and worldly universe, the idea is unknown, or receives insufficient attention. Hence, it is important to stress it.[2]

We find in the schema an echo of the nineteenth century revival of the theology of the mystical body. It draws attention to the supernatural mystery of the Church, in face of representations which centred too exclusively on its external and hierarchical structure.

1. Latin text in Mansi, *Sacrorum conciliorum nova et amplissima collectio*, vol. 51, col. 539, with all the scriptural references relevant to the schema.

2. Cf. Mansi, vol. 51, col. 553, where these remarks are followed by a detailed vindication of the plan of the chapter.

The two great initiators of this revival were Johann Adam Möhler (1796-1838), whose studies in ecclesiology were never completed, and Carlo Passaglia (1812-1887), professor at the Roman College and author of a remarkable *De Ecclesia Christi,* two volumes of which appeared in 1853 and 1854.[1] These labours did not go on in parallel, without any contact. There was a real link between Möhler and the Roman theologians over the doctrine of the mystical body, though it is hard to specify just what it was.[2] We know that Schrader played a decisive role in the preparation of the schema: he was a disciple of Passaglia and for long his close collaborator, particularly in the drafting of his *De Ecclesia Christi.* We know moreover that Schrader was entrusted with putting the finishing touches to the schema to be submitted to the Vatican Fathers.[3] So it is not surprising that this important document began with the doctrine of the mystical body.

How was this first chapter received? We know it was never discussed, either in the deputation on faith or in general congregation. Alone among its contents, Chapter XI on the primacy (with the cor-

1. Secularized at his own request in 1859, Passaglia was soon won over to the cause of Cavour and became the head of the liberal clergy in Italy. He died reconciled with the church.

2. On this subject, see A. Kerkvoorde, 'La théologie du Corps mystique au XIXe siècle', in *NRT*, 1940-1945, vol. 67, pp. 1025-1038. The article quotes some interesting passages from Passaglia's treatise. See also the same author's introduction to M. J. Scheeben, *Le mystère de l'Eglise et des sacraments*, Paris, 1946 (the English translation, *The Mysteries of Christianity*, London, 1947, does not have this introduction).

3. On the literary activity of Passaglia and Schrader, see H. Schauf, *Die Einwohnung des Heiligen Geistes*, Freiburg-im-Breisgau, 1941. On Schrader's part in the drafting of the schema, see Mansi, vol. 49, cols. 626, 628, 633 and 696. But it should not be forgotten that Perrone was the prime author of the whole of the first ten chapters. We know that the theologians of the Theologico-dogmatic Commission adopted as the basis of their work the *Syllabus* and *Quanta cura*. On the doctrine of the Church, Father Perrone was responsible for paragraph 5 of the Syllabus: *Errores de Ecclesia ejusque juribus:* see Mansi, vol. 49, col. 622. Examination of Father Perrone's votum went on for several sittings. The author revised his text after it had been considered by the special deputation (cols. 622, 626, 628-629). A small and quite incidental indication enables us to stress the link between Möhler and the Roman theologians. In his *Théologie dogmatique* (second ed. of French translation, 1859), Chapter IV, *On the qualities of the Church*, Perrone quotes Möhler with high praise four times in the space of twenty pages: pp. 468, 480, 486, 492. We know from another source that Möhler was quoted three times in the notes to the schema: Mansi; vol. 51, cols. 553, 555, 575. I owe these details to J. P. Torrell, *La théologie de l'épiscopat au premier concile du Vatican*, Paris, 1961, p. 57.

responding canons), and an additional chapter on pontifical infallibility, which were detached from the rest, served as a basis for the discussions which gave birth to the constitution *Pastor Aeternus.*[1] But we do possess the written comments of a large number of Fathers on the first chapter.[2]

Among the opponents of the terminology employed in Chapter I were a number of French prelates. Here are one or two characteristic examples. The Bishop of St Brieuc, Mgr David, calls for the elimination of this section which: '1. does not correspond with the aim of the schema but, if anything, comes under mystical theology; 2. gives rise to confusion by doing away with the classical distinction between the body and the soul of the Church.' The Bishop of Perpignan, Mgr Ramadie, thinks the same. He wants something other than 'considerations destined to maintain the ardour of mystical life'. Why state that the Church is the mystical body, asks the Archbishop of Marseilles, Mgr Place, who 'does not understand what use this will serve' (*Cui bono enim hoc fiat, non perspicit*). Mgr Grimardias, Bishop of Cahors, asks for a 'clear definition of the Church of Christ'. Mgr Lyonnet, the Bishop of Albi, proposes that they should adopt purely and simply the definition which is to be found 'in every manual of theology and in duly approved catechisms'. The Bishop of Sens, Mgr Bernadou, suggests that the chapter should be given the title: *Ecclesia est societas spiritualis supernaturalis . . .*, and that the text should be modified to conform with the title. The Bishop of Orleans, Mgr Dupanloup, would like to have the chapter, which he regards as 'unprofitable' and even 'somewhat empty', removed; he does not think it expedient to base the whole schema on a 'metaphorical idea'.

These French bishops showed that they were principally concerned with clarity and exactness of thought. Fears of another sort were expressed by Cardinal Trevisanato, Patriarch of Venice, and thirteen bishops, twelve of them Italian (mostly Piedmontese) and one Brazilian. They asked whether, in order to consolidate dogma, it was prudent to adopt that 'doctrine of the mystical body which the Jansenists made use of to introduce their own errors'. One of the Fathers in this group put forward a definition of the Church directly inspired by that of Bellarmine. Among the Council Fathers who

1. Denz. 1821-1840.
2. See Mansi, vol. 51, cols. 751-763.

expressed their reservations, a number would have preferred to use the term kingdom of God, or society—in a word they would have liked a more manageable definition of the Church.

The reservations had their effect. Father Kleutgen produced a second draft for a discussion which never took place.[1] Would this draft have been accepted? It was never examined by the deputation on faith, still less by the Fathers in general congregation. The latter did not even have the opportunity of making written comments on it. However that might be, the order of presentation was reversed. The new draft began by defining the Church in the accepted theological vocabulary as *coetus fidelium atque vera societas*. The image of the mystical body was still there, but it had fallen into the background. Father Kleutgen had been closely concerned in the work of the Council, and his reason for adopting this new doctrinal presentation was to conform with the wishes of the Fathers.[2]

Though Chapter I of the first schema possessed no authoritative value, yet it undeniably had historical effects. The Franco-Prussian war prevented the continuance of the dogmatic discussions on the nature of the Church, and it is highly probable that any definition which had emerged from them would have been inspired by Kleutgen's theological formulation rather than by Schrader's. The time was not ripe. But the doctrinal gain of the first schema was not lost. Leo XIII's teaching on the Church showed striking resemblances to that first chapter of the schema. What is more, the encyclical *Mystici Corporis* explicitly takes its stand on Leo XIII's two ecclesiological encyclicals *Satis Cognitum* (1896) and *Divinum Illud* (1897).[3] Much, too, can be learned from the different attitudes of the bishops towards the theological and pastoral use of the biblical theme of the mystical body. We shall find almost identical attitudes adopted at the time of Pius XII's encyclical in 1943.

1. Cf. Mansi, vol. 53, cols. 308-317, followed by a *Relatio de schemate reformato*, cols 317-332.

2. He says this in his *Relatio:* 'Multis rev. patribus in priore schemate displicuit, definitionem ecclesiae symbolicam, qua corpus Christi dicitur, tanquam caput doctrinae et fundamentum eorum, quae sequuntur, proponi. Hoc igitur mutatum est' (col. 319).

3. Cf. F. Malmberg, *Een lichaam en een geest. Nieuwe gezichtspunkten in de ecclesiologie*, Utrecht, 1958, p. 19. This book has been translated into German under the title: *Ein Leib ein Geist. Vom Mysterium der Kirche*, Freiburg-im-Breisgau, 1960.

II. The Theological and Pastoral Atmosphere just prior to the Encyclical

Before describing the atmosphere up to the time of the encyclical, we should emphasize the astonishing revival of interest in the concept of the mystical body between the two wars. An American Jesuit, J. J. Bluett, doing research into the question, wrote in 1942: 'A period of extraordinary growth began in 1920. Between 1920 and 1925, as much was written on the subject as during the whole twenty years previously. Between 1925 and 1930, this output was doubled. In the five following years, we are confronted with five times what had been written in the corresponding period a decade earlier. The peak of acceleration seems to have been reached in 1937. The growth went on after that year but at a more moderate rate.'[1] At this period two important and characteristic works appeared: *Le Corps mystique du Christ,* written by a Belgian Jesuit, Emile Mersch, who died in 1940, and *Corpus Christi quod est Ecclesia,* whose author was a Dutch Jesuit, Sebastian Tromp, professor at the Gregorian university in Rome.[2] The similarity between Tromp's work and *Mystici Corporis* has been noted by more than one author.[3]

Tentative investigations and probings, with occasional confusion, is a fair comment on the theological situation in Germany in these years. In 1939, Karl Pelz, a parish priest in Berlin, published in manuscript form a work entitled *Der Christ als Christus* (the Christian *qua* Christ). 'He pushed to its limits the relationship between Christ and the Christian, Christ and the Church, going so far as to deny all distance between them and assert a real identity between them. The Roman Congregation considered this dangerous,

1. Quoted by F. Malmberg, *Een lichaam . . .* p. 220. Bluett's inquiry was confined to a review article, 'The Mystical Body of Christ: 1890-1940', in *Theological Studies,* 1942, vol. 3, pp. 261-289.

2. E. Mersch, *Le Corps mystique du Christ. Etudes de théologie historique,* Paris and Brussels, 1933. S. Tromp, *Corpus Christi quod est Ecclesia. I. Introductio generalis,* Rome, 1937. The second and third volumes of this work appeared quite recently: *Pars altera: De Christo Capite Mystici Corporis,* Rome, 1960, and *III: De Spiritu Christi anima,* Rome, 1960.

3. See C. Lialine, 'Une étape en ecclésiologie. Réflexions sur l'encyclique *Mystici corporis.*' Excerpt from *Irenikon,* 1946-1947, vols. 19-20, pp. 54 and 83. F. Malmberg, *Een lichaam . . .,* pp. 24-26.

and put it on the index of forbidden books.'[1] This book marks the extreme position in the tide of ecclesiological discussion which eddied round the image of the body of Christ, with the principal emphasis on the spiritual aspect. The juridical aspect commanded very little attention—it was thought to be settled. Karl Pelz went so far as to compare the unity realized in the mystical body with transubstantiation in the eucharist. Not everyone was so sweeping; far from it. But we must admit that a salient feature of German Catholic ecclesiology at this period was what has been described as its 'anti-intellectual, mystical, organic, biological, "feminine" in Przywara's sense of the word) aspect'.[2] Father Przywara described this manner of thought as 'romantic', to distinguish it from the Lutheran and Gallican approaches to the same subject. Certain German Catholic theologians reacted vigorously to this tendency. They included, in addition to the celebrated Jesuit we have just mentioned, L. Deimel and M. D. Koster. Let us for a moment consider Koster's position.

M. D. Koster, professor at the Dominican Study House of Walberberg, and a pupil of Rademacher of the Bonn faculty, published at Paderborn in 1940 a work which attracted a lot of attention, *Ekklesiologie im Werden* (Ecclesiology in the making).

He made a complete inventory of the ecclesiology of his time, and was particularly severe on the movement we have just described. His conclusion was forthright: 'The whole of present-day ecclesiology is still in the pre-theological stage. It is a far cry from proper theological status. . . . The work of compiling a genuine ecclesiology has still to be undertaken' (p. 142). German ecclesiology, influenced by the incomplete and pre-theological views of St Augustine, saw in the mystical body no more than an aggregate of individuals sanctified and united with Christ by grace. Now to St Paul the body of Christ is above all a *corporative reality* (*Körperschaft,* p. 51), which is itself identical with the people of God. The starting point for the theological work which must be undertaken has to be the teaching of the magisterium and particularly the ordinary magisterium. In the pronouncements of the ordinary magisterium the most frequently

1. N. Oehmen, 'L'ecclésiologie dans la crise' in 'Questions sur L'Eglise et son unité' (*Irenikon,* wartime edition), pp. 1-11. This extract is set at the head of the article.
2. Lialine, *Une étape* . . . p. 22.

used term is 'the people of God'. Father Koster sees undeniable advantages in an ecclesiology of the people of God, the most obvious being that it makes apparent the continuity of the two Testaments; the one people exists under two different dispensations.

The people of God, of the old covenant, becomes the Church, the body of Christ (p. 151). 'As for the "Body of Christ", this is *one name* for the Church among others, and neither more nor less. It is an expression which can never be the *definition* of the Church' (p. 122, our italics).

The practical repercussions of this theological debate began to disturb those with pastoral responsibility. In 1941, Father M. Kassiepe published a book on 'the impasses and wrong turnings of contemporary spiritual life'.[1] In his view, the aberrations and deviations of the time led to 'a semiquietism which minimizes man's part in the work of grace'.[2] Certain doctrines, excellent in themselves, such as that of the mystical body, were over-emphasized from lack of prudence. 'It is regrettable that this sublime doctrine should so often be misunderstood and wrongly interpreted'.[3] The Archbishop of Freiburg-im-Breisgau, Mgr Conrad Groeber, sounded the alarm in a letter and questionnaire addressed to the members of the German episcopate on 18 January 1943, five months before *Mystici Corporis* appeared. He expressed his concern over an ecclesiology conceived in terms of spiritual biology, masked by the vague term 'mystical body', whose moral tendencies converged towards a bogus mysticism where the frontiers between created and uncreated disappeared. The document ended with an appeal to the Pope to intervene : 'When I think of my pastoral responsibilities, I feel bound to ask how much good is being done to the faithful by inundating them with the mystical theology of the body of Christ (. . .). Bishops of greater Germany as we are, can we be silent? Can Rome be silent?'[4]

1. *Irrwege und Umwege im Frömmigkeitsleben der Gegenwart.* I do not know where this work was published.
2. Lialine's expression, *Une étape* . . ., p. 26.
3. M. Kassiepe, quoted by Lialine, *Une étape* . . ., p. 27.
4. See Lialine, *Une étape* . . . p. 27.

III. The Doctrinal Impasses noted by the Encyclical

Rome was not silent. The encyclical *Mystici Corporis* was promulgated on the feast of the Apostles Peter and Paul, 29 June 1943.

How did the Pope use it to denounce doctrinal errors? The head of the Church found himself faced with a mentality that was dangerous, vague, diffuse and hard to pin down. He did not embark on a scientific analysis of this situation. His aim was not to make a precise diagnosis of the spiritual mentality at a given moment, as the historian of doctrine would do. His reaction was essentially pastoral. In the prevailing confusion, the Church took the lead and vigorously denounced certain major doctrinal tendencies which she considered full of danger for the flock which was her responsibility.

Quite deliberately, the Church denounces tendencies but not individuals. She seems to be saying : 'I have just issued a warning against certain errors which I have carefully defined. If you recognize these views as being your own, you have strayed from the truth of which I am the depository and the guardian. Those who hunt for the names of the people at whom such pronouncements are aimed will always be disappointed. They will probably feel that all have not grasped the full implications of the positions of these authors. They are responsible for their own disappointment in looking to a document for something it was never intended to provide.' In brief, this encyclical, like any other, reflected a specific historical situation. It was no part of its aim to undertake punctilious analyses of individual positions but to react vigorously to the actual situation. Finally, we must remember that its purpose went beyond the occasion that led to its issue : the problem had arisen principally in Germany; but it was to the universal Church that Pius XII addressed his encyclical.

His warning concerned three major dangers :

1. An erroneous conception of the unity attained in the mystical body. This was the principal error the encyclical set out to denounce : 'A false mysticism (which attempts . . .) to obliterate the inviolable frontiers between things created and the Creator' (p. 197; p. 9).[1]

1. The first page reference is to the pagination of the *Acta Apostolicae Sedis*, vol. 35. The second page reference is to the English translation published by the Catholic Truth Society, from which we quote.

Certain people were putting forward a mistaken idea of unity: 'According to them the divine Redeemer and the members of the Church are united to form one physical person, . . . and consequently while attributing divine properties to human beings, they make Christ our Lord subject to error and human frailty (p. 234; p. 51).

2. Neglect of the external and visible aspect of the mystical body by stressing its exclusively and onesidedly interior aspect—union with Christ and charity—leads to a conception of 'the Church as something interior and invisible . . . a society nurtured and shaped by charity, with which it disparagingly contrasts another society which (is called) juridical' (pp. 223-224; p. 39). Two consequences follow inevitably. Those who subscribe to these views can no longer understand

(a) either the visible and normal role of the Pope: 'It is a dangerous error to hold that one can adhere to Christ as Head of the Church, without loyal allegiance to his Vicar on earth' (p. 211; p. 25).

(b) or the authentic unity of the Church in which unity and visibility are inseparably coupled. This may end up in a certain indiscriminate approach to the various denominations: 'It is therefore an aberration from divine truth to represent the Church as something intangible and invisible, as a mere "pneumatic" entity joining together by an invisible link a number of communities of Christians in spite of their difference in faith' (pp. 199-200; p. 12).

3. A trend of thought that leads to an unhealthy quietism. We must beware of 'the dangerous error which endeavours to make our mysterious union with Christ the basis of an unsound system of quietism, attributing the whole spiritual life of Christians and their advance towards virtue solely to the action of the divine Spirit, to the exclusion and neglect of the cooperation which we must provide' (p. 234; p. 51).[1]

1. The encyclical also issues a warning against certain errors concerning confession and prayer. But these last are only indirectly connected with the whole and do not concern ecclesiology. In addition to Father Lialine's work, there are two other useful commentaries: L. Malevez, ' Quelques enseignements de l'encyclique "Mystici Corporis Christi" in *NRT*, 1945, vol. 67, pp. 996-1015 and L. Bouyer, 'Oû en est la théologie du Corps mystique?' in *Rev. des sciences religieuses*, 1948, vol. 22, pp. 313-333.

IV. Points Specially Emphasized

Confronted with these tendencies, the Church could have reacted in two different ways. It might have followed Father Kleutgen's drafting of the second schema and Father Koster in the controversy oulined above, abandoning the image of the mystical body as central to any account of the Church and substituting for it a concept which was not as prone to the same disadvantages.[1] On the other hand, it could provide a doctrinally precise and closely-reasoned elaboration of the biblical image, with a view to making impossible in the future the dubious interpretations which had been current in certain theological and spiritual circles in Germany. The encyclical followed this second course which was, it must be added, the only reasonable attitude. If the Pope had acted in any other way, the doctrinal confusion would have remained and the concept of the mystical body would still have been shrouded in an aura of suspicion.

Mystici Corporis' first step, then, was to define the Church. This definition can be regarded as central to the encyclical : 'To describe this true Church of Christ—which is the Holy, Catholic, Apostolic, Roman Church—there is no name more noble . . . than "the mystical body of Jesus Christ"' (p. 199; p. 12). What the Pope meant to assert here, of course, was that the mystical body and the Roman Catholic Church are one and the same thing. This very fact led him immediately to emphasize the visibility of this body, which must be concrete and perceptible to the senses, as Leo XIII stated : 'By the very fact of being a body the Church is visible' (p. 199; p. 12). By way of this reminder the encyclical was able to bring into its doctrinal exposition an aspect which the Germans had overlooked, whose first expression is found in I Cor. 12 :12-27 and Rom. 12 :3-8, which deal with charisms in the Church : here we find all that the opponents of the mystical body image had sought for in other terms with a more sociological overtone. The mystical body is constituted 'organically' and 'hierarchically'; it is endowed with means of sanctification, i.e. sacraments; it is composed of specific members. This emphasis on visibility also makes it

1. Father Kleutgen saw it as a 'gathering of the faithful' and a 'society'; Father Koster as the 'people of God'.

possible to reveal the Pope's role in the Universal Church and the bishops' role in individual Churches, and also the 'juridical and social elements' with which the Church is provided for perpetuating on this earth the salutary work of the Redemption' (p. 224; p. 39).

Faced with 'false mysticism', it became essential to say precisely what the adjective 'mystical' does mean. That was the second major undertaking of the encyclical. To start with, the word was not abandoned, though Father Koster and L. Deimel regarded it with marked disfavour.[1] 'The body of Christ, which is the Church, must be called "mystical". This word, employed by several ancient writers, is endorsed by a number of Papal documents '(p. 221; p. 36). But besides this argument from usage and authority, there are inherent reasons for the use of the word. The use of 'mystical' makes it possible to distinguish between the social body of the Church and the physical body of Christ, born of Mary and present in the eucharist; it also enables one to distinguish it from any other natural body, whether physical or moral.

We can summarize this teaching in the form of the following table (pp. 221-223; pp. 37-39):

Distinction between mystical body and physical body:

From the point of view of 'subsistence':
—physical body: unity of 'subsistence' for the body as a whole, separate 'subsistence' for the parts;
—mystical body: each member possesses its own separate personality.[2]
From the point of view of the relation between the whole and the parts:
—physical body: each member exists for the good of the organism as a whole;
—mystical body: the Church is ordained for the good of the faithful (it is also designed for the glory of God and of Jesus Christ).

1. See Lialine, *Une étape . . .*, p. 24.
2. The word 'subsistence' here is borrowed from the technical vocabulary of scholastic philosophy. The 'subsistent' being is one which exists in an independent manner (which is therefore neither the accident of a subject nor the intrinsic co-principle of a substance). The person is pre-eminently a 'subsistent' being.

Distinction between mystical body and moral body:

—moral body: the only principle of unity is a common end;
—in the mystical body, in addition to this common aspiration there is another internal principle of the supernatural order: the Spirit of God, which is responsible for the unity of the Church.

We have selected from the encyclical those points which are a direct answer to well-defined historical difficulties, which can be dated and placed. Have we distorted the document as a whole by making this selection? There is no special pleading, nothing one-sided about the encyclical. It is a calm and comprehensive exposition of the doctrine of the mystical body. A great deal of it is devoted to teaching which is accepted and undisputed and which we have, therefore, not thought it necessary to go into. The encyclical must be studied as a whole for one to have a full idea of its teaching.

V. What Authority has this Encyclical, and the Pronouncements of the Magisterium in General?

Before we examine more closely the doctrinal value of *Mystici Corporis* and the acceptance it demands, we should perhaps consider this particular problem in a wider perspective: what is the right way to understand the question of the teaching authority of the Church?

When we consider the Christian's attitude of mind towards the magisterium, it is the relationship between master and disciple that commands our attention. Strictly speaking, it is a matter on one side of *discipline* or teaching (the action of the master), and on the other of *docility* (the disposition and action of the disciple). It is the latter we shall discuss here. Docility lies in the intelligence; it is concerned with the acquisition of knowledge (II, II, q. 48, a. 1).[1] It qualifies a man 'to digest teaching well' (q. 49, a. 3). That is its object. It accepts the opinion of competent men (q. 53, a. 3). It develops by study and mental exercise applied 'with care, assiduity and respect to the teachings it receives', and refrains from 'neglecting them out

1. The references in brackets are to the *Summa Theologica* of St Thomas. To avoid unduly multiplying footnotes, we shall give brief cross-references to St Thomas and Scripture in the text.

of laziness or despising them out of pride' (q. 49, a. 3, ad 2). What is more, there are degrees in docility : it will be proportionate to the distance that lies between the qualifications or doctrinal authority of the teacher and the knowledge of the pupil. In short, to be docile is to accept as a guiding rule the 'mastery' of someone else. Whoever deliberately evades such a rule will be on the contrary indocile, hasty and rash (q. 53, a. 3, c. and ad 2).

This docility should be confused neither with obedience nor with faith. As a virtue of the intelligence, whose object is knowledge, it differs from obedience, which submits the will to the precept of the superior; though in concrete behaviour these virtues often go hand in hand, docility can exist without obedience entering into the matter. On the other hand, docility is not faith. Its object is teaching, the teaching of the 'masters' whom Christ has given us. It is not a theological virtue, whose object is none other than God himself.

Docility presupposes discernment. Has the 'master' who is speaking to me the right to teach me? Has he the intention of doing so? To what degree does he commit his authority? These questions arise when we consider all the implications of the exercise of the magisterium of a professor of theology in a given university, of a single bishop, the bishops of the Church under the direction of the successor of St Peter, or of the Supreme Pontiff. The quality and intensity of the docility will differ appreciably in each case. An analysis of the pronouncement under consideration is therefore essential. Faced with a pontifical statement, for instance, we must ascertain in what manner the Pope meant to exercise his authority as pastor and teacher and what sort of compliance he expected from the faithful. We must know whether we are faced with a warning, advice, the settling of a controversy, a caution, or a doctrinal pronouncement in the strict sense of the word. The internal assent which docility towards the ecclesiastical magisterium implies should correspond exactly to the nature and importance of the act of the teaching authority.[1] At the highest point, when the exercise of the magisterium fulfils all the conditions necessary to be infallible, it is not just docility that will be expected from believers, but pure and simple faith. Docile assent to the ecclesiastical magisterium *will be accompanied* by assent to God himself, to the primal truth, the

1. On internal assent, see proposition 7 of the Decree *Lamentabili*, of 3 July 1907 (Denz. 2007).

object of the virtue of faith. It is thus not a question of the *transformation* of docility into faith. In the act of faith, docility to the magisterium remains unchanged. In the economy of salvation, the Church is at the constant service of the object of faith. She is the 'servant of the object', *ministra objecti fidei.*[1]

When, then, is the magisterium infallible? The Church is infallible in its definitive decisions on faith and morals. The two subjects of this charism are on the one hand the episcopal college under the authority of its head, the Pope, and on the other the Pope himself. The divine assistance which infallibility presupposes directly affects the *acts* of the magisterium. It is granted to persons only in view of these acts. With regard to the Supreme Pontiff, Mgr Gasser, spokesman for the deputation on faith at the First Vatican Council, specified this clearly: 'By his papal authority, the Pontiff is always the supreme judge in matters of faith and of morals, the father and the teacher of all Christians; but he benefits from the divine aid which was promised him and prevents him from being mistaken solely in the real and actual exercise of his responsibility as supreme arbiter of controversies concerning the faith and as teacher of the universal Church. Consequently, the phrase "the Roman Pontiff is infallible" is certainly not false, since Christ promised his assistance to the person of Peter and to that of his successor; it is simply incomplete, since the Pope is infallible only when he lays down a definition on matters of faith and morals by a solemn pronouncement to the universal Church'.[2] There is every reason for believing that this clarification is valid also of the magisterium of the episcopal college united with the Pope. The episcopate as a whole is infallible when, either meeting in a general Council (formal magisterium) or scattered all over the earth (ordinary magisterium) the bishops propose a definite teaching on faith and morals as obligatory on all the faithful.[3]

1. There are also occasions when the Pope does not commit his authority in any way. When, speaking to a group of sportsmen, he praises the effects of physical exertion, no one is bound by the opinions he expresses. The only object of such fatherly words is to show a cordial interest in a particular group of believers.

2. We are here quoting a passage from the *relatio* of 11 July 1870 on Chapter IV of *Pastor aeternus:* Mansi, vol. 52, col. 1213.

3. On this, see proposition 23 of the *Syllabus* (Denz, 1723), Chapter III of the dogmatic constitution *Dei Filius* (Denz. 1792); and compare with a passage of the letter *Tuas libenter,* of 21 December 1863 (Denz. 1683).

The Pope is infallible under the conditions clearly defined by the First Vatican Council. 'When he speaks *ex cathedra,* that is to say when, fulfilling his responsibility as pastor and teacher of all Christians by virtue of his supreme apostolic authority, he defines a doctrine concerned with faith and morals as one that must be believed by the universal Church, the Roman Pontiff benefits from that infallibility with which the Divine Redeemer wished his Church to be endowed in the definition of doctrine concerning faith and morals'.[1] Four conditions are required: 1. The subject of the infallibility is the Roman Pontiff as pastor of the universal Church, assuming his supreme apostolic authority, and in no way as a private teacher. 2. Infallibility extends to the whole field of faith and of morals, but is limited to this. 3. The Pope's teaching must be addressed to the entire Church. 4. The intention to lay down a definitive and irrevocable decision must be manifest from the nature of the statement or from the circumstances. Outside these conditions, there is no *ex cathedra* definition.[2]

All the same we should note that these four conditions may *a priori* be fulfilled in widely varying circumstances. The Pope is not bound to adopt any one particular literary form or oratorical manner when he issues an infallible doctrine. The Immaculate Conception was defined in the bull *Ineffabilis Deus* of 1854, the Assumption in the apostolic constitution *Munificentissimus* of 1950. But the Pope could just as well have recourse to less formal methods, such as an address or even a radio message. There is no limitation on his power to select whatever means seem to him most opportune and most efficacious; he is not bound by any precedent. Before we go any further, it should therefore be stated that an encyclical *can* contain an infallible piece of teaching.

Did the Pope let it be understood, in *Mystici Corporis,* that he wished to bind the faith of believers by an *ex cathedra* definition? There is nothing to show he did. The doctrinal implications of the document are nevertheless considerable. Pius XII says clearly: 'It

1. Dogmatic constitution *Pastor aeternus,* Chapter IV (Denz. 1839). The text concludes with the famous formula: 'Consequently we teach and define that the definitions of the Roman Pontiff are irrevocable of themselves, not by virtue of the assent of the Church, *ex sese, non autem ex consensu Ecclesiae*'.

2. This point is stressed also by the Code of Canon Law. Nothing is considered dogmatically declared or defined except insofar as there is manifest proof that it has been. See can. 1393, 3.

is chiefly our *pastoral concern* (*pastoralis sollicitudo*) which prompts Us to expound this sublime doctrine in detail at the present time'. (p. 196; p. 9). Further on he is even more explicit: 'We have deemed it our *pastoral duty* to set forth ... *to the whole Christian flock* (*universo christiano gregi*) (...) the doctrine of the mystical body' (p. 198; p. 10). The teaching given us by virtue of this encyclical thus requires of us that inner religious assent which we described earlier when discussing docility. We are confronted with one of those cases to which allusion was made later, in the encyclical *Humani generis* of 1950: 'Nor is it to be supposed that a position advanced in an encyclical does not *ipso facto* claim assent (*assensum*). In writing them it is true the Popes do not exercise their teaching authority to the full. But such statements come under the day-to-day teaching of the Church'.[1] *Humani Generis* then applied to this point the decisive question in *Mystici Corporis*: 'That the mystical body of Christ and the Catholic Church in communion with Rome are one and the same thing is a doctrine based on revealed truth, and as such was set forth by Us in an encyclical a few years back; some imagine, nevertheless, that they are not bound to hold it'.[2] Finally, a duty of obedience corresponds to this assent from docility: 'And when the Roman Pontiffs go out of their way to pronounce on some subject which has hitherto been controverted, it must be clear to everybody that in the mind and intention of the Pontiffs concerned, this subject can no longer be regarded as a matter for free debate among theologians'.[3] Nevertheless, on the present point, neither docility nor obedience possess that definitive and irrevocable character with which the Christian must respond to an *ex cathedra* definition which binds nothing less than the divine faith of the believer.

What we have said up to now answers the question of what authority belongs to the encyclical *Mystici Corporis*. But now, in order to see all the ramifications of the contemporary problem, we think it necessary, at the risk of appearing to stray from our subject, to tackle a related question. Can we, in addition to the infallibility of the solemn magisterium of the Pope, talk of the infallibility of his ordinary magisterium? We remain at the heart of the problem, for

1. *AAS*, 1950, vol. 42, p. 568; C. T. S. translation, p. 11.
2. *AAS*, p. 571; C.T.S. translation, pp. 14-15.
3. *AAS*, p. 568; C.T.S. translation, p. 11.

those who answer in the affirmative see the encyclicals above all as the specially chosen vehicle for the exercise of this kind of infallibility.[1]

Let us examine the writings of two contemporary authors who defend this thesis, a Spanish Jesuit, Father Joachim Salaverri, and a French Benedictine, Dom Paul Nau. Let us first of all dispose of an argument that might be based on a passage of *Humani generis* which, dealing with the ordinary magisterium, declares that it 'is covered by the promise, "He who listens to you listens to me" '. It is quite clear from the context that there is no question here of an *infallible* ordinary magisterium.[2] Nor will we linger over the conclusions which Father Salaverri feels able to draw from the dogma of primacy. The Pope possesses the plenitude of supreme power (Denz., 1831); and a blow would be dealt to this plenitude if the Pope could not exercise his infallible magisterium at once *modo extraordinario* and *modo ordinario*. This argument is not convincing. The ordinary magisterium of the bishops is a collegial magisterium. The magisterium of the Pope is exercised by a single person. What is appropriate to the first is not necessarily appropriate to the second.

Father Salaverri's principal argument is based on a comparison of two major texts of the Vatican Council, the first coming from Chapter IV of *Pastor aeternus* and the second from Chapter III of *Dei Filius*. Its author presents it in the form of a syllogism, which runs as follows. The Roman Pontiff enjoys the infallibility with which the Divine Redeemer willed to endow his Church (Denz., 1839). Now the Church exercises her infallibility, not only through the formal and extraordinary magisterium, but also through the ordinary magisterium (Denz., 1792). It is thus clear that the Pope likewise enjoys infallibility in the exercise of his ordinary magisterium. The argument looks a weighty one. But does it take into account the implications of the tests it uses, implications which from

1. The fullest critical study of this problem appears to be that of H. Stirnimann, O.P., 'Magisterio enim ordinario haec docentur. Zu einer Kontroversstelle der Enzyklika "Humani Generis" ' in *Freib. Zeitschr. f. Phil. und Theol.*, 1954, vol. 1, pp. 17-47. This provides a full bibliography, particularly on the writings of J. Salaverri. The only work of this latter writer to which we will refer the reader is his manual 'De Ecclesia Christi', in *Sacrae theologiae summa*, vol. 1., *Theol fund.*, Madrid, 1955, principally numbers 645-649. References may also be made to a more recent and well-documented work, M. Caudron, 'Magistère ordinaire et infaillibilité pontificale d'après la constitution "Dei Filius" ', in *ETL*, 1960, vol. 36, pp. 393-431.

2. *AAS*, p. 568; C.T.S. translation, p. 11.

a study of the acts of the Council we are able to define precisely?

The first text, which lays down an equivalence between the infallibility of the Pope and of the Church, is concerned solely with the *object* of Papal infallibility; it teaches that the extent of the infallibility is exactly the same in the two cases; it does not attempt to consider the way in which this charism is exercised.[1] The second text, which distinguishes in the Church between a *solemne judicium* and an *ordinarium et universale magisterium,* lends itself just as little to the use which Father Salaverri makes of it. There is no question here, either explicitly or implicitly, of a twofold method of exercise of the magisterium on every subject. On the contrary, when it defines here the role of the ordinary magisterium in propounding the material object of faith, the Council deliberately excluded the question of the personal magisterium of the Pope.[2] Mgr Conrad Martin, speaking for the deputation on faith, was led to clarify the matter. Several Fathers of the Council found the formulae used obscure. 'Thus Martinez, Bishop of Havana, thought that the *magisterium ordinarium* was the infallible magisterium of the Sovereign Pontiff, and therefore believed that the text of the draft sought to distinguish between the formal definitions of Councils and this Papal magisterium. Disputing the validity of such an interpretation, the Archbishop of Trebizond, Errington, urged that the vital question of the infallibility of the Sovereign Pontiff could not be dealt with in this chapter, particularly not *oblique et sine discussione*'.[3] All these doubts were removed by Mgr Martin's statement. The sole purpose of the deputation on faith was to describe briefly the material object of faith, without any direct or indirect allusion to papal infallibility, which question was reserved for another schema.[4] The formula submitted to the Council had no other implications than those contained in Pius IX's letter to the Archbishop of Munich-Freising: 'Divine faith should not be limited to points expressly defined by decrees of Oecumenical Councils, or of Roman pontiffs and the apostolic see; but it should extend also to points which are described as divinely revealed *by the ordinary magisterium* of the whole Church scattered all over the world'.[1] Which goes to show

1. See H. Stirnimann, *Magisterio* . . ., pp. 29-32.
2. See H. Stirnimann, *Magisterio* . . ., pp. 32-33.
3. Caudron, *Magistère ordinaire* . . ., p. 406.
4. Mansi, vol. 51, col. 223.

how hard it was to find support in the Vatican Council for the idea of an infallible ordinary magisterium as applied to the person of the Sovereign Pontiff.

On this point, Dom Paul Nau maintains a different position, personal to himself.[2] In the encyclicals the aim of the Popes is to ensure unanimity in the world in the profession of the one faith. Leaving aside formal pronouncements, this unity will be achieved not by an isolated assertion, but by a body of such statements. In every correct sense of the word, infallibility should not be used except of this body. Dom Nau draws from this idea of an infallible ordinary magisterium, whose characteristic marks are the 'material repetition of the same truths' (p. 407) and 'the internal cohesion of doctrinal development' (p. 408). Here is how he defines its nature: 'It is not that of a judgment or of an act to be considered in isolation, as if we could expect complete illumination from it alone. It is on the contrary that of a plurality of assertions or expositions none of which taken on its own can provide us with absolute certainty. That should be understood only of their entirety. But they all combine to form that whole. Consequently, none of them can be treated lightly, as the simple opinion of a private teacher' (p. 401).

To avoid repeating ourselves, we will not discuss here the positive grounds which Dom Nau presents in support of his thesis. Let us get right down to the main issue. Three things are of prime importance. 1. Before considering the various affirmations of a single truth in terms of a continuous whole, each must first be considered in itself. Each has a precise value and demands from us an appropriate response. On this point, Dom Nau pays too little attention to the doctrine of 'assent from docility' which we have already discussed and which is fundamental.[3]—2. The value of the whole depends on the value of the parts. If each of the affirmations, frequently repeated in a perfectly coherent sequence, demands no more than the mere *assensus interior* of which we have spoken, the whole cannot require

1. *Tuas libentur*, 21 Dec. 1863 (Denz., 1683).

2. P. Nau, *Une source doctrinale. Les encycliques. Essai sur l'autorité de leur enseignement*, Paris, 1952. This is the republication in booklet form (89pp.) of three articles which appeared in *La Pensée catholique* in 1950 and 1951. See *RSPT*, 1953, vol. 37 pp. 734-735 for review by Father Congar. We are using here a more recent study by the same author, 'Le magistère pontifical ordinaire, lieu théologique', in *RT*, 1956, vol. 56, pp. 389-412.

3. Cf. how the author deals with one aspect of this problem, pp. 406-407.

an assent which is more binding and of another order.—3. Dom Nau has not made clear the real function of the pronouncements of the ordinary magisterium of the Pope in concert with the ordinary magisterium of the episcopal college.

For we often lose sight of the doctrinal role proper to the Pope within the context of an episcopal college, the whole of which is called to fulfil the function of judge and teacher. In its solemn form, the Oecumenical Council, the Pope presides, in person or by delegate, superintends the discussions and confirms the decisions. He also exercises his office as head of the episcopate, whose definitions of faith are infallible. The prologue of the constitution *Dei Filius* shows clearly how the bishops of the whole world sit and pass judgment with the Pope.[1]

Other things being equal, the Pope exercises a similar role in the doctrinal activity of the ordinary magisterium of the whole Church scattered over the world, a role of active guidance at the heart and at the head of an episcopal college endowed with the charism of infallibility. It is true that this function is harder to grasp and to define than that of the Pope in a Council. It is nevertheless incontestable that the encyclicals have a definite role here. They contribute, for example, to the progressive creation of common convictions which, *as they deepen,* may eventually be put forward as truths of faith by the episcopal college as a whole. A teaching on faith proposed by the ordinary magisterium of the episcopate scattered throughout the world has *in itself* the same irrevocable character as the solemn definition.[2] In the *consensus* of the scattered episcopate, the Pope occupies a primary and decisive place.[3]

Thus we have no grounds for asserting that the infallibility of the personal magisterium of the Pope extends beyond *ex cathedra* definitions, as they were described in the dogmatic constitution.

1. Nunc autem, sedentibus Nobiscum et judicantibus universi orbis episcopis . . . (Denz., 1781).

2. It is for this reason that I find it hard to understand the following sentence of Caudron's: 'The act of the ordinary magisterium is the non-definitive act proper to the scattered magisterium' (*Magistère ordinaire* . . ., p. 429). It seems to me moreover to contradict several passages in the immediate context. Thus a few lines earlier, the author had said: 'The Fathers of the Council have often stressed that the ordinary magisterium is in fact a form of teaching dogmas on the same basis as definition.'

3. On all this, see Appendix II, *The episcopal body united with the Pope*, particularly the conclusions.

We have said—and we deliberately repeat this—that the conditions of such definitions can be fulfilled in circumstances and spoken and written forms which vary greatly. It is important to stress this, for once this fact has been settled, discussion of the ordinary magisterium becomes much clearer. The infallible magisterium of the Pope is always a solemn or extraordinary magisterium, whatever the context in which it is exercised. On this point, there is no reason to diverge from the vocabulary of the Vatican Council, which is repeated clearly and firmly by ecclesiastical law, in canon 1323 of the Code. It is probably unnecessary to emphasize that the adjective 'solemn' in this context does not refer to any external ceremonies or setting, but solely to the precise objective requirements laid down in the stated conditions. In the same sense we speak of a 'solemn vow' in canon law and of a 'solemn contract' in jurisprudence.

It may be interesting, at the end of this discussion, to note that the first author to have put forward the thesis of the infallibility of the ordinary magisterium of the Pope was J. M. A. Vacant, in a book published in 1887.[1] What is more, he did not conceal the novelty of his assertion : 'Consequently I am going to put forward a proposition which I have not hitherto read, in so many words, in any work. I cannot base this assertion on authorities, and I shall, therefore, have to base it on reasons'.[2]

This fairly broad discussion of the ordinary magisterium completes our general exposition of the historical setting, content and doctrinal implications of *Mystici Corporis*. This is without doubt the most complete document concerning the doctrine of the Church that the magisterium has given us. We recognize its very real value. Moreover, we must not forget the statement of *Humani generis*, which is particularly applicable to the present case : 'For the most part the positions advanced, the duties inculcated by these encyclical letters are already bound up, under some other title, with the general body of Catholic teaching'.[3] We have here an impressive synthesis, which covers a wide field of the facts about the magisterium. It is an important stage in the development of ecclesiology. It is in the context of this encyclical that we must prosecute our search for a definition of the Church.

1. J. M. A. Vacant, *Le magistère de l'Eglise et ses organes*, Paris, 1887.
2. *Le magistère ordinaire . . .*, p. 96.
3. *AAS*, p. 568; C.T.S. translation, p. 11, our italics.

II

BIBLICAL VOCABULARY AND IMAGES

THERE are a great many different presentations of the biblical vocabulary and imagery and these are used to a greater or lesser extent by different authors. We will confine ourselves to the principal terms, which are also those to bring out most clearly the form of sociability proper to the Church. Any definition of the Christian community must be rooted in these scriptural data.

I. 'CHURCH'

A glance at a concordance shows that the word *ekklesia* is most unevenly distributed in the New Testament. It appears in only two places in the gospels—both in St Matthew—though both are important. Its use is especially frequent in the Acts, in the writings of St Paul and in the Apocalypse.[1]

1. The usage and meaning of the word *ekklesia* have been studied particularly among Protestants by K. L. Schmidt, in *Die Kirche des Urchristentums, Festgabe f. A. Deissmann*, second ed., Tübingen, 1932, and in his article 'Ekklesia' in Kittel's *Theol. Wörterbuch z. N.T.*, vol. III. These writings are interesting, but should be read with discrimination. Among Catholic works, references may be made to F. Braun, *Aspects nouveaux du problème de l'Eglise*, Fribourg, 1942 (the German edition, *Neues Liche auf die Kirche*, Einsiedeln, 1946, is fuller); L. Cerfaux, *La théologie de l'Eglise suivant Saint Paul*, Paris, first ed. 1942, second ed. 1948 (The second edition is somewhat different from the first; we will specify each time to which we are referring. English translation, from the second ed., *The Church in the Theology of Saint Paul*, Edinburgh, 1959); H. Schlier, *Le temps de l'Eglise, Recherches d'exégèse* Tournai and Paris, 1961; P. Tena, *Ekklesia, Historia y teologia de la palabra en la Sagrada Escritura y en los documentos cristianos primitivos*, Barcelona, 1957; Idem, art. 'Eglise (I. Ecclesia dans l'Ecriture et les premiers temps apostoliques)', in *Dictionnaire de Spiritualité*, vol. 4, section 25; R. Schnackenburg, *Die kirche im Neuen Testament*, Freiburg-im-Br., 1961. Reference can also be made to B. D. Dupuy, 'Le Mystère de l'Eglise', in *La vie spirituelle*, 1961, vol. 104, pp. 70-85. The *LTK* provides the best recent documentation on the Catholic side. On the Church in the New Testament, see R. Schnackenburg's excellent article in vol. 6, col. 167-172.

From the many meanings of the word 'Church', New Testament lexicons distinguish the two principal ones: the individual local community and the community as a whole, the entire body of the faithful. Various scholars arrive at a far from uniform classification of the texts: it is not always easy to know whether a text should be placed in the first or the second category. But the real problem lies in the mutual relationship between the two meanings. Does one have the priority over the other? Should they simply be set side by side? There was a time when the first meaning was accepted as historically the older by many exegetes, including, among Catholics, Batiffol and H. Leclercq. They were influenced by the usage of the hellenic world, in which *ekklesia* always meant the assembly of people convened within a single city. Thanks to the researches of K. L. Schmidt, the second interpretation is becoming more and more accepted.[1]

1. *The Acts of the Apostles*

A first series of important and significant texts is to be found in Acts 2:47[2], 5:11, 7:38, 8:1, 8:3 and 9:31. All these texts use the word in the singular. At first, the Church in Jerusalem is meant. In Acts 8:1 this is explicitly stated, but in 7:38, in contrast with the other passages, the word 'Church' is used of the assembly in the desert, the people of Israel led by Moses. This is very characteristic. Though not a verbatim quotation, the passage recalls Deut. 9:10, where the *qahal* of the Masoretic text corresponds to the *ekklesia* of the Septuagint. In 9:31, according to the Alexandrine text, which Nestle's critical edition prefers, it no longer refers only to the community in Jerusalem, but to the community spread all over Judaea, Galilee and Samaria. One and the same term, used in the singular, can therefore designate at once the community of the city of Jerusalem, the Israelites assembled in the desert and the whole body of Christian believers over a fairly wide area.

In a number of places, the plural is found alongside the singular.[3] The singular, however, predominates, whether it is used of the com-

1. On this point, see F. Braun, *Aspects nouveaux . . .*, p. 33.

2. See the critical apparatus of E. Nestle, *Novum Testamentum graece et latine*, eleventh ed., Stuttgart, 1932.

3. In 9:31 in the Western text and the Antioch text. The plural has better warrant in 15:41. It is absolutely certain in 16:5.

munity in Jerusalem (11:22), of Antioch in Syria (11:26, 13:1, 14:27, 15:3), of Caesarea (18:22) or again of that of Ephesus (20:17). We shall single out at once one particularly meaningful passage, because it too reveals the Old Testament background of the term: this is Acts 20:28, which speaks of 'God's Church ... which he won for himself at the price of his own blood'. Nestle finds a parallel for this text in Ps. 73:2: 'Bethink thee of the company thou hast gathered long ago', where, however, the word used is not *ekklesia* but *sunagoge*.

These passages enable us to bring out the distinctive characteristics of the idea of the Church in the New Testament. In the various texts cited, the local Christian community is called purely and simply 'the Church'. The local link is not essential or decisive, for we read also of the Church in Judaea, Galilee and Samaria (9:31). In 20:28 it is the Church only, without any local limitation; here it is a question of the Church and nothing more. The fact that sometimes the singular and sometimes the plural is used is also significant.

From all this it seems perfectly permissible to infer that:

1. We must discard any explanation that would regard the *ekklesiai* as a splitting into parts of the *ekklesia* or look on the *ekklesia* as the sum of the *ekklesiai*.

2. The formula which best tallies with reality would seem to be the following: the Church exists in a number of places. Or, to put it more precisely: the word 'Church' designates *the people of God as a whole and the manifestation of this people in a particular place.*

The word 'Church' contains within itself its whole value and strength. All qualification is superfluous. Without any sort of addition, the same word designates both the Judaeo-Christian community and the Pagan-Christian community. The genitive *tou Theou,* which occurs in Acts 20:28 has no kind of restrictive sense. It merely renders explicit the normal content of the concept of the Church. Every Church is of God. It is precisely this that distinguishes the Christian assembly from pagan political assemblies.

It is true that Acts uses the word *ekklesia* not only to designate the Christian community but also to signify a meeting of the people in the pagan city (see 19:32, 39, 40). It is interesting for our purposes to note what there is in common between the two ideas and what distinguishes them.

If we had to choose a word which would do duty automatically for the term *ekklesia,* we should, following K. L. Schmidt,[1] suggest *assembly* (*Versammlung*). This word admirably expresses what there is in common between the various acceptations of the term : the fact of gathering, of meeting, of coming together and of remaining together.

But the Christian assembly is not just any random assembly. It is the *ekklesia tou Theou* (Acts 20 :28). That is its distinguishing mark. It is God who gathers the assembly together, and those whom he gathers are his. In his farewell to the presbyters of Ephesus, Paul does in fact say : 'Keep watch over yourselves and over God's Church, in which the Holy Spirit has made you bishops; you are to be shepherds of that flock which he won for himself at the price of his own blood' (20 :28). It follows that the theological concept of the Church cannot be thought of in a quantitative sense but in a qualitative sense. The more numerous the people who attend a public meeting, the more right it has to be called an 'assembly'. Such is not the case with the Christian community. What constitutes it a 'Church' is nothing to do with larger or smaller numbers, but the intervention of God who gathers his own together.[2]

2. *The epistles of St Paul*

What are the relationships between the community as a whole and the local communities? We shall adopt here, as a hypothesis to be proved, the conclusion which has emerged from our inquiry into Acts : that the general community which constitutes the Church does not take its being from an adding together of local communities, but that each community, however small it may be, represents the whole Church.

The assembly within a household already bears the title of Church. That is significant. 'My greetings, also, to the church in their household' (Rom. 16 :5). In I Cor. 16 :19 a simple assembly meeting in a private house is cited alongside great communities : 'A greeting to you from all the churches of Asia, and many greetings, in the Lord's name, from Aquila and Priscilla, as well as the church in their household'. In Col. 4 :15, Paul keeps to the same usage,

1. In Kittel, vol. III, p. 507.
2. In 20:28, certain Mss have *tou kuriou* instead of *tou Theou.* This does not affect the basic meaning.

although this is an epistle in which he deepens the theology of the Church.

'The Church of God set up in Corinth.' This expressions occurs twice, in I Cor. 1 :2 and II Cor. 1 : 1. The phrase as we have translated it renders the sense of the Greek expression very well.[1] Crampon gives an even more literal translation, as does Knox in II Cor. 1 : 1 : 'The Church of God which is at Corinth'. Brevity might tempt us to say: The Church of Corinth. That would be inexact. Paul means the Church as it is at Corinth, as it is present at Corinth. Thus, when someone in this kind of assembly is rebuked (I Cor. 6 :4), when its members meet for the eucharist (I Cor. 11 : 18), when women are told to be silent (I Cor. 14 :34), when advice is given for keeping down the community's expenses (I Tim. 5 : 16), it is of the Church as such, beyond the local group, that Paul is thinking.[2]

St Paul uses the formula 'Church of God' more often than the author of Acts does. The expression is used sometimes in the singular and sometimes in the plural.[3] This transition from one number to the other is more important than might appear. It is extremely revealing of Paul's thinking. Since we are accustomed to distinguish quite clearly between the entire community and the local community, we often find ourselves using the expression 'Church of God' to designate the first, but it will rarely occur to us to apply it to the second. For Paul, the local community deserves this qualification on the same grounds as the entire community.

As in Acts, the expression in its complete form, *ekklesia tou Theou,* does not mean anything more than the single word *ekklesia.* The genitive adds no new idea, and therefore wherever it is missing, it must be understood. From this angle, it is interesting to note that in certain manuscript traditions it has simply been added, so normal did it seem and so much in line with Paul's thought (I Cor. 14 :4; Phil. 3 :6). It is indeed God who acts in and with the Church: 'God has given us different positions in the Church; apostles first ...' (I Cor. 12 :28).

God acts in Christ. That is the reason why Christ is expressly mentioned. The fullest formulation is that of I Thess. 2 : 14 : 'You took

1. *Te ekklesia ... te ouse en Korintho.*
2. Cf. K. L. Schmidt, 'Ekklesia,' in Kittel, vol. III, p. 508.
3. The singular in I Cor. 1 :2, 10 :32, 11 :22, 15 :9, Gal. 1 :13, I Tim. 3 :5, 15; the plural in I Cor. 11 :16, I Thess. 2 :14, II Thess. 1 :4.

for your model, brethren, the churches of God which are assembled in Judaea in the name of Christ Jesus'. In Gal. 1:22, Paul speaks of 'the Christian churches of Judaea' (without the genitive *tou Theou*). Rom. 16:16 has 'all the churches of Christ send you their greeting'. Here the genitive has the same sense as *en Christo*.

We have not yet found in all this, any more than in Acts, a really developed doctrine of the Church. It is as an assembly of God in Christ that the Church reveals itself. But hitherto no additional element has come to enrich the subject we are discussing, except for the contribution of I Tim. 3:15, in which the Church appears as *oikos tou Theou* : 'Thou mayest be in no doubt over the conduct that is expected of thee in God's household. By that I mean the Church of the living God'. This apposition corresponds with the theme of I Cor. 14:4, 12, where spiritual gifts are more highly regarded insofar as they 'strengthen the faith of the Church'.

It is in the captivity epistles that the great doctrinal developments are to be found. Since we shall have to return to the ecclesiological epistles, we will not appeal here to these great texts. A mere glance at the major passages will show their accord with those we have just been considering.

It remains to say a word or two about the epistle to the Hebrews, which occupies a place apart in the Pauline writings. There are two passages to be considered : 'I will proclaim thy name to my brethren; in the midst of the congregation I will praise thee' (Heb. 2:12; R.S.V. text). This is a quotation from Ps. 21:23 where, it is interesting to note, the corresponding Hebrew word is *qahal*; and 'The scene of your approach now is mount Sion, is the heavenly Jerusalem, city of the living God; here are gathered thousands upon thousands of angels, here is the *assembly* of those first-born sons whose names are written in heaven' (Heb. 12:22-23)—this passage is important, for it is the only one where the word *ekklesia* is used to designate the heavenly Jerusalem. K. L. Schmidt therefore asks whether we are really still up against the technical use of the term. He suggests that we should see in the word a synonym of the preceding word, *paneguris*, festal gathering. Nothing, however, forces us to follow this suggestion, which is based on a hardly convincing argument.[1]

1. What are these first-born sons? For the principal hypotheses, see C. Spicq, *Epitre aux Hébreux*, vol. II, p. 407.

3. *Other New Testament writings*

The two most important texts which it remains for us to tackle are those of the Gospel according to St Matthew (16:17-19; 18:17). There can be no question of examining them closely here. The first demands exhaustive consideration in the framework of a theology of Peter and his primacy. We will simply indicate the problems. 'My church' (16:18), says Jesus. What is the Semitic expression behind this word? The Jews spoke Aramaic. Hebrew was, however, the language of worship, so we may credit them with a certain familiarity with its vocabulary. If the word is Hebrew it can only be *qahal* or a term with a similar connotation. If, on the contrary, it is an Aramaic expression, the word *kenista* would seem the obvious solution. Now this term can be used either of the community as a whole, or of a limited community attached to a synagogue.[1] This last hypothesis is worth considering. K. L. Schmidt asks whether we must not regard the Christian community as a particular group within Judaism, as a 'sect, without the pejorative overtones of this word, a "synagogue" with a particular point of view'. Groups of this kind appear in the first book of Machabees (2:42, 7:12). Pursuing his argument, he asks whether we may not see here an allusion to the idea of a 'remnant of Israel' (see Rom. 11:5).[2] This last line of interpretation would provide us with a further piece of evidence concerning the way in which the Christians regarded themselves in relation to the mass of the people of God: they were the chosen 'remnant'. In conclusion, we should note that on this 'remnant of Israel' depends Israel's permanent position as God's people. The second text, Matt. 18:17, raises fewer problems. It obviously refers to the local community, whereas the first concerns the Church as such. It is difficult to draw sweeping conclusions from these two passages. We should simply note St Matthew's overall conformity with the usage of Acts and the Pauline writings. Here, only two chapters apart, we find that double usage of *ekklesia* which we considered above.

The other uses of the word in the New Testament are not of a nature to add much to our knowledge. In the Apocalypse, the term *ekklesia* appears only in the framework which is the setting of the book, at the beginning and at the end. The plural is employed thirteen times. The singular is employed once to designate each of the

1. See Kittel, vol. III, p. 529.
2. One can see the comparisons which may be made with the Qumran texts.

seven churches. The third epistle of St John uses the word three times (vv. 6, 9 and 10). The epistle of St James employs it once (5 : 14) in the sense of the entire community.

4. *The bases of the interpretation given*

Let us start by setting down quite clearly the interpretation we have followed : *ekklesia tou Theou* is the exact parallel, the synonym, of *qahal Jahveh* in the Hebrew Bible, the people of God. We must turn to the Old Testament, and not to the classical languages, for an explanation of the use of the word *ekklesia* in the New Testament. We have followed the Basel exegete K. L. Schmidt in his reading of Acts and St Paul with reference also to the work of F. Braun. The German ecclesiologist M. Schmaus takes the same line.[1] Here is a summary of the arguments on which the equation is based :

1. The usage of the Septuagint : 'Whenever there is question of translating *qahal* (. . .) it is *ekklesia* that comes naturally to the minds of the translators. Why? Nobody knows exactly. The fact remains that a close relationship existed between the two terms'.[2] Christians, many of whom had come from Judaism and who continued to turn their eyes to the Old Testament, quite naturally adopted this term with the specific meaning it had already acquired in the Greek Bible.

2. The early Christian literature in Latin : how are we to explain that writers contented themselves with transcribing the Greek word? If it was to render the exact sense of the *ekklesia* of classical Greek this transcription is inexplicable, for the Latin language possessed two exact equivalents, *curia* and *contio*. This procedure is, however, easier to understand if, 'on account of its relationship with the established Old Testament expression, *ekklesia* in Christian parlance possessed an untranslatable technical sense'.[3]

This is confirmed by the investigations of Mlle. Christine Mohrmann, a specialist in Christian Latin. In a suggestive article, she wrote : 'When Christianity made its entry into the Roman world, the new doctrine had to be formulated in Latin. That language, as an

1. M. Schmaus, *Katholische Dogmatik*, vol. III, 1 :'Die Lehre von der Kirche', Munich, 1958, pp. 26-37.
2. F. Braun, *Aspects nouveaux* . . ., p. 34.
3. F. Braun, *Aspects nouveaux* . . ., p. 35.

agency of human thinking, had got to adapt itself to its new task. This is where we find that Christianity exercised a direct influence on Latin.'[1]

'Generally speaking, we can say that it was above all more or less concrete things and institutions that made their entry into the West under their foreign names. In this way an entire technical vocabulary, composed of borrowings, became habitual in Christian circles. It includes such words as *apostolus, ecclesia, evangelium, baptisma, catechumenus, diaconus, episcopus* and a host of others. We find that words linked with heathen worship were excluded: thus Christians used the word *propheta* and avoided words like *vates* and *fatidicus,* associated as they were with the pagan religion'.[2]

5. *Theological aspects*

Our concern here is not to draw conclusions, but to make comparisons in order to show the interest of the question. We shall simply indicate the lines of research. What has been said hitherto may shed light on a particular theology of the individual church.

Starting from other premises, J. Anger wrote not long ago: 'The diocese would be, on a small scale, what the entire Church is on a larger. We should nevertheless beware of seeing in individual churches mere administrative areas set up solely with a view to efficiency of management; of seeing in the bishop a sort of provincial governor or prefect of a department; or finally of regarding the single and universal Church as the sum of individual churches. With regard to the individual Church the bishop does not bring it a shrunken Christ, but the wholeness of the mystery entrusted to the united episcopate. The priestly work of Jesus Christ is restricted only in the area of its application; but within its field of action, the whole

1. 'Quelques traits caractéristiques du latin des chrétiens'. This article first appeared in the *Miscellanea G. Mercati,* vol. I, 1956. It was later republished with other writings under the title of *Etudes sur le latin des chrétiens,* Rome, 1958. The passage quoted is on p. 22 of *Etudes.* See also B. Botte, 'Les anciennes versions de la Bible', in *La Maison-Dieu,* no. 53, 1958, pp. 89-109. The number of words borrowed from Greek and Hebrew by the Vulgate and the early versions 'is well over a hundred' (B. Botte, p. 93).

2. *Etudes . . .,* p. 62. Since all this is bound up with the missionary problem of the early Church in the pagan world, we may note in passing a work by the same author, published in the same compilation, which tackles the above question from a strictly missionary viewpoint: 'Le problème du vocabulaire chrétien. Expériences d'évangelisation paléochrétiennes et modernes'.

of it is at work. . . . How are we to explain that the individual Church is worthy to possess in its entirety the mystery of the universal Church, and is not merely a division or a province of it? By this fact, that in substance it is everything the universal Church is, that is to say Jesus transmitted to men.'[1]

Karl Rahner takes his stand directly on the exegesis we have followed. He asks how are we to reconcile these two well-established facts : on the one hand the primacy of the Pope's universal and immediate jurisdiction, on the other the divine institution of the episcopate which although it is not an independent power, does at least exist in its own right, and cannot therefore be done away with :

'The historical and theological answer to this question seems to lie in the fact that an individual "church" is not just an administrative district of the whole Church, but bears a unique relationship to the universal Church, one based on the nature of the Church and on her differentiation from natural territorial societies. . . . The layman in these questions will see this most clearly if he remembers that by "Church", in the New Testament, is meant both the universal and the local Church. . . . In order to develop this basic thought more systematically we can also say that the Church as a whole, where she really becomes an "event" in the full sense of the term, is necessarily a local Church. In the local Church the whole Church becomes tangible.'[2]

II. 'People'

The biblical background of the word 'Church' prompts us to a

1. J. Anger, *La Doctrine du Corps mystique de Jésus-Christ*, fourth ed., Paris, 1934 pp. 262-266. (English translation, *The Doctrine of the Mystical Body of Christ, according to the principles of the theology of St Thomas*, London, 1932, pp. 181-4.)

2. 'Primat und Episkopat', article republished in *Sendung und Gnade. Beiträge zur Pastoraltheologie*, Innsbruck, 1959 (English translation, 'The Episcopate and the Primacy', in *The Episcopate and the Primacy*, Freiburg, 1962, pp. 20-3). It appeared again, even more recently, as the first part of a work written in collaboration, K. Rahner and J. Ratzinger, *Episkopat und Primat*, Freiburg-im-Br., 1961 (English translation, *Episcopacy and the Primacy*, Edinburgh, 1962). On the same subject, it is important to see how the New Testament position, as we have explained it, differs from all the congregationalist positions. The primary thing is the community as a whole, the people of God. On this point, I cannot share the views of the Protestant J. L. Leuba, *L'institution et l'événement*, Neuchâtel, 1950, p. 93 (English translation, *New Testament Patterns*, London, 1953.

careful study of the term 'people', *laos*. The theology of the people of God, which ranges over the two Testaments, makes it possible to emphasize an essential dimension of the Church, its historical dimension. But it does not stop there.[1]

In the Septuagint, the word *laos* came in its characteristic sense to mean the people of Israel. In the New Testament, we notice a shift in meaning. Henceforth the Christian community is considered as the *laos*.

'God has looked with favour on the Gentiles (*ethne*), and chosen from among them a people (*laos*) dedicated to his name' (Acts 15:14). St James's declaration here was based on the experience of the Church since the conversion of the Roman centurion Cornelius (Acts 10). Peter's speech, which preceded James's, pointed the lesson of this missionary experience: God has given the Holy Spirit to the pagans. He has made no distinction between them and us. Why should we impose on them a yoke which God has not thought necessary? (15:8-10). From this the conclusion could be drawn that if God had made no distinction, it was because he looked on these pagans as his people. In all this the prophecy of Amos was fulfilled (9:11-12).[2]

What we are dealing with here is an absolutely revolutionary event in Jewish religious life. Despite the preparation of the prophets, *ethne* and *laos* were in diametrical opposition. Yet here was God drawing the second out of the first. Alongside Israel had appeared a new *laos* in which faith alone was the determinant. And not only converts from paganism but also those who came from the Jewish world belonged to the *laos* on the last grounds, i.e. faith. We see here a shift in the meaning of the concept *laos*, which was henceforth severed from its national and biological ties. The Christian people took over the succession from the Jewish people and on these grounds received its inheritance, without in return ensuring

1. Short bibliography: A. Vonier, *Le peuple de Dieu*, Lyons, 1943 (English translation, 'The People of God' in *Collected Works of Abbot Vonier*, London, 1952, Vol. II, pp. 137-225); A. Chavasse, 'Du Peuple de Dieu à l'Eglise du Christ' in *Maison-Dieu*, 1952, no. 32; H. Strathmann (Protestant) article 'Laos' in Kittel, vol. IV, pp. 29-57; A. Oepke (Prot.), *Das neue Gottesvolk*, Gütersloh, 1950; C. Dillenschneider, '*L'Eglise, peuple de Dieu*' (part of an article on 'Toute l'Eglise en Marie'), in *Marie et l'Eglise*, III (*Etudes mariales*, 1953, eleventh year), Paris, pp. 76-79.

2. This text had already been interpreted by the Septuagint in a more universalist sense than the Hebrew text.

its material continuation. 'I have many people in this city' God tells St Paul in a vision at Corinth (Acts 18:10; R.S.V. text). We find here the same concept of people. All future Christians coming from the pagan world (cf. 18:6) constituted this people.

The most important passage for our present purpose is two verses of the epistle to the Romans (9:25-26), which should be seen in their context. Verses 23 and 24 state the thesis: 'We are the objects of his mercy, we whom (God) has called, Jews and Gentiles alike'. Verses 25-29 provide the proof: two texts from Osee and two from Isaias. From verse 30 on, we have the conclusion. The two texts from Osee concern us indirectly. In Osee, they refer to Israel, at whom they are *directly* aimed. In the words: 'Those who were no people of mine, I will call my people', Paul sees a prophecy of the conversion of the pagans. God has transferred to the Gentiles the love with which he used to pursue Israel.

'I will be their God and they shall be my people' (II Cor. 6:16). This text, inserted into a composite quotation, is used to prove that we are the temple of the living God. It takes us back to Lev. 26:12 and Ez. 37:27: it is the formula of the covenant between God and his people. The covenant itself henceforth passes to the Christian community. This passage recalls the testament of Exodus which makes Israel the people of God.

'A people set apart for himself' (Tit. 2:14). Here we note a further advance on the texts we have already examined. Paul transfers to the Church the concept of *laos periousios,* borrowed from Ex. 19:5, 23:22 (Septuagint), Deut. 7:6, 14:2.[1] It is for God a 'special', a 'particular' people. 'I, to whom all the earth belongs, will single you out among its peoples to be my own' (Ex. 19:5). Israel had been the object of a quite special affection on the part of Jahveh. Today, the Church is the beneficiary of this affection.

'You are a chosen race, a royal priesthood, a consecrated nation, a people God means to have for himself' (I Peter 2:9). This text transfers to the Christian community, in addition to the title 'special people' on which we have just commented with reference to the preceding text, all the other honours of Israel.

In the epistle to the Hebrews (4:5, 13:12), to attribute the word

1. In his commentary on I Peter 2:9, where a similar expression occurs, E. G. Selwyn (*The First Epistle of St Peter*, London, 1955, pp. 166-167) makes very clear what this formula means: 'A people for God's own possession'.

'people' to the Church no longer raises a problem. So there is no further need for explicit justification. This was the spirit in which the author of the epistle read the Old Testament.

In a passage from the Apocalypse (18 :4) : 'Come out of her, my people', an Old Testament text which had directly designated the people of Israel (Jer. 51 :45) is given a new application to the Church. Further on, there is a new use of *laos* : 'He will dwell with them, and they will be his own people' (Apoc. 21 :3). Here the reference is to the heavenly Jerusalem considered as the people of God foretold by the prophets Zacharias and Ezechiel.[1]

We are now in a position to draw together the elements provided by this exegetical inquiry. In the Old Testament, the idea of the people of God held two components : national community and religious conformity. On the one hand was membership of an ethnical social group, founded most often on hereditary continuity, to which people usually belonged through biological links, though in exceptional cases through voluntary accession; on the other God expected from his people an attitude of faithfulness. These two aspects are conveyed in the promise of the covenant in Ex. 19 :3-5 : first, the 'race of Jacob' and 'Israel's sons' and then respect for the covenant are involved. There was to be constant tension between these two elements, which reached its climax in Osee's words : 'Call his name Not my people, for you are not my people . . .' (1 :9; R.S.V. text). The prophets put forward the reconciliation of these two elements as the object of eschatological hope, in which some part would be played by the 'nations'.

What the prophets had foretold, what the facts had shadowed forth, what there had been a tendency to forget, was completely fulfilled in the New Testament. As a social community, the people was henceforth severed from its national, ethnic and hereditary links. Its foundation was of an exclusively religious nature. If we consider the manner of its recruitment from a *physical* point of view, this people has derived from various national and ethnic communities. But all are fused in a single people, for now the religious relationship alone is *constitutive*. Only the divine act of salvation in the

1. 'I am coming to dwell in the midst of thee' (Zach. 2 :10). 'I will set up my sanctuary in their midst for ever. My tabernacle over them; they my people, and I their God' (Ezech. 37 :26-27). For a complete study, we should have also to consider the text of Luke 1 :17. The precursor's mission is to prepare a 'people' for the Lord.

mission of Jesus and in faith in him counts. Thus everything is summed up in Gal. 3:26-29 and its parallels (I Cor. 12:13, Col. 3:11). You are one in Christ: there is no more Jew, nor Greek, nor Barbarian, nor Scythian, nor circumcision, nor uncircumcision, nor slave, nor freeman, nor male, nor female. And yet in Christ you are descendants of Abraham.

Although in Christ the variety of national affinities may be transcended, it must not be concluded that St Paul intends to deny its existence on its own proper plane. It is and remains legitimate. Paul does not ask Jew to become Greek or Greek to become Jew, but that the one, like the other, should abandon his particularisms in Christ. The formula of the epistle to the Galatians (3:26-29) is clear enough: unity in Christ, which does not abolish the physiological and psychological difference between the sexes, does not do away with national or ethnical, cultural or social distinctions either.[1] Paul's message is from the Church and on the Church.

What is more, no harm can be done to the unity of the Church's community because of the variety of national affinities. Any levelling-down of nationalities was alien to Paul, but he was equally strongly opposed to a confusion of planes, to religious nationalism. That was why Paul demanded that meals (and the eucharist) should be taken in common. Here the values of communion, the values of the Church, were at stake. It was on this plane that Paul was to stand up to Peter over their difference at Antioch (Gal. 2:11-14). Paul was asking Christians of Jewish origin to make a very painful decision. For a Jew, there was never any question of eating a meal in the company of a non-Jew. A religious prescription of this kind must have become second nature to all convinced Jews. Paul would not compromise. The point was an essential one. National differences remained, but they no longer had any religious significance. 'There are no special national ways of belonging to God'.[2]

1. On this last point, see I Cor. 7:20-21.
2. H. Strathmann, in Kittel, vol. IV, p. 56. We have drawn considerably on this author for our analysis of texts and conclusions.

III. 'Body'

The idea of the Church in the New Testament was enriched by successive, complementary, contributions. It is therefore out of the question to paint a violent contrast between 'people of God' and 'Body of Christ'. That would create problems which excite the curiosity but distract the mind from its real tasks. Certain authors, while acknowledging that 'people of God' and 'Body of Christ' are the same actual reality, fancy that they can be distinguished in virtue of their relationships of container to contained, of sensible significant to spiritual signified, of outward regulation according to the generation of grace and inner regulation according to the life of grace. Though valid in themselves, these distinctions do not correspond to the biblical expressions to which they are attributed.

In the New Testament, the 'people of God' as well as the 'Body of Christ' designates the reality of a community which is *at once* exterior and interior, significant and signified. So the way in which they can be distinguished is not in terms of these categories, but rather according to two ways of illuminating that mode of unity which is proper to the Church. 'People' shows how human diversity is absorbed back into Christ, in the heart of a unity whose sole constituent is religious affinity. 'Body' reveals how sacramental unity with Christ is the source of all unity, but at the same time stresses how a new diversity, that of charisms and functions, emerges at the heart of Christian unity.

The doctrine of the Church as the body of Christ belongs to St Paul. Nevertheless, even in the captivity epistles, where it attains its final form, this doctrine remains a complex one.[1] In the epistle

1. There is a plentiful bibliography. We put first the article of P. Benoit, 'Corps, tête et plérôme dans les épîtres de la captivité', in *Revue Biblique*, 1956, vol. 56, pp. 5-44. This article quotes all the important works which had appeared up to 1955. It was republished in a collection of the writings of Father Benoit, *Exégèse et théologie*, two vols., Paris, 1961. This article will be found in vol. II, pp. 107-153. We shall also use the two books of L. Cerfaux, *The Church in the Theology of St Paul* (op.cit.) and *Le Christ dans la théologie de saint Paul*, Paris, 1951, (English translation, *Christ in the Theology of St Paul*, Edinburgh, 1959). Mgr. Cerfaux's arguments are discussed by T. Zapalena, 'Vos estis Corpus Christi, I Cor. 12:27' in *Verbum Domini*, 1959, vol. 37, pp. 79-95 and 162-170. A disciple of Cerfaux, J. Havet, examines the criticisms of T. Zapalena in 'La doctrine paulinienne du

to the Colossians, the Church is in one place the *body* of Christ (1 :24 : 'In this mortal frame of mine, I help to pay off the debt which the afflictions of Christ still leave to be paid, for the sake of his body, the Church') while in another Christ is the *head* of the body (1 :18) : 'He too is that head whose body is the Church'). The image is more homogeneous in the epistle to the Ephesians : 'He has put everything under his dominion, and made him the head to which the whole Church is joined, so that the Church is his body' (Eph. 1 :22-23).

In certain texts, Christ and the Church are, as it were, on the same plane : 'May he be glorified in the Church, and in Christ Jesus' (Eph. 3 :21); 'Those words are a high mystery, and I am applying them here to Christ and his Church' (Eph. 5 :32). Elsewhere the Church is represented as subordinated to Christ. This happens in the context where the Church appears as a wife : 'Women must owe obedience at all points to their husbands, as the Church does to Christ' (Eph. 5 :24); 'It is unheard of, that a man should bear ill-will to his own flesh and blood; no, he keeps it fed and warmed; and so it is with Christ and his Church' (Eph. 5 :29). So these texts tally with those where Christ is represented as 'head'.

The terminology is not uniform. The images are not homogeneous. One point, however, is absolutely plain; christology and ecclesiology go hand in hand, the Church is completely dependent on Christ. We might apply the familiar phrase to their relations and say that ecclesiology is nothing more than developed christology.

We should not be surprised by this unexpected succession of images. We are faced with a mystery, as St Paul explicitly states (Eph. 3 :2 ff) : 'You have heard how the mystery was made known to me by revelation, as I have written briefly. When you read this you can perceive my insight into the mystery of Christ' (R.S.V. text). St Paul is the messenger chosen to make public this mystery, which nevertheless remains beyond human reach—a revelation on

'"Corps du Christ". Essai de mise au point', in *Littérature et théologie pauliniennes* (*Recherches bibliques V*), Bruges and Paris, 1960, pp. 185-216. See further Y. Congar, 'Corps Mystique', in *Catholicisme*, vol. III. For a Protestant viewpoint, see P. Bonnard, 'L'Eglise corps du Christ dans le paulinisme', in *Rev. de théol. et de phil.*, 1958, vol. 8, pp. 268-282. Other important works used here include L. Malavez, 'L'Eglise corps du Christ. Sens et provenance de l'expression chez S. Paul', in *Science religieuse*, 1944, pp. 27-94 and J. Reuss, 'Die Kirche als "Leib Christi" und die Herkunft dieser Vorstellung bei dem Apostel Paulus', in *Biblische Zeitschrift*, 1958, vol. 2, pp. 103-127.

God's part, a mystery in the eyes of men. Hence the difficulty of approximating to the reality. 'The mystical identification leaves enough that is vague and nebulous in the concepts to dispense us from rigid conceptions with precise outlines.' To be too insistent and to emphasize too forcefully 'is to be lacking in tact and reserve with regard to formulae which, because they are *mystical,* have a right to remain unfinished'.[1] Need we add that mystical identification does not abolish separate existence? We are confronted with a mystical language which jibs at details. Doctrinal theology must provide this identification with a formulation acceptable to minds trained in philosophy and accustomed to its categories. But the place for this is not here.

The theme of the Church as the body of Christ appears as early as the great epistles. What is new in the captivity epistles is the role of Christ as head in relation to the body. 'The head does indeed appear in the exposition of I Cor. 12 :12-27, in verse 21, but with a very different value indeed : this is not Christ, the aggregate of the *soma,* but only one of the organs, no doubt more dignified but of the same order as the others, one which can argue with the feet on the usefulness of their respective functions. If we wanted to allegorize the imagery of this passage, we might say that here the head represents a governing organ in the life of the Church, the head of a community or, with a touch of anachronism, the bishop.'[2]

Which brings us to consider a two-fold equivalence : 1. The Church = Body of Christ (Col. 1 :24); 2. Christ = Head of the Church (Col. 1 :18; Eph. 1 :22, 5 :23).

1. *The Church is the Body of Christ*

Whence came the foundation of the body of Christ which is the Church? Father Benoit, in the article we have already quoted, replies : from the 'sacramental union of the body of Christians with the risen body of Christ'.[3] This holds true for the whole body of Paul's writings and therefore of epistles as early as those to the Corinthians and Romans. On this point Father Benoit differs from the view which, at the stage of the great epistles, would see no more in the

1. L. Cerfaux, *La théologie de l'Eglise selon S. Paul* (first ed.) p. 265. I have not found this text in the second edition (nor is it in the published English translation).
2. P. Benoit, *Corps* . . . p. 23.
3. *Corps* . . ., p. 43.

expression 'body of Christ' than a metaphor 'indicating the moral union of Christians with Christ and among themselves'.[1] The view which Father Benoit criticizes today was his own in the recension he earlier made of a work by A. Wikenhauser.[2]

Father Benoit thus adopts a position which had been championed principally by L. Cerfaux, and of which a brief summary will be found in the following passage: 'For it happened, in fact, that Christians actually did have a human (and sacred) body which was for them the source of a real, supra-physical unity. This was Christ's body, which they received sacramentally in the eucharist, in which they were allowed to participate because they were baptized. Thus Christian unity, realized in the Church, was specially bound up with their sharing in Christ's body.'[3] This view has today been widely adopted by many authors.[4]

This doctrine of the Church as the body of Christ falls into a well-defined framework of ideas concerning the physical realism of our union with Christ. That is one of Paul's basic ideas: he expresses it in his frequent formula, *en Christo*. But how is this union effected? By faith and baptism, two things as inseparable as mind and body in man. Chapter 6 of the epistle to the Romans (1-11) bears witness to the profound and *realistic* conception Paul had of baptism as a means of union with Christ. 'At the root of this key passage is a *conception of salvation whose physical realism* our modern way of thinking is too prone to water down'.[5] The anthropological monism characteristic of Semitic and Biblical thinking leads to the assertion that sin represents not only the death of the soul, but of the body too. It follows logically that return to life by salvation demands the restoration of human integrity through the return to life of the body itself. This doctrine should be compared with that of Greek dualism, taken up by the gnostics, which sees salvation in the liberation of the soul from the tangible and evil matter of the body.

It is immediately obvious how Christ's resurrection and union with his glorious body have the decisive role to play in this salva-

1. *Corps . . .*, p. 6.
2. A. Wikenhauser, *Die Kirche als der mystische Leib nach dem Apostel Paulus*, Münster Westf., 1937. Used by P. Benoit in *Revue Biblique*, 1938, vol. 47, pp. 115-119.
3. L. Cerfaux, *Christ in the Theology of St Paul*, *op. cit.*, p. 351.
4. J. Havet gives an impressive list in *La doctrine . . .*, p. 187.
5. P. Benoit, *Corps . . .*, p. 8.

tion which extends to the body. Belief in genuine immortality is only affirmed if we approach it by way of the resurrection of the body. What is more, the way of salvation was only thrown open when life was restored to Christ's body; life was restored to him by the gift of the Spirit at the moment of his resurrection (Rom. 1 :4). Henceforth the body of Christ, spiritual and life-giving (I Cor. 15 :44 ff.), is the bearer of the regenerated life of salvation. It is by uniting with him, in his body, that the Christian will be clothed in the image of the heavenly man : the risen Christ (I Cor. 15 :49). There lies the meaning of the rite of baptism : physical and sacramental union of the body of the Christian with the body of Christ in death and resurrection.

In another study,[1] Father Benoit stated more explicitly this essential teaching on the physical realism of salvation. Here are a few excerpts :

> 'The Word did not take a human body *merely to communicate* with men on their own level of sense experience but also, and primarily, to *take over* man entire, body and soul, and totally to recreate him, body and soul . . . When he communicates his life to his faithful, then, it is their body and soul alike that he joins to himself in order to refashion them. He puts his body and soul alike in contact with theirs so that they may share his 'passover' from death to life. . . . Salvation works through faith and through the sacraments of faith : faith alone would have been enough for disembodied spirits; the sacraments of faith are necessary to reach, at its own level, the body which contains the soul. Note that this is something quite different from that means of expression . . . which enlightens the mind by making use of the understanding of the senses. Here it is a question, short and simple, of making life new, recreated, pure, flow from the risen body of Christ into the contaminated flesh of the sinner. *This demands a contact quite different from a spiritual contact: a bodily contact, belonging to the physical order, which works according to its own laws,* (our italics).

Concurring with a finding of Mgr Cerfaux, Benoit adds :

1. 'Les recits de l'institution et leur portée' in *Lumière et Vie*, Feb. 1957, no. 31. The passages quoted appear on pp. 67-69. This article was republished in the collection *Exégèse et theologie*, by P. Benoit, Paris, 1961, vol. I, pp. 210-239. (English translation, 'The accounts of the institution and what they imply', in *The Eucharist in the New Testament*, London, 1964. The passages quoted are on pp. 87-88.)

'Such a contact eludes rational appraisal by the intelligence : it is experienced rather than defined.'

So we have found a formulation in terms of biblical theology of what we express in doctrinal theology by the theme of the physical instrumentality of the humanity of Christ (a Greek theological theme taken up by mediaeval thinking) and by the physical causality of the sacraments. In order to grasp exactly what Benoit means by 'physical' realism, we must remember the meaning of the word 'physical' both in the language of theology and in current contemporary parlance. In the language of theology, physical causality is that of the efficient cause properly so called, the cause which is an agent; this cause is distinguished from the moral cause, which is of the order of finality, and which acts by presenting a good as an end to be pursued, either by advice, invitation, precept or threat. In common parlance, 'physical' as opposed to 'moral' means what appertains to matter—physical excitation or physical pleasure. The technical terminology of theology has also found a certain echo in contemporary parlance, in the sense that 'physical' means 'effective' or 'real', as in 'this is a physical impossibility'.

The theology of the body of Christ in the great epistles is contained in four capital passages.

(a). 'Have you never been told that your bodies belong to the body of Christ? And am I to take what belongs to Christ and make it one with a harlot? God forbid' (I Cor. 6 :15). In warning against fornication, St Paul reminds the Christian that his body is sacred. The context makes clear both the origin and the realism of this expression. Our bodies have been ransomed by Christ, an allusion to his death with which we have communion (I Cor. 7 :23, Gal. 3 :13, 4 :5); they participate in the resurrection of Jesus, the certain pledge of which is the presence of the *pneuma* that sanctifies (cf. Rom. 8 :11-23). The union in question is very real and physical, since it is compared to sexual union. The formula 'one spirit' (I Cor. 6 :17) does nothing to diminish the realism of thought. The logical conclusion in the context should be : the man who unites himself to the Lord becomes one body with him. Paul uses the word 'spirit' here, solely because he has just used the word 'body' in connection with sin. But the meaning remains clear : we are a single body with the Lord. Father Benoit has no difficulty in showing that this 'Spirit' is not disincarnate. 'This is the spirit which gives life to the spiritual body of Christ, and through him the body of the regenerated Christian' (I Cor. 15:44-49).[1]

I should like to stress the importance of this text for the interpretation of the Pauline doctrine of the body of Christ. Dom O. Casel had previously noted that the image of marriage is one of the principal components of the theme of the Church as a body.[2] In his view, the key to the exegesis of our passages lies in a comparison with Gen. 2:24: 'The two become one flesh'. Read in this light, the text of Eph. 5:22-32 is very illuminating on St Paul's whole thinking on this subject. Casel's suggestion has been verified, confirmed and cleverly developed in two articles by Father A. M. Dubarle.[3]

(b) 'We have a cup that we bless; is not this cup we bless a participation in Christ's blood? Is not the bread we break a participation in Christ's *body*? The one bread makes us one body, though we are many in number; the same bread is shared by all' (I Cor. 10:16-17). Paul shows that it is an act of apostasy to take part in the ritual meals that accompany pagan sacrifices. V. 17 makes his realism perfectly clear: 'The one bread makes us one body'. According to Benoit and Cerfaux, the word 'body' is not simply an image to evoke collective unity in Christ. The word *soma* cannot mean in verse 17 something different from what it meant in the preceding verse: 'The inference from one verse to the other is noteworthy: when they receive into their bodies, by the sacramental rite, the body of Christ, they "are", all together, one body, that is to say this body, individual to start with, yet assumes into itself all the bodies of those whom it unites'.[4] J. Reuss considers this interpretation put forward by Benoit 'more likely' than others. In summing it up, he ends by quoting a phrase from Wikenhauser: 'Christians eat this bread in which the "spiritual" Christ is present; for this reason they become one body, that is to say the body of Christ'.[5]

Personally, I am not entirely convinced that the word *soma* in

1. *Corps* . . ., p. 13.
2. *Jahrbuch für Liturgiewissenschaft*, 1935, vol. 13, pp. 290-291.
3. 'Les fondements bibliques du titre marial de nouvelle Eve', in *RSR*, 1951-1952, vols. 39-40, *Mélanges Lebreton*, pp. 49-64; 'La conception de l'homme dans l'Ancien Testament', in *Sacra Pagina, Miscellanea biblica Congressus internationalis catholici de re biblica*, Gembloux, 1959, vol. I, pp. 522-536. In the first article particular attention should be paid to pp. 52-55, in the second to pp. 529ff.
4. P. Benoit, *Corps* . . ., p. 14.
5. A. Wikenhauser, *Die Kirche* . . ., p. 108.

verse 17 must be understood in the individual sense. I would postulate a transition from the individual sense (of verse 16) to the collective sense through the medium of *koinonia.* I should be inclined to present matters in the following equation: the body (which we make, v. 17) = communion in Christ's body (v. 16). It is the word 'communion' that permits this widening of meaning, while retaining its unique reference to the individual, sacramental body of Christ.[1] In this way we remain within the bounds of a strictly realistic, physical exegesis, while eluding the difficulties of the interpretation put forward by Benoit and Cerfaux. How can we be the *individual* body of Christ? It should be noted that this explanation, which I advance with reservations, maintains the general line of Benoit's exposition. We do not look for the justification of the collective sense in the theme of moral solidarity.

Cerfaux's philological argument remains. In the language of the day, the word *soma* could not carry the sense of a moral body, of society. That meaning was only to develop much later. 'In all the hellenic texts where the comparison with the human body is made, even though the comparative particle is often enough omitted, this comparison is always understood and the metaphor always remains a discernible metaphor'.[2] We will confine ourselves here to noting that Father S. Lyonnet is of a different opinion. In a note in an exegetical review, he quotes a text of the period where the word *soma* is incontestably taken in the collective sense.[3]

In a recent work, J. de Fraine has discussed this philological argument. Back in 1936, T. W. Manson had drawn attention to the expression *Hellenon somati,* the class of Hellenes, in an edict of Augustus. In his view, one cannot say that *soma* was never used by pre-Christian authors in the sense of corporate body or society. De Fraine concludes his inquiry by saying: 'Even had we to admit that *soma* in its *profane* sense is never 'social body', we should in any case remember the fact that the idea of the collective body was com-

1. In *koinonia,* as the word is employed here, the 'horizontal' relation is only a secondary sense, the primary sense being participation. But it is a real sense. See A. R. George, *Communion with God in the New Testament*, London, 1953, p. 172.

2. L. Cerfaux, *Théologie . . .*, first ed., p. 220. This idea has been considerably developed in the second ed., pp. 208-210.

3. Cicero used the word in Greek to designate the collection of his oratorical works which he sent up to Atticus. *Biblica*, 1951, vol. 32, p. 285.

pletely general in Judaism. In the eyes of Jahveh, the people of Israel always remained a single person'.[1]

(c) 'A man's body is all one, though it has a number of different organs; and all this multitude of organs goes to make up one body; so it is with Christ'. This verse opens that great passage in which St Paul deals with the body of Christ in connection with spiritual gifts (I Cor. 12 :12-27). If we are to grasp the thought of the present passage aright, we must bear in mind the exegesis of the first two. We know that for a long time people sought to explain the dissertation on the charisms along the lines of classical allegory.[2] This explanation can no longer be admitted once it is realized that *St Paul already possessed* a doctrine of the 'Body of Christ'. 'He knew and he had already said that Christians are all united with the risen body of Christ and form only one body with him'.[3] But if Paul was here using allegory in order to illustrate a major conviction of his faith and of his theology, that was because this beautiful metaphor was well suited to *show the consequence of a conviction he had already acquired*. The allegory lays an opportune stress not only on the union of Christians with Christ, but *with each other*.

Sacramental realism finds expression in the various parts of verse 13. Baptism has plunged us into one and the same body. We have all been given to drink of one Spirit. Is this a second allusion to baptism? Benoit thinks rather that this 'drink' evokes another great rite of incorporation, the eucharist. Comparison with I Cor. 10 :3 is illuminating : there the subject is the types of the Old Testament and there too baptism and spiritual feeding follow each other, as in chapter 12.[4] Starting from verse 14 of chapter 12, St Paul methodically applies the profane metaphor to the theme we have just outlined. When he concludes the passage, in verse 27, the Apostle does not simply bring to a close the drawing out of the allegory—for that, it would have sufficed to say : 'You form one body in Christ'—but returns to the major theme by saying : 'You are the body of Christ'.

(d) The key to the interpretation of Rom. 12 :3-8 lies in its depen-

1. J. de Fraine, *Adam et son lignage*, Bruges and Paris, 1959, p. 206. See also the whole context.
2. On this allegory and the part it has played in the biblical theology of the body of Christ, see *Corps* . . ., p. 5-6; J. Dupont, *Gnosis*, Louvain, 1949, pp. 427-438.
3. P. Benoit, *Corps* . . ., p. 14.
4. P. Benoit, *Corps* . . ., p. 15.

dent relationship to the more explicit passage we have just been discussing. 'We form one body in Christ' (12:5) might very well suggest nothing more than a community united with Christ by a moral link. But when we consider that this passage was written shortly after I Cor.; that its context is in the same train of thought, i.e. the diversity of charisms; and that the brief recall of the classical allegory can only be the summary of the more explicit dissertation of I Cor., then there can be no further justification for isolating this text. What is more, the formula *en Christo* in St Paul conveys a very pronounced meaning, which is far more than a moral link. It sums up the whole system of our union with Christ with the utmost realism.

This survey of the great epistles has enabled us to make the following points:

1. That the theology of the body of Christ in these writings must be explained in terms of physical reality, and not solely of moral solidarity. This physical realism, apparent in the captivity epistles, is present also in the ecclesiology of I Cor. and of Rom.

2. That this interpretation is based (a) on St Paul's faith in the death and resurrection of Christ as a source of salvation for the faithful who join themselves to him; (b) on the anthropological monism of biblical thinking, which leads to a 'bodily' conception of salvation.

The theme we have just expounded gains fresh prominence in the captivity epistles. We shall say very little about them, for we shall be returning to them soon. In these epistles, the theme does not merely crop up occasionally, but occupies a central place. It designates the group of the saved.[1] What is there in these texts which is radically new? The body of Christ is personified to a greater extent and is more clearly distinguished from the individual Christ (the role of *kephale*). But for all that, we still find in them the physical and sacramental union of Christians with the risen body of Christ. Exegetes as a whole see ontological and not merely moral union in these writings.

As to the great epistles, we have already emphasized the importance of Rom. 6:1-11, which shows us how deep and realistic was the conception Paul had formed of baptism as a means of union with Christ, and with his death and his resurrection. The expression 'body of Christ' is not yet used; but the theme has already been stated. The same is true of Col. 2:11-13. It is interesting to note the paral-

1. P. Benoit, *Corps . . .*, p. 19.

lelism with Romans, since this shows that we are in the same mental context. In the baptismal union, the Christian divests himself completely of his fleshly body and is 'buried with him', 'united with his burial, united too with his resurrection' by the faith that gives the physical rite its saving value in union with Christ.

'The very condition of your calling as members of a single body' (Col. 3 :15). 'Both sides, united in a single body, he would reconcile to God through his cross, inflicting death, in his own person, upon the feud' (Eph. 2 :16). The setting of the second text is particularly illuminating. This single body is not just a moral or social body, but first of all and above all the body of Christ, in which hate has been killed. In his flesh Christ has done away with hate (2 :14).

In Eph. 4 :4-6 the major themes are taken up again. 'You are one body, with a single Spirit; each of you, when he was called, called in the same hope; with the same Lord, the same faith, the same baptism; with the same God, the same Father, all of us, who is above all things, pervades all things and lives in all of us.' Let us stress, for a start, the strongly baptismal character of this beautiful passage. One single God is at the summit; as means of access to him, there is the same Lord; we are linked to him by the same faith, the same baptism; to advance in this direction as one body, with a single Spirit. We should detract from the full significance and the cohesion of this text if we saw no more in the word 'body' than the purely moral reality we have already eliminated. What is involved in fact is at once the individual body of Christ and the body constituted by Christians. 'It is the two together, indissolubly linked : the individual body of Christ augmented by all the Christians who are dependent on him, in their very bodies, through faith and baptism; the Spirit flowing into the individual body of Christ and through him all the members of his great body.'[1] We will deal with the other texts on the 'body' in the next section. In each of them, the image of 'body' is more or less linked with that of 'head'.

2. *Christ is the head of the Church*

In order to set the problem in a wider context, I should like to start by citing two passages from an important work. 'The New Testament expresses . . . the relationship existing between Christ and the Church along two lines which, it must be added, do not diverge.

1. P. Benoit, *Corps . . .*, p. 21.

The synoptic gospels represent the relationship of Christ to his disciples as being first and foremost one of authority or power. St John shows him establishing between himself and his followers a relationship of mystical identity (chapter 15). These relationships are united in the ideas of bride and of body of which Paul is fond. The apostle on one hand represents the Church as the Body of Christ, having a mystical, that is to say a spiritual and hidden head or chief of this body, Lord of the Church.' In a note, the authors specify the theme we take as the object of our discussion : 'The idea of *Kephale* in its application to Christ is not introduced by Paul as an elaboration of the comparison of the body, as if Christ were, *in the complete body,* what the head is in our organism. It is dependent thematically on another context and another concern : to assert that Christ is *above* the Church, *above* the Powers.'[1]

What are the possible meanings of *Kephale* in St Paul? Besides the usual physiological sense—the head as part of the body—*Kephale* may have a hierarchical sense : chief, authority, first, principal. We have only to refer to I Cor. 11 :3-10. This hierarchical meaning is also to be found in the captivity epistles. To appreciate this, we have only to compare Eph. 5 :23 and I Cor. 11 :3 : 'The head to which a woman is united is her husband,' and to refer to Col. 2 :10, where Christ is portrayed as the fountain head from which all dominion and power proceed. Within the physiological sense, closer scrutiny of the role of the head in relation to the body led to the emergence of the idea of vital principle. According to Benoit, the hierarchical sense is biblical, whereas the vital principle sense is hellenic.

Did one meaning evolve from the other? Benoit believes that we can find a transition from the hierarchical sense to the vital principle sense. The investigations of J. Dupont[2] and Schlier[3] have shown that in the Semitic and particularly in the biblical world the first is the normal sense of the word. 'It thus seems *a priori* probable that this term was first accepted in the same sense when it appeared in the captivity epistles.'[4] Benoit thinks he can demonstrate this *a posteriori*. This evolution is of completely secondary

1. Extract from an article entitled 'La Seigneurie du Christ sur l'Eglise et sur le monde', by a group of theologians of the 'Catholic conference on ecumenical questions', published in *Istina*, April 1959, vol. 9: see pp. 139-150.
2. *Gnosis*, pp. 446 ff.
3. In Kittel, vol. III, pp. 674ff.
4. P. Benoit, *Corps* . . ., p. 25.

importance in my view. What matters is to distinguish the different doctrinal implications of the word 'head'.

Let us arrange the texts according to their meaning. The political or hierarchical sense seems obvious in Col. 2 :10 and Eph. 5 :23. I think it probable in Col. 1 :10 and Eph. 1 :22. From the physiological angle, the sense of vital principle is vouched for in Col. 2 :19 and Eph. 4 :16.[1] Certain Catholic exegetes, however, maintain that only the text of Eph. 4 :16 carries the sense of vital principle.

Why should Christ have been represented with such insistence as head, and particularly in the hierarchical sense? Paul was led to do so by circumstances. In Colossae, the danger lay in speculations which attributed to the powers governing the universe a role calculated to compromise the supremacy of Christ. Paul was thus led 'to assert more vigorously the celestial residence of the glorified Christ, *above* all the cosmic and celestial powers whose importance the Colossian doctors wished to over-rate'.[2]

We have drawn attention to the Semitic origin of the political or hierarchical meaning. What is the origin of the other meaning? Following Lightfoot and Dupont, Benoit thinks that we can detect here an echo of the teaching of doctors like Hippocrates or Galen 'who sought in "*egkephalon*" *the source of the nerve impulses which control all the organs*'.[3] This connotation was not stressed by Semitic thought, which regarded the heart instead as the seat of life. Aristotle himself considered the heart as the seat of sensations. In Plato and the Stoics, the role of the head was better understood. In the sense of vital principle, the head played a new role, 'no longer only of control, but of animation: (from it) there flowed out through joints and ligaments the vital impulse which supplied the

1. *Corps . . .*, p. 27. See by way of comparison the viewpoint of an Anglican theologian. Writing on 'The Meaning of *Kephale* in the Pauline epistles', in the *Journal of Theological Studies*, 1954, pp. 211-215, S. Bedale maintains that in *all* the texts of the captivity epistles, the *principal* if not the exclusive sense is that of 'first', 'beginning'. Therefore there is nothing remarkable about the meaning of Col. 2:19 and Eph. 4:16. The only concession the author makes is the following: 'Of course it seems hardly possible that St Paul could use "Kephale" in the immediate context of "Soma" without any conscious reference at all to the anatomical image thereby evoked. It is suggested, rather, that there is something in the nature of a *double-entente* in his use of these passages' (p. 214). In that case the sense of vital principle would not be explicit; it is simply an implied allusion to it.

2. P. Benoit, *Corps . . .*, p. 23.

3. *Corps . . .*, p. 27.

body with energy, ensured its cohesion and produced in its harmonious growth'.[1]

The synthesis is arrived at in the epistle to the Ephesians (5 :22-32).[2] Here we find a fusion of the themes we have noted in St Paul : the Church as body of Christ, Christ as head. The basic concept of the 'body of Christ' and historically the first is to be found in verses 30 : We are limbs of his body; 26 : this incorporation is brought about by baptism; 23 : it is the body that Christ has saved. The idea of 'head' is used here in its twofold meaning. First comes that of superiority : 'Christ is head of the Church ... The Church owes obedience to Christ' (vv. 23-24). Then comes that of close union; nevertheless St Paul does not have recourse to the term 'head' but to the perhaps even stronger image of the relationship between husband and wife (vv. 25, 29).[3]

Cerfaux comments : 'The metaphor of the head came to superimpose itself on the image of the Church as body; it did not mingle with that image to the point of transforming it. The body of Christ with which the Church is mystically identified remains his real and complete body (without distinction or opposition between head and members).'[4] 'Yet St Paul avoids thinking of the body as opposed to the head, in terms of a trunk alone, for he still speaks of "the whole body". The imagination must not form the outline of a well-defined image.'[5] Benoit is of a different opinion, and uses weighty arguments : 'It is difficult not to perceive in Col. 2 :19 and Eph. 4 :16 an echo of the psychology of which Paul had been told, perhaps by the "beloved physician" (Col. 4 :14) ... Thus was effected the combination of the theme of the head (of the Powers) with the theme of the Body of Christ, and it is a very happy adaptation.'[6] The notion of head, understood exclusively in the sense of supremacy, might have injected the idea of a separation between Christ and the Church; on the other hand, the close union of Christians with Christ might have been wrongly understood in the sense of an absolute identity. The blending of the two images into a single one safe-

1. *Corps* . . ., p. 27
2. Cf. P. Benoit, *Corps*, p. 28; J. Reuss, *Die Kirche* . . ., p. 126.
3. See on this point the articles of A. M. Dubarle already quoted on p.55, note 3 above.
4. *La théologie* . . ., first ed., p. 307.
5. *The Church in the Theology of St Paul*, p. 335.
6. *Corps* . . ., p. 27.

guards at once the ideas of superiority and of vital contact.

A Protestant exegete has attempted to formulate Protestant objections to Catholic biblical theology of the body of Christ. 'Roman Catholic doctrine and pastoral teaching,' he says, 'tend inexorably towards a confusion of the head and the body . . . It is not possible, on the basis of the biblical texts, to transfer to the body the perfections of the head'.[1] 'Catholic thinking is here the prisoner of an implacable logic which, in one way or another, leads to the transfer to the Church of the "glory" which belongs only to Christ, and, according to I Cor. 15, to those who are risen with him.'[2] 'While, in Paul, the theme of the Church as the body of Christ is always used to glorify Christ or to exhort the faithful, in the Catholic interpretation, it is used to exalt the Church.'[3] According to Bonnard, the New Testament position is : 'The body of the Church is attached to the head for ever, but it is a recalcitrant body.'[4] I do not think that the line we have taken here and that of the authors we have followed deserves this reproach. The idea of head implies supremacy, and consequently *transcendence*. There can thus be no question of purely and simply assimilating the body to the head, while we admit that all the body has of value it owes to the head. Moreover there is no exaltation of the Church which is not purely Christological.

A biblical image cannot exhaust the reality of the Church : we have just seen how the image of 'body' complemented the idea of 'people'. We are far from sharing the view of Father Koster. 'People' and 'body' are not contrasted with each other as external reality and spiritual reality; there is no question of any dialectic of the social and the mystical. As we recalled at the start of this third section these are simply two complementary ways of representing the unity of the Church. A complete panorama would demand a consideration of a whole series of further metaphysical designations. The Church is not only the people of God and the body of Christ, but the flock, the plantation of God, the vine, the temple, the city, the Kingdom, the virgin (wife, woman and mother) etc. All these metaphors complete each other, partly overlap and mutually enrich

1. P. Bonnard, *L'Eglise corps . . .*, p. 269.
2. *L'Eglise corps . . .*, p. 280.
3. *L'Eglise corps . . .*, p. 282.
4. *L'Eglise corps . . .*, p. 269.

each other. Here, we have taken into account only those that are most important for our purpose. It still remains for us, however, briefly to consider the relation of the Church with the Kingdom.

IV. A Point of Reference: The 'Kingdom'

The Church is not identical with the Kingdom, although it is uniform with it. So there is no need for us to discuss the Kingdom in detail. Nevertheless, the Church cannot be understood except in terms of this Kingdom. We shall content ourselves here with setting out schematically the essential data from the whole of the New Testament.[1]

The power of admitting people to the Kingdom or of barring them from it has been entrusted to the Church: Matt. 16:18-20.[2] The same truth, less explicitly stated, is to be found elsewhere.[3] Must we distinguish between the Kingship of Christ and the Kingdom of God? We should note in passing that Kingship summons up first and foremost the exercise of power (reign), whereas Kingdom presupposes the coming into being of a people. The difference of meaning is however minimal in the present context. Most of the time the verbal distinction between a Kingdom of the Son of Man and a Kingdom of God has no correspondence to a real distinction. There are nevertheless signs of differentiation in Matt. 13:41, 43.

In St Paul, the distinction is clear. The Kingship (Kingdom) of Christ is a present reality to which the members of the Church belong. As from now, we are 'transferred to the kingdom of his beloved

1. Short bibliography: Y. Congar, 'Royaume, Eglise et Monde' in *Recherches et débats*, July 1951, pp. 2-42; the collective article 'La Seigneurie du Christ', already referred to; J. Mulders, 'De Verhouding Rijk Gods kerk in de katholieke theologie', in *Katholiek Archief*, July 1957, cols. 709-728 (this is an excellent publication); David M. Stanley, 'Kingdom to Church: The Structural Development of the Apostolic Christianity in the New Testament', in *Theological Studies*, 1955, vol. 16, pp. 1-29; R. Schnackenburg, *Gottes Herrschaft und Reich*, Freiburg, 1959 (English translation, *God's Rule and Kingdom*, Edinburgh, 1963); see also the summary of a lecture by the same author, 'Kirche und Reich Gottes', in *Una Sancta*, April 1957, pp. 42 ff. For the kingdom of God parables, cf. C. H. Dodd (Prot), *Parables of the Kingdom*, London, 1935.

2. See also Matt. 18:18.

3. Luke 12:32: 'Do not be afraid, my little flock. Your Father has determined to give you his kingdom'; 22:29: 'As my Father has allotted a kingdom to me, so I allot to you a place to eat and drink at my table in my kingdom'. See Matt. 28:18-20.

son' (Col. 1:13).[1] What should we take this to mean? By his resurrection, Christ has been enthroned by God as Lord. Through him, the rule of God is exercised now, in this era. Though still hidden in heaven (Col. 3:1-4), Christ has already subjected the world of spirits to himself; he exercises his power over the whole universe. Nevertheless, the Church is at the heart of the sovereignty of Christ; she is the special field of action for his abundant graces, his efficacious organ. Christ is head of the universe and of the Church. But the Church alone is the body of Christ, and his pleroma.

The relationship between the present reign of Christ and the future divine reign is to be seen in I Cor. 15:24-28. The Kingship of Christ described by St Paul has an aspect of struggle, of a victory to be rounded off and to be revealed. After having dispossessed every other sort of rule, authority and power, Christ must still overthrow death, the last enemy. At the moment of the parousia and the resurrection of the dead, Christ will hand over the Kingdom to the Father.

It is desirable for us too to follow the usage of the early Church and to distinguish, without separating the two, between the present Kingship of Christ and the Kingdom of God in its complete manifestation. The two concepts cover the same objective content. The difference between them is of a temporal nature. It should be noted, however, that God reigns, even now, in Christ, and that the Kingdom of Jesus will never have an end (Luke 1:33).

What is the most suitable phrase we can find to express the relationship of the Church with the Kingdom? Some of the authors quoted by Professor Schnackenburg see the Church as the 'bearer' (*Trägerin*) of the Kingdom (Meinertz), some as the 'present form' (*Jetzgestalt*) of the Kingdom (E. Walter).[2] For Schnackenburg, along with a number of other exegetes, the dynamic formulae carry the day: there is, as it were, an irruption of the powers and the good things of the future era into the Church and, through the Church, into the world. In short, we are faced with realities united yet in tension, for which no entirely satisfactory phrase has yet been found. The realities of salvation are present in the Church, but they have not yet attained their eschatological dimensions. The Church's condition is still that of a pilgrim. A passage from the *Didache* conveys this tension: 'Remember, Lord, thy Church, to deliver it from evil

1. See also Eph. 1:20-23; 2:5-6; 4:11-16.
2. See the summary of his lecture.

and perfect it in thy love. Gather it together from the four winds, this hallowed Church, into thy kingdom that thou hast prepared for it' (10, 5).

Two other formulae to express the relationship between the Church and the Kingdom deserve mention. Braun[1] sees as it were a perichoresis, a reciprocal interpenetration between the two : 'The Church is the Kingdom insofar as it is possessed here below with the force of the Kingdom, insofar as, with all its being, it strives towards the glorious and final Kingdom of the ages to come.' In the same way the Kingdom is the Church : its virtue, in the form of grace and of eternal life, is active principally in the Christian community. As Mulders sees it : 'The Church is . . . the *sacrament* of the kingdom on earth. The kingdom is present in it as is the grace of God in the sacraments. . . . The aim of the Church is to render sacramentally present on earth the single kingdom of God, expressed in the signs adapted to the time between the resurrection of Christ and the parousia.'[2]

The direction the inquiry on which we have been engaged in these first two chapters, and which we shall continue in the remainder of the book, is clear : to determine what is the nature of the Church. We shall do this by means of a critical examination of the definition of the Church. The criteriological principles that we shall use must be supplied to us by theology, *intellectus fidei,* which is founded on the *auditus fidei,* revelation and the magisterium. With this end in view, we began with the most important pronouncement of the magisterium : *Mystici corporis.* We then turned to Scripture, source of the magisterium, which is *proxima et universalis veritatis norma,*[3] to make a comparison. From this two things should emerge : 1. The manifestation of the conformity of the magisterium with Scripture; 2. an enrichment of our knowledge of the Church, for the magisterium has not said everything and is not able to say everything.[4]

Countering the ecclesiological trends which insist with one-sided emphasis on the mystical and inner unity of the Church, *Mystici Corporis* set out to give a fair place to visibility. The mystical body

1. F. Braun, *Aspects nouveaux . . .*, p. 166.
2. J. Mulders, *De Verhouding . . .*, col. 722.
3. Denz., 2313
4. Denz., 2314.

is concrete and perceptible to the senses. Its organic, hierarchical and sacramental character follow from this.

In Scripture, we found behind the word 'Church' the people of God in its entirety and the manifestation of this people in a particular place. The gain was twofold : the discovery of a type of unity peculiar to the Church—the part as the presence of the whole—and the fact that behind the word 'Church' lies the theme of the 'People',

The Church is the real 'people of God', foretold by Osee, a people henceforth constituted exclusively by the religious link of faith. The term 'people of God' brings clearly to the fore the historical dimension of the Church : its uninterrupted continuity with the Old Testament, in a homogeneity which is still there despite the rupture. This concept is therefore particularly suited to account for eschatological tension. The Church is the 'Body of Christ', the result of the sacramental union of Christians with the risen body of Jesus. For the Church, the kingdom is an end and a goal. The values of the kingdom are already present in her and aspire to their fulfilment.

In the New Testament, each of the designations of the Church has its own shade of meaning. No theology can be exclusive in this field. 'It is impossible to construct a theology of the Church starting solely from the ideas of body, of wife, of people, of temple or of kingdom, for no image exhausts the reality of the Church as a whole.'[1] To be sure, theology may lean more heavily on one or another of these images. But it will then have to try and incorporate in the doctrinal elaboration of one theme the essential data of the others. We shall now investigate the theology of St Thomas Aquinas and inquire how he understood the Church in his reflection on the datum of faith.

1. G. Thils, *Orientations de la théologie*, Louvain, 1958, p. 96.

III

ST THOMAS, THEOLOGIAN OF THE MYSTICAL BODY

We are now approaching a key point. Was St Thomas, when he discussed the mystical body, a completely faithful interpreter of Scripture? Did he weigh equally all aspects, including the sociological, of the mystical body? And is St Thomas able to shed light on our search for a definition of the Church and our examination of what form its sociability takes and what its principle of coherence and unity is? These very questions lead us to the further question of the relationships between St Thomas's teaching and that of the magisterium in *Mystici Corporis.*

I. Origin of the Expression 'Mystical Body' to Designate the Church[1]

The Fathers remained faithful to the biblical vocabulary. They talk of the 'body of Christ', which is the Church. A ninth century author, John Scotus Erigena, was to call the Church *corpus spirituale;* but despite the similarity between the meaning of the two terms, he does not go so far as to talk of *corpus mysticum.* 'This last expression does not appear in any author of Christian antiquity

1. Bibliography: H. de Lubac, *Corpus Mysticum. L'eucharistie et l'Église au moyen âge*, Paris, 1944 (except where indicated, quotations are from first ed.; second ed., 1949), *Catholicisme. Les Aspects sociaux du dogme*, Paris, fourth ed., 1947 (English translation, *Catholicism*, London, 1950), *Méditation sur l'Eglise*, Paris, 1953 (English translation, *The Splendour of the Church*, London, 1956); F. Holböck, *Der eucharistische und der mystische Leib Christi in ihren Beziehungen zu einander nach der Lehre der Frühscholastik*, Rome, 1941. On this last work, as on the first de Lubac referred to, see a review by Y. Congar in *RSPT*, 1947, p. 83 ff.; F. Malmberg, *Een Lichaam . . .*, pp. 72-76.

nor of the early middle ages.'[1] In the long discussion aroused by Paschase Radbert's treatise *De Corpore et sanguine Domini,* published in 844, 'the *corpus* par excellence, the one which first sprang to mind and which it was not necessary to designate in any other way was the Church'.[2]

Corpus mysticum, on the contrary, was used for a fairly long time of the eucharistic body 'in contrast to *corpus Christi quod est Ecclesia,* which was pre-eminently the *verum corpus.* Was it not indeed completely natural to describe as "mystical" this body whose hidden presence was due to the "mystical prayer" and which the faithful received in a "mystical banquet"? This body, offered under species which "mystically" signified the Church?'[3]

We will find nothing to surprise us in this if we recall the early use of the word 'mystical'. In the common Christian tradition, in the liturgy and in theological works, 'everything which has to do with the mystery of the altar is copiously and almost indifferently described as mystical. Nothing therefore could seem more normal.'[4] In the second half of the twelfth century, the Church began to be called *corpus mysticum,* and the usage was to spread quite rapidly.[5]

What was the reason for this inversion of the two formulae? It resulted from the controversy against Berengarius (1000-1088). Since the end of the patristic period (St Isidore), theological thought had ranged side by side the three realities which the Bible designates by the name of the 'body of Christ': the body born of Mary, the eucharistic body and the Church. This threefold use had been regarded as three ways of understanding the single body of Christ: 'Three forms of which the first led through the second to the third: the last, since it designated what was aimed at and procured by the other two, received the name *corpus verum,* whereas the eucharistic reality received that of *sacramentum corporis,* or again of *corpus*

1. H. de Lubac, *Corpus mysticum,* p. 12.
2. H. de Lubac, *Corpus mysticum,* p. 29.
3. H. de Lubac, *Catholicisme,* p. 73.
4. H. de Lubac, *Corpus mysticum,* p. 45. On the three senses of the adjective, see L. Bouyer, ' "Mystique". Essai sur l'histoire d'un mot', in *La Vie Spirituelle,* Supplement no. 9, 15 May 1949, pp. 1-23.
5. In the *Tractatus de sacramentis* of a certain Master Simon, between 1145 and 1160, we read: ' In sacramento altaris duo sunt: id est, corpus Christi verum, et quod per illud significatur: corpus ejus mysticum, quod est Ecclesia' (quoted in H. de Lubac, *Corpus myst.,* p. 120).

mysticum.'[1] We find a similar expression of this sacramentarian synthesis, in line with the ontological symbolism of the Fathers, in such an author as Guillaume de Saint-Thierry, who died about 1148.[2]

This sacramentary synthesis became the object of dialectic onslaught. When attacked by Berengarius, it fell to pieces. 'On the one hand, a real body—earthly or heavenly—which could only be understood *sensualiter;* on the other, a spiritual body. . . . On the one hand, the idea of a substantial presence, which has ceased for us since Christ has ascended into heaven; on the other, a "virtue" bereft of the pregnant meaning it still had for the theologians of the preceding age. On the one hand, finally, Christ himself in his personal reality or, in the sacrament, his virtue; on the other, the Church which we are . . . Others might be tempted to over-identify Christ and his Church, the Head and the members of the body; Berengarius, on the contrary, had not even retained the feeling of their mutual immanence.'[3] To counter Berengarius, theology proceeded henceforth to emphasize the substantial identity of the body present in the sacrament with the body born of Mary, and to reserve to them the term *corpus verum,* while carefully distinguishing them from the body of the Church or the communion which were shortly to be designated by *corpus mysticum*.[4]

From our present point of view, the application of the expression *corpus mysticum* to the Church denotes the homogeneity of the theology of the mediaeval Church with that of the Fathers and of St Paul. The threefold aspect of the body of Christ remained, as did the study of the relationships between the three realities designated by 'body of Christ'. In the mystical body, the eucharistic, sacramental reference stands out clearly. *We must take care to retain it.* It is a major element in the Christian tradition. We must beware of giving way to the dissociation which did come about later when, faced with the Protestant Reformation, a theology of the Church was worked out without prime regard to the fundamental position

1. Congar, Encyclopedia *Catholicisme,* vol. 3, col. 212.

2. *Sur le Sacrement de l'Autel,* chap. 12, *PL,* vol. 180, cols. 361-362; in translation in H. de Lubac, *Catholicism,* p. 226, where a series of interesting references to other authors are given in a note.

3. H. de Lubac, *Corpus mysticum,* p. 260.

4. On the two factors which conditioned this evolution, Berengarius and the birth of scholasticism, see chap. X of *Corpus mysticum.*

of the eucharist. There is therefore, as de Lubac says, every indication that we should study the mutual relationship of Church and eucharist. One can say that they act one on the other as reciprocal causes. Each has been entrusted to the other so to speak, by Christ; it is the Church which makes the eucharist, but it is also the eucharist which makes the Church.[1]

II. Is it still possible today to take our stand on St Thomas?[2]

Any theology of the body of Christ which is to take into account the requirements of Pauline teaching must fulfil three conditions. It must show:

1. How union with Christ explains the doctrine of the Church as the body of Christ;

2. That this union is sacramental and that it forms part of a 'physical' or 'corporal' conception of salvation;

3. That in the corporal structure resulting from this, there is room for an interior organization and a variety of functions.[3]

In general, authors stress how closely the encyclical *Mystici Corporis* corresponds with Pauline teaching. But some are not quite so positive that this is the case with St Thomas. What then are we to think of the synthesis outlined at the centre of the treatise on Christ? Is it adequate? Is St Thomas still a reliable guide today?

The theological authority of Father Tromp, as well as the affinity between his book and the contents of the encyclical, is acknowledged. Now Tromp, without directly alluding to St Thomas, shows that he is disconcerted by a trend of thinking of which almost the whole of the middle ages forms part. 'The concept of *Ecclesia ab Abel,* of the universal Church in the sense of St Gregory, or of the mystical

1. Cf. H. de Lubac, *The Splendour of the Church*, p. 92.

2. Bibliography M. D. Koster, *Ecclesiologie . . .*; A. Mitterer, *Geheimnisvoller Leib Christi nach St Th. v. Aquin und nach Papst Pius XII*, Vienna, 1950; appreciations on Mitterer's book will be found in *BT*, vol. 8, 1947-1953, pp. 363-373 by C. Journet, and in *RSPT*, 1951, vol. 35, pp. 633-634, by Y. Congar; J. Beumer, 'Die Idee einer vorchristlichen Kirche bei Augustinus', in *Münch. Theol. Zeitschr.*, 1952, vol. 3, pp. 161-175; Y. Congar, 'Ecclesia ab Abel', in *Abhandlungen über Theologie und Kirche. Festschrift für Karl Adam*, Dusseldorf, 1952, pp. 79-108.

3. I Cor. 12:28 and parallel texts.

definite mystical personality, is almost forced by that very fact to body considered as the assemblage of all the saints who, from the origin of the world to its end, are justified by faith in the Redeemer, is of key importance for an understanding of the evolution of ecclesiology as a whole. This concept seems to preoccupy the minds of a considerable number of scholastics to such an extent that the more defined (*strictior*) concept, as it appears in the writings of St Paul, comes to take a completely secondary place. This cannot occur without danger for the doctrine. Indeed, we must note firstly that the union of the saints is an invisible reality and next that anyone who, in the manner of St Augustine, considers the *Ecclesia ab Abel* as a definite mystical personality, is almost forced by that very fact to consider the organization of the mystical body willed by Christ as an almost (*quodammodo*) accidental thing: Suarez himself has not definitely broken free from these ideas in his ecclesiology.'[1]

A few years later, in 1940—the first edition of Tromp's book appeared in 1937—it was a Dominican who questioned the manner in which ecclesiology made use of the key question of the grace of Christ in the *Summa*. In Koster's view, it is certain that IIIa, q. 8 does not properly speaking fall within the realm of ecclesiology. The vocabulary used is revealing enough. 'The word *ecclesia* here includes angels and men since their beginnings. This is clear evidence that we are not dealing with the *ecclesia* in the Pauline sense. In the present context, *ecclesia* and "body of Christ" acquire a meaning which is not authentically ecclesiological but authentically Christological. This meaning is not to be found in St Paul. It goes back to St Augustine.'[2] Here is how Kostern summarizes and appraises St Augustine's position: 'In St Augustine, it is not "corporeity" (*Leibhaftigkeit*) but on the contrary "non-corporeity" that the expression "body of Christ" stresses. The Church is thus this "invisible body of Christ", the "non-corporal" body of Christ.'[3]

A Viennese theologian, Albert Mitterer, devoted a whole book, published in 1950, to demonstrating the opposition between St Thomas and the encyclical *Mystici Corporis*. In his view, the Summa's teaching on this point belonged to a bygone age; the encyclical, on the contrary, had opened a new age. He ends his study

1. S. Tromp, *Corpus Christi*, second ed., 1946, p. 127.
2. M. D. Koster, *Ekklesiologie im Werden*, p. 41.
3. *Ekklesiologie* . . ., p. 57.

with these words: 'There is an extremely interesting evolution from the teaching of St Paul, who used the predicate "body of Christ" to designate a subject which was none other than the Church of his time, through St Thomas, who hesitates between the visible Church and the invisible Church, to the encyclical which establishes clearly that the Roman Catholic Church is the mystical body of Christ.'[1] He goes even further: he believes himself justified in asserting that the expression 'mystical body *of the Church*' in St Thomas means the invisible Church as opposed to the visible Church.[2]

Similar criticisms will be found in F. Malmberg's study, published in 1959. He sees the crux of the question 'in the idea St Thomas formed of the *grace of Christ*. The stress was so firmly laid on the inner and spiritual nature of this grace that its essentially "incarnational" character and consequently its essentially "corporal" character ceased to find adequate expression. The ecclesiology of *Mystici Corporis* presents theologians with an authentic doctrine of the Church, on the basis of which they can overcome this one-sided spiritualization of Christian grace'.

In varying forms and with varying degrees of tact, the same complaint has been recurring regularly for twenty-five years: St Thomas may have shown the influx of the life of Christ into the Church, but he did not give sufficient place to the corporeity of the 'mystical body'. How can this visible side of the Church, and all its external organization be emphasized in a 'body' which includes the just men of the old dispensation and the angels? Must we not challenge St Thomas's theology of grace as too spiritual and too 'disincarnate'? The question is a serious one and it calls for serious examination. We propose to answer it by setting out the broad lines of St Thomas's synthesis in the subject.

III. The Basis of the Theology of the Mystical Body

What is the theological basis of the doctrine of the mystical body in St Thomas? The plenitude of personal grace, surely. St Thomas, commenting on John 1:16 says so plainly: 'Christ is our head be-

1. A. Mitterer, *Geheimnisvoller Leib* . . ., p. 339.
2. A. Mitterer, *Geheimnisvoller Leib* . . ., p. 340.
3. F. Malmberg, *Een Lichaam* . . ., p. 144.

cause he possesses the plenitude of grace.'[1] But can this line of argument be carried to its logical conclusion? Surely that would mean, in the end, making this plenitude of grace to be a principal cause? Now this seems impossible. Even at its highest point, grace is and remains a *participation* in the divine nature. God alone can be its cause.[2]

Consequently, St Thomas never says that the grace of Christ is the principal cause of grace: just the opposite. Christ in his humanity is an instrumental principle.[3] But here we are up against a new difficulty. Christ's humanity is only an instrument. This being the case, it is difficult any longer to see what role remains for grace. To explain how a bad minister can nevertheless administer a sacrament, St Thomas recalls the general principle: 'The instrument does not act according to its own form or virtue, but according to a virtue belonging to the one who handles it. It is therefore indifferent for the instrument *qua* instrument to have this or that form, this or that virtue, outside what is required by its object as an instrument.'[4] The virtue of the minister does not enter into the composition of the sacrament, although it does constitute the inner disposition consonant with the holiness of the sacrament.[5]

The problem does not take the form of a dilemma. St Thomas passes from the explanation through the plenitude of grace to that through the instrumentality of humanity without the least hesitation or incoherence. He does so because, as he sees it, the one necessarily implies the other: the one is not adequate without the other. The final proof, it seems to me, is rooted in the *ratio instrumenti,* in what makes the instrument, in what is required for it to be able to fulfil its task.

When Christ enters the question, it is his complete humanity that is included in the *ratio instrumenti,* that whole living and active humanity, hypostatically united with the Word for the purpose of the salvation of all mankind. So that the plenitude of grace, which is the immediate consequence of the hypostatic union, pertains essentially to the *ratio instrumenti.* It is in this sense that St Thomas can say categorically: the actions of Christ are salutary to

1. III, q. 8, a. 5, sed c.
2. The *maxime tale* of grace is beyond grace; it is God himself.
3. III, q. 8, a. 1, ad 1; q. 27, a. 5; q. 64, a. 3; I-II, q. 112, a. 1, ad 1., etc.
4. III, q. 64, a. 5, c.
5. Ibid, ad 3.

us, causing grace in us.[1] It is the *holy* actions of Christ that are the instruments of his divinity.

What I have called *instrumental*[2] corresponds exactly with *actio propria* in the following text:

> 'The instrument has a twofold action: an instrumental action in which it works not through its own virtue but through the virtue of the principal agent; and a proper action (*actio propria*) which falls to it by reason of its own proper form. . . . The instrument does not perform its instrumental action except when it exercises its own proper action.'[3]

In purely human affairs, this instrumental support can occupy a place of varying importance. The mind is more involved in the work of the sacred writer who composes an historical book like the Acts of the Apostles than in the work of a schoolboy who is taking dictation from his teacher. In sacramental causality, if the part of the minister is considered, instrumental support is relatively small: he is required to make a definite sign, with the intention of doing what the Church does; nothing more. On the contrary, in the instrumentality of the humanity of Christ, his complete human life is committed, just as it is, its most precious part being the grace which unites it to God by theological activity and makes it specifically responsive to divine impulses. It is for this reason and in this framework that all the *acta et passa* of Christ have an efficacity for our salvation.[4]

For St Thomas, the theological basis of the mystical body is the plenitude of Christ's grace as instrumental support of the divine causality of grace and salvation.[5]

1. III, q. 8, a. 1, ad 1.
2. *Ratio instrumenti*: III, q. 64, a. 5, c.
3. III, q. 62, a. 1, ad 2.
4. See Prol. of IIIa and of q. 27.
5. We must appreciate the force of an expression like the following: 'Actus personalis gratiae, qui est sanctum facere formaliter habentem, est ratio justificationis aliorum, quae pertinet ad gratiam capitis' (III, q. 8, a. 5, ad 2). On this whole question, I have benefited from the invaluable help of Father A. Patfoort, Professor of dogmatic theology at Le Saulchoir.

IV. The 'Corporeity' of the Mystical Body. Ecclesiology and Anthropology.[1]

When St Thomas raised the question : is Christ head of men with regard to their bodies or only with regard to their souls? he knew that the answer had already been given by the faith.[2] His whole approach intends simply to account for this datum by theological argument that will demonstrate its appropriateness. 'Have you never been told that your bodies belong to the body of Christ?' (I Cor. 6 : 15). St Paul's assertion is clear enough. To explain it, St Thomas has recourse to a line of argument which St Augustine had set out in full. St Augustine, commenting on I Cor. 6 : 15, declared : 'His body is the Church. If our Lord Jesus Christ had been united only to a human soul, our souls alone would be his members; but he also united himself to a body in order to be likewise our head in this respect, since we are composed of soul and body : our bodies are thus his members as well.'[3] This may serve to clear St Augustine of certain accusations brought against his ecclesiology by Father Koster and other writers, without sufficient research.[4]

St Thomas's line of argument is thus based on the fact that man is composed of soul and body, not as the result of some accidental association, but in virtue of the unity of a single essence. That is the reason why the soul differs in kind from the angel, why it is united with the body as *forma,* and why this union with the body is for the good of the soul.[5] On this basis we can begin to understand the fitnesses or harmonies of the incarnation, of the sacramental order

1. Bibliography: G. Philips, 'La grâce des Justes de l'Ancien Testament', in *ETL*, 1947, vol. 23, pp. 521-556; 1948, vol. 24, pp. 23-58; A. M. Hoffmann, 'Die Gnade der Gerechten des Alten Bundes nach Th. v. Aq.', in *Divus Thomas*, Fribourg 1951, vol. 29, pp. 167-187.

2. III, q. 8, a. 2.

3. 'Profecto illius membra sunt et corpora nostra'. *Sermo* 161, 1; *PL*, vol. 38, col. 878.

4. In the same order of ideas, see also *In Primam epist. Joan.*, 2, 2, *PL*, vol. 35, col. 1990: 'Omnis enim Ecclesia sponsa Christi est, cujus principium et *primitiae* caro Christi est'. In his *flesh* Christ is not only the cause but the *first fruits* of the Church.

5. I, q. 75, a. 7, c. et ad 3.; q. 76, a. 1; q. 89, a. 1.: 'Propter melius animae.' This is of course the scholastic analysis of the anthropological monism which we discussed above.

in our earthly state and of the resurrection of the body. 'Man had strayed away from spiritual realities in order to devote himself entirely to corporal things. On the basis of these last he could not, through his own efforts, bring about his return to God. That is why the divine wisdom which had made man assumed a corporal nature and came to visit him where he was, submerged in corporal things, in order to bring him back to spiritual realities by the mysteries of his body.'[1] In the same line of thinking, in order to establish the fitness of the sacramental order, St Thomas's first argument is drawn

> 'from the characteristics of human nature, whose peculiarity it is to be led to the spiritual and the intelligible through the corporal and the sensible'[2]

To the objection that the state of the soul separated from its body is the most perfect that can be conceived, and therefore that the resurrection of the body will be a retrograde step, St Thomas replies: 'The state of the soul in the body is more perfect than out of it, for it is part of a composite whole.'[3] Here again it is the unity of human nature, body and soul, which accounts theologically for the dogma of the resurrection of the body.

The 'corporeity' of the mystical body is a truth of faith, made theologically manifest by the 'corporeity' of human nature. But we may wonder whether this 'corporeity' really obtains at every moment of the history of salvation. For St Thomas as for St Augustine, there is only one mediator: every grace comes through Christ and the Church and hence all the righteous of the old covenant belong to the same Church as we do. All this is true. But how can these righteous ones belong to the same Church as we do except through a purely invisible link? To answer this objection, which is not without cogency, we must show how this corporeity existed in the various states of the Church, in its various periods. St Thomas very rightly says that the Church 'is of a child's age in Abel's days, is young with the patriarchs, has grown up with the apostles; she will attain old age at the end of the world'.[4] But at none of these periods is 'corporeity'

1. 'Ut per sui corporis mysteria eum ad spiritualia revocaret'. *Comp. theol.* chap. 201.
2. III, q. 61, a. 1.
3. *Suppl.*, q. 75, a. 1, ad 4; see also a. 2, in c.
4. *In Ps.* 36: 18.

absent. The sacraments of the Old Law played a role in the divine economy. They belonged to the Church *in the making*. As images of future realities, they acted as the support of faith.

> 'The holy Fathers did not look on the sacraments of the Old Law as realities, but as images and foreshadowings of what was still to come.... That is why the early Fathers, in observing their legal and sacramental practices, were drawn towards Christ by the same faith and the same love by which we ourselves are carried away. So they really belonged, like ourselves, to the same body of the Church.'[1]

Is the 'corporeity' of the Church to be regarded as a property of its earthly condition? The sacraments will disappear in the beatific vision. The hierarchy of the Church, as an office, has no reason to exist except here on earth. We can employ a variety of images to explain the transitory nature of the sacramental order and the Church's ministry: the scaffolding which a temple needs while it is building, the bandages which secure a fractured limb till it has set, the mould which the modeller uses to make a work of art.[2] But these comparisons would be misunderstood if these provisional structures were identified with the status of mediation which is inherent to the nature of the Church.

In heaven, the Church's hierarchy will serve no further purpose. It is undoubtedly merely a temporal element, conditioned by man's state between the resurrection and the *parousia*. But the economy of mediation of which it forms part will remain forever. As Mgr Journet very rightly observes

> 'The strength by which they know God as he knows himself and love him as he loves himself still comes to them mediately by way of the human nature of Christ, the eternal king of men and angels.'[3]

1. III, q. 8, a. 3, ad 3. See III, q. 61, a. 3, for how St Thomas explains the necessity of the sacraments in the Old Covenant.
2. See A. Liégé, in *Initiation théologique*, ed. A. M. Henry, vol. IV, pp. 388-389.
3. *L'Eglise du Verbe Incarné*, vol. I, Bruges, 1942, p. 21 (English translation, *The Church of the Word Incarnate*, London, 1955, vol. I, p. 15). See III, q.22, a. 5, ad 1; *Suppl.*, q. 92, a.3, ad 12.

So St. Thomas's assertion, qu. 8, a. 2, remains absolutely exact concerning the state of beatific vision. The twofold 'corporeity' is present there. It is the complete humanity of Christ (not only his soul but his body) that exerts an influence on the complete humanity of the elect (not only their souls, but their bodies too). We should point out in passing that it is because of this glorification of bodies that an eschatological *innovatio mundi* is necessary.[1]

The angels' membership in the mystical body does not affect anything we have said. It is not a sign that St Thomas has a theology of the Church in which 'corporeity' does not hold its real place. The angels belong to the mystical body, but in another fashion from men. And this 'other fashion' is based on the fact that there is no *conformitas naturae* between the humanity of Christ and the angels (*Comp. theol.*, chap 214). Christ is head of the angels, St Thomas asserts elsewhere, but not in exactly the same sense that he is head of men.[2] The theology of the mystical body depends on the theology of the motive of the incarnation. For St Thomas, this motive is the redemption of *men*.[3] Christ did not save the angels, who anyway had no need to be saved. He did not merit the grace they have. Since they were not the object of the incarnation, the angels only experience its benefits as an indirect consequence.[4] Our ecclesiology of the mystical body thus remains closely dependent on our anthropology.[5]

V. The Mystical Body and the Eucharist[6]

The relationship established between the visible species of bread and wine (*sacramentum*), the body and blood of Christ (*sacramentum et res*), the mystical body and its unity (*res*) is of funda-

1. See *Suppl.*, q. 91. These texts need to be stripped of their mediaeval cosmological imagery, but their teaching still has genuine value.
2. 'Non tamen ita proprie': III *Sent.*, d. 13, q. 2,a. 2, sol. 1.
3. Whence the assumption of a soul and of a *body* by the Word.
4. On these benefits, see H. Bouessé, *Le Sauveur du Monde*, 2, *Le Mystère de l'Incurnation*, Chambéry and Paris, 1953, pp. 352 ff.
5. This is the import of III, q. 8, a. 2.
6. Bibliography: In addition to the works noted at the beginning of this chapter, see those named by Y. Congar in a note on p. 87 of *Esquisses du Mystère de L'Eglise* (English translation, *The Mystery of the Church*, London, 1958), and by H. de Lubec on p. 50 of *Catholicism*; also A. M. Roguet, 'L'unité du Corps mystique dans la charité. "Res sacramenti" de l'eucharistie', in *Maison-Dieu*, 1950, no. 24, pp. 20-45.

mental importance for an understanding of the way in which the middle ages saw the relationship between the body of the Church and the eucharistic body. This relationship was clearly formulated in these three terms by Peter Lombard; Innocent III returned to it in 1202 in a reply to the Bishop of Lyons.[1] It was simply the theological implementation of I Cor. 10:17.

The Church is thus the final spiritual reality signified and effected by the eucharist.[2] We meet very frequently with the expression *sacramentum ecclesiasticae unitatis*.[3] Since, moreover, the uniting bond of the Church is a union of charity, St Thomas was to say that the eucharist is the sacrament of unity and of peace, the sacrament of charity, whereas baptism is the sacrament of faith.[4] The eucharist effects the unity of the Church; more strictly, it establishes the mystical body, because it contains the real body of Christ.[5]

In our earthly condition, the eucharist is thus the proper cause of the mystical body and the unity of the Church. Baptism, whose link with the eucharist is a close one, effects entrance into the Church only because it is inseparable from the *votum eucharistiae*.[6] St Thomas lays special emphasis on this doctrine of baptism's connection with the eucharist. How can this sacrament confer grace since it is already necessary to have grace to receive it? To this question, St Thomas replies:

> 'This sacrament confers grace of itself. Before receiving this sacrament, nobody possesses grace, except in the sense of desiring the sacrament, a personal desire where adults are concerned, the desire of the Church when it comes to children.'[7]

Since the eucharist, in our earthly condition, is the proper cause of the Church, it will be interesting to verify the relation to that sacrament of all those who belong to the mystical body in various

1. IV *Sent.*, d. 8, chap. 7-8, Quaracchi ed., 1916, vol. II, p. 792; Denz., 415.
2. 'Res hujus sacramenti est unitas corporis mystici'. III, q. 73, a. 3. 'Corpus mysticum', q. 73, a. 1, arg. 2, etc.
3. Cf. for example q. 73, a. 2, sed c. See also q. 83, a. 4, ad 3.
4. III, q. 83, a. 4, in fine corp.; q. 73, a. 3, ad 3; q. 79, a. 1, etc.
5. 'Eucharistia continet aliquid sacrum absolute', III, q. 73, a. 1, ad 3; 'In hoc sacramento totum mysterium nostrae salutis comprehenditur', III, q. 83, a. 4.
6. Cf. III, q. 67, a. 2; q. 73, a. 3, c.
7. III, q. 79, a. 1, ad 1.

ages and conditions. St Thomas distinguished two ways of eating the body of Christ, a *manducatio sacramentalis* and a *manducatio spiritualis*. In the first, the Christian receives the sacrament without necessarily perceiving and benefiting from the effect of grace; in the second, he receives the effect of the sacrament, spiritual union with Christ through faith and charity.[1]

The *manducatio spiritualis* of the body of Christ is necessary for everyone. It is nothing other than incorporation into Christ. But it includes the wish or desire to receive the sacrament itself. Hence this desire also is necessary for salvation. It would be ineffectual if it were not put into practice when the appropriate occasion arose. Consequently the Christian is obliged to receive this sacrament by virtue of the Lord's precept, and not only in pursuance of the ordinances of the Church.[2] This then is the position of the Christian who is living in the Church today, between the resurrection and the *parousia*.[3]

What is the position of the righteous who lived before the institution of the eucharist? Again, we shall find here a special application of the principle. In their case what happened was a *manducatio spiritualis* of the *sacrament* of the eucharist *propter figuram* in the images which the manna and the water from the rock constituted for them (I Cor. 10:3).[4]

When it comes to the angels, St Thomas introduces a valuable and extremely enlightening distinction. *Manducatio spiritualis* can be understood in two ways, according to whether it is a question of Christ *in propria specie*, as he is in heaven, or of Christ 'under the species of this sacrament'. The *manducatio spiritualis* of the angels must be explained in the first way. The angels are united with Christ by perfect charity and by the beatific vision. The sacrament is not a part of their own spiritual economy. They have no cause to desire it. The sacramental economy forms part of the imperfect order of faith.

1. III, q. 80, a. 1.
2. III, q. 80, a. 11.
3. For infants, see q. 73, a. 3, c.: 'Ex intentione Ecclesiae desiderant eucharistiam', and q. 80, a. 9, ad 3, et in c.: they lack the *sacramenti devotio*.
4. III, q. 80, a. 1, ad 3. In this passage, St Thomas's theological formulation is definite: they really do eat the *sacrament* spiritually. In *IV Sent.*, d. 9, a. 2, sol. 4, ad 2, his thinking is still fluid: there St Thomas practically assimilates the position of the righteous of the Old Testament with that of the angels.

What we have said is aimed simply at shedding light on the eucharist as the proper cause of the mystical body. We were dealing with the sacrament so far as, in our earthly condition, it is the intermediary through which we attain the real body of Chrst. But of course it is this real body which, in the background, is the proper cause of the mystical body as a conjoint instrument (the sacrament being a separate instrument) whatever the period in the history of salvation.

This brief exposition of some salient points in St Thomas's teaching on the mystical body shows that the apprehensions of certain authors have little foundation and that they are based on inadequate information. We can regard St Thomas as a faithful and perceptive interpreter of New Testament data, and one who is in substantial agreement with the teaching of *Mystici Corporis,* the commentary of the magisterium on the same data.

IV

AN ATTEMPT AT A DEFINITION OF THE CHURCH

We embark now on a critical search for the definition of the Church, with the aid of the criteriological principles resulting from our scriptural inquiry and our study of St Thomas's doctrine, in particular the relationship between ecclesiology and anthropology in his theology of the mystical body. Our analysis of the position of the magisterium in *Mystici Corporis* enabled us to place the problem. This examination should lead us to a reasoned choice. Bellarmine (1542-1621) gave a celebrated definition which towers over the whole discussion. It is to be found in *De controversiis Christianae fidei adversus nostri temporis haereticos.*[1] The translated text we quote appears in the second part of a chapter which began by recording a series of definitions put forward by heretics, both in ancient times and contemporaries of the author.

I. Bellarmine's Definition

Cardinal Bellarmine ends his exposition of the various heretical positions by a definition which he attributes to Calvin and which can be stated in three propositions: 1. The Church is composed of the predestined righteous alone; 2. Only God knows the real Church, whose basis is election; 3. There exists additionally an external Church in which the good and the evil are mixed. It is this distinction of a twofold Church—a Church of the predestined and an external Church—that Bellarmine attacks; his first words are: '*Ecclesiam unam tantum esse, non duas.*'

1. The first volume of the *De Controversiis* appeared at Ingolstadt in 1586. This definition appears in vol. II, *Prima Controversia generalis*, liber III, *De Ecclesia militante*, Caput II, 'De definitione Ecclesiae', 1601 edition, Ingolstadt, cols. 137-138.

Here is the passage from Bellarmine: 'There is only one Church, not two. And this one true Church is the community of men brought together by profession of the true faith and communion in the same sacraments, and under the administration of recognized pastors and especially of the sole vicar of Christ on earth, the Roman pontiff.' This definition thus comprises three elements: 1. profession of the true faith (which corresponds with the magisterium); 2. communion in the sacraments (which corresponds with the power of order); 3. submission to recognized pastors (which sums up the power of jurisdiction).

From this it is easy to deduce who belongs to the Church and who does not. The first element rules out the infidels who had never been members of the Church—Jews, Turks and pagans—and those who have left it: heretics and apostates. The second element excludes catechumens and the excommunicated, and the third schismatics. Everyone else belongs to it, including reprobates, criminals and the ungodly.

The characteristic note of this definition is its insistence on visibility. 'All other definitions call for inner virtues in order to declare anyone a member of the Church, and consequently say that the Church is invisible.' Naturally Bellarmine acknowledges that 'all the virtues are to be found in the Church: faith, hope, charity etc.'. But he does not think it necessary to include them for a definition of the Church to be consonant with the Scriptures: 'Nevertheless, for anyone to be able to be declared a member of this *true Church, of which the Scriptures speak, we do not think that any inner virtue is required of him.*' The outward profession of the faith and communion in the sacrament suffices, and these are things which the senses themselves can establish. Bellarmine does not hesitate to liken membership of the Church to membership of a particular nationality: 'The Church is indeed a community (*cœtus*) of men, as visible and palable as the community of the Roman people, or the kingdom of France or the republic of Venice.'[1]

1. To what extent does Bellarmine retain an Augustinian idea of the Church which he explicitly mentions in the passage we are examining? 'Notandum est ex Augustino in breviculo collationis, collatione tertia, Ecclesiam esse corpus vivum, in quo est anima et corpus. Et quidem anima sunt interna dona Spiritus Sancti, fides, spes, caritas, etc. Corpus sunt externa professio fidei et communicatio sacramentorum'. According to this definition, the Church is composed at once of inner gifts and of an external structure. But in the end Bellarmine does not adopt this

II. Value and Limitations of Bellarmine's Position

In the New Testament, the Church appears as a local community —Jerusalem, or the Church of God established at Corinth—and at the same time as a comprehensive community: the aggregate of the faithful in a wider area.[1] These communities, local and universal alike, were visible and palpable. Their members and their leaders were known, and they were organized by ministries.[2] This whole aspect of an organized society is admirably conveyed by Bellarmine's definition.

But another aspect, even more important, is left in the shade. This organized society exists with a view to something else. Bellarmine omits from his definition what is the whole object of the teaching of the Pauline epistles and St John. The union of Christians with Christ is a union of life. That is what we must understand from the texts in the captivity epistles which say that the Church is the body of Christ, and that Christ as head plays the part of vital principle in relation to the body. This conviction is already present, although under another form, in the great epistles. The same theme is to be found in St John: the vital union of the vine and its branches: The encyclical *Mystici Corporis* means to sum up the whole of this scriptural teaching when it says: 'Although the juridical grounds upon which also the Church is built have their origin in the divine constitution given her by Christ and although they contribute to the achievement of her supernatural purpose, nevertheless, that which raises the Christian society to a level utterly surpassing any order of nature is the Spirit of our Redeemer, the source of all graces, gifts,

position as his own. He takes only its 'corporal' element. He thus contents himself with the minimum requirement for anyone 'to be described as a visible part of the Church'. The phrase in question does not occur either in the *Breviculus*, or, it seems anywhere else in St Augustine's works. It should be noted, however, that Bellarmine does not say 'sicut dicit Augustinus', but 'notandum est ex Augustino: he does not represent this as a verbatim quotation. There is in fact in the *Breviculus*, col. III, 10, 20 (*PL*, vol. 43, col. 635) a passage on the inner man and the outward man that may perhaps have been Bellarmine's source. Apart from this, the nearest text to the formula is probably *Ep.* 185, 11, 50; *PL* 33, 815. See also the 'visibile sacramentum' set over against the 'invisibilis unctio caritatis', in *Contra litt. Petiliani*, II, 104, 239; *PL*, vol. 43, cols. 342-343.

1. Acts 9:31: 'The church, all through Judaea and Galilee and Samaria.'
2. Apostles, prophets, teachers . . . see I Cor. 12:28.

and miraculous powers, perennially and intimately pervading the Church and acting in her.'[1]

Bellarmine is a saint; he was not unaware of the mystical character of the Church; he merely omitted discussing it. But this omission, which reveals the precise intention of an apologist whose intention was to stress visibility in opposition to the Protestants, hampered his ecclesiology and was to have regrettable effects.

This inner communion was present to his mind. But his firm determination not to introduce into his own formula any allusion whatsoever to inner virtues *was later to give many people the idea that the Church is for us reduced to the sensible.* This would probably not be cause for concern, were it not that Bellarmine's formula, by reason of its attractive simplicity and its practical character, won over many theologians and canonists. Not a few catechisms have adopted its essential features.

One of its effects, which we will note first, was that it hampered controversy with the Protestants. In Bossuet's day, controversialists such as Claude and Jurieu were, it seems, convinced that the complete definition of the Church put forward by Catholics was restricted to externals.[2] This conviction still underlies the criticisms that various people make of the Church. It is obvious from this that in the end Bellarmine's apologetic plan resulted in a somewhat disappointing form of apologetics. In discussion with Protestants, who will turn it to their advantage, it is unfortunate to understate the spiritual in order to stress only the visible.

Another consequence to be noted is the difficulty we find in assimilating formulae with a spiritual orientation, such as that of Khomiakov, who defines the Church as: 'a living organism, the organism of truth and love, or more precisely, truth and love as an organism.'[3] Catholic theology is able to give this formula its full import—provided that it extricates itself from the limitations imposed by Bellarmine's definition.

In face of difficulties such as those I have just detailed, theologians

1. Encyclical *Mystici Corporis*, A.A.S. vol. 35, p. 223; C.T.S. translation, p. 38.
2. See Journet, *L'Eglise du Verbe Incarné*, vol. II, Bruges and Paris, 1951, pp. 23 and 53.
3. G. Samarine, preface to *Oeuvres théologiques de A. S. Khomiakov*, translated from the Russian, Gratieux, Paris 1939, p. 58.

feel the need to complete Bellarmine's definition.[1] It is obvious that it cannot be maintained as a complete ontological definition, for all that it is a perfectly valid and accurate empirical description. We must go beyond it.[2]

III. The Sacramental Definition of the Church[3]

This definition is obviously favoured by theologians today. Here it is in O. Semmelroth's formulation: 'Here below, the Church is the sacrament of Jesus Christ, as Christ in his holy humanity is the sacrament of God.'[4] The notion of sacrament employed by Semmelroth is that which the Council of Trent borrowed from St Augustine, the 'visible form of an invisible grace.'[5] The New Testament shows us the humanity of Christ as a sacramental epiphany, not only of the second person of the Trinity, but of God himself. It was in this humanity that the grace of God manifested itself in the most perfect manner. We can thus consider Christ in his humanity as the *primordial sacrament* (*Ursakrament*), a title which is due also, in a derivative and secondary sense, to the Church as body of Christ.

1. See for example Scheeben, quoted by Journet, vol. II, p. 23. 'One need only have the true Church before one's eyes to be held soul as well as body, for in as much as it is the mystical body of Christ, it is not a dead body, but a living body. In a community where all publicly profess the same faith, participate in the same means of grace and submit to the same visible head, inner faith, charity and inner justification will also be found etc.' (*Dogmatik*, vol. 4, p. 294).

2. Note the aptness of a passage of the Bellarmine text which we are discussing here: 'Omnes aliae requirunt internas virtutes ad constituendum aliquem in Ecclesia, et propterea Ecclesiam veram invisibilem faciunt'. To introduce inward elements into the notion of the Church in no way implies admitting that the Church is invisible. When we say that Christ is God, we in no way admit that Christ is invisible. The visibility of Christ and of his Church is a *sui generis* visibility, wholly in relation to a spiritual element, at once as a sign and as a means of grace. The inward element is, as it were, presupposed by the outward marks.

3. Short bibliography: O. Semmelroth, *Die Kirche als Ursakrament*, Frankfurt-a.-M., 1953 (reviewed by Y. Congar in *RSPT*, 1953, vol. 33, p. 752), and 'Die Kirche als sichtbare Gestalt der unsichtbaren Gnade' in *Scholastik*, 1953, vol. 28, pp. 23-39; and 'Um die Einheit des Kirchenbegriffes', in *Fragen der Theologie heute*, ed. Feiner, Einsiedeln, 1957, pp. 319-337; G. Hoffmann, 'Die Kontroverse über den Kirchenbegriff', in *Trierer theol. Zeitschr.*, 1956, pp. 109-114, 174-182; B. Willems, O.P., 'Der sakramentale Kirchenbegriff', in *Freib. Zeitschr. f. Phil. u. Theol.*, 1958, vol. 5, pp. 274-296.

4. Quoted by G. Hoffmann, *Die Kontroverse . . .*, p. 175.

5. Denz., 876.

The seven sacraments are the extension of the sacramentality of Christ and of the Church. Semmelroth often compares the Church to the palm of the hand. The individual sacraments are its fingers: it is by means of them that the hand can grasp.

In itself, the sacramental picture is enlightening. The mystical body is at once an inner and an outward reality. This inseparable duality can fittingly be expressed by *sacramentum* and by *res*. But in this case, we must keep firmly in mind that the Church is constituted by both; the Church is not only the sacrament (the sign and the cause) but also the *res* (the reality signified and caused). Now sacramental language, if employed indiscriminately, runs the risk of reducing ecclesiology to the study of outward elements. What is true of the Church-as-institution is not true of the Church without further qualification. As Congar has observed: 'The Church visible, the Church institutional, is the ministry of faith and of the sacraments of faith, by which men are grafted into Christ and realize the Mystical Body which is the Church in its inward substance.'[1] 'The Church-as-institution is the sacrament, the minister, in brief the instrument of the work done.'[2] But in its living whole, the Church is more than the *sacramentum;* it is also the new life of humanity.

The danger we have just exposed is not imaginary. Semmelroth, for example, lays far too much stress on the outward components. Proof of this lies in his view that secret heretics and schismatics should be considered members of the Church. B. Willems, one of those who follow him on this point, gives as a reason for this: 'as long as they still profess the true faith outwardly . . . , they have a part in the sacramental function of the Church in the universe.'[3] After the scriptural and theological inquiry we have carried out, this opinion is astonishing. It is nevertheless in line with the *material* application to the Church of the sacramental scheme.

For St Thomas, the sinner belongs to the mystical body in an imperfect manner, through the faith unformed which still, in a certain way, unites him to Christ.[4] But when the heretic destroys this faith within himself by heresy and apostasy, he severs the last

1. *Esquisses du mystère de l'Eglise,* second ed., Paris 1953, p. 85 (English translation, *The Mystery of the Church,* London, 1960, p. 114).
2. p. 84.
3. B. Willems, *Der sakramentale Kirchenbegriff,* p. 290. On the same page there is a note on other contemporary authors who hold the same point of view.
4. III, q. 8, a. 3, c. et ad 2.

link which still binds him to Christ; by the same fact, he cuts himself off from those who at that moment form the mystical body. According to St Thomas, the heretic is cut off from the Church, whatever his outward behaviour, even if, out of pure hypocrisy, he continues to profess in public the faith he has repudiated in his heart. This position is perfectly logical in St Thomas. The external elements are to be judged by the inner reality, which is the principal and decisive one, just as the soul preponderates over the body.[1]

We have noted certain weaknesses in Semmelroth's position. Our own position is not without its difficulties. The argument generally urged against it does not lack force : an undisclosed heretic could continue to exercise a jurisdiction of whose nullity he alone was aware, and the result for the Church would be a serious state of uncertainty. Various answers have been given to this objection. Turrecremata, basing himself on a passage in St Thomas, asserts that the Holy Spirit will provide what is necessary to salvation, either by permitting the discovery of the undisclosed heresy or by making good what has not been done.[2] Journet holds a different position : undisclosed heresy excludes a man from the Church, but does not *ipso facto* entail the cessation of his jurisdictional powers.[3]

1. I know of no place where St Thomas has explicitly discussed membership of the Church by secret heretics. But the viewpoint we have stated follows naturally from the principles of his ecclesiology.

2. *IV Sent.*, d. 24, q. 1, a. 2, sol. 3, ad 2. Turrecremata discussed this problem in a wider setting. He asked whether a prelate is debarred from his prelacy by the fact that he is a heretic. He was confronted with two opinions. The first replied in the affirmative; second in the negative: if they become heretics, the pope or any other prelate *ipso facto* loses his powers of prelacy—of papacy, where the pope is concerned. After stating his personal agreement with the first opinion, Turrecremata refuted the four arguments advanced on behalf of the second. In refuting the last of these arguments he stressed the role of the Holy Spirit in preserving the Church from the disastrous potential effects of undisclosed herecy. '*Cum universalis Ecclesia regatur a Spiritu Sancto nunquam deficiet in his quae necessaria sunt ad salutem*, licet in aliis deficere posset. Unde si papa esset occultus haereticus, et per consequens papatu privatus, et ideo illa quae jurisdictionis exercere non posset, quamvis posset facere ea quae sunt ordinis, Deus Ecclesiae suae provideret revelando ei perfidiam papae, vel praeservando aliquos episcopos per alium modum sibi possibilem licet nobis ignotum. Et ideo *nullus ordo ecclesiasticu necessarius ad salutem Ecclesiae universalis confunderetur* licet multa sine quibus potest esse salus possent esse confusa; praeservaret enim Deus ne confunderentur illa quae universali Ecclesiae sunt necessaria ad salutem.' (*Summa de Ecclesia*, Lib. IV, pars 2, cap. XX, Venice 1560, f. 394.

3. See C. Journet, *L'Eglise du Verbe Incarné*, vol. II, p. 575, note 3; p. 656; p. 1063, note 1.

Is the undisclosed heretic still a member of the Church or not? The two opposing theses both have their obscurities. The second should all the same be preferred to the first: it takes into account scriptural teaching, which the first cannot entirely do.

The positive value of the sacramental explanation by comparison with Bellarmine's position lies in the unity it establishes between all the realities which constitute the sacramental order: the humanity of Christ, the Church, sacramental rites. But it has not succeeded in incorporating all the inwardness of the mystery of the Church into its theological systematization, at least in a number of its most outstanding representatives, among whom is Father Semmelroth.[1]

1. Karl Rahner takes the same position, and we therefore cannot agree with certain important passages of his well-known article 'Die Gliedschaft in der Kirche nach der Lehre der Enzyklika Pius XII *Mystici Corporis Christi*' published in English translation in *Theological Investigations*, vol. II, London, 1964. After convincingly demonstrating, following Leo XIII (*Satis cognitum*), that the Church is at once *a visible society*, juridically organized, and *an inner community* of all those who are united with God in Christ and through the Spirit, Father Rahner concludes: 'These two dimensions of the Church are essentially related to one another' (p. 15). He proceeds to show how this relationship has been studied in the light of the relationship which exists between 'the sacramental sign and its effects of grace', and reaches the following two conclusions: 1. 'Now the sacramental sign can be validly posited without there being effected the supernatural grace signified by it' (p. 15); 2. in ordinary ecclesiastical parlance, the word sacrament designates *in recto* the' sacramental sign (i.e. the plane of the public, historical and tangible proceeding) and only indirectly also the sacramental grace' (p. 16).

Up to this point this is beyond dispute. One might expect Rahner to deduce that the sacramental explanation—interesting and enlightening though it may be—cannot be applied just as it is to the Church, and that it must be submitted to an analogical transposition. Not a bit of it; we remain on exactly the same plane: 'The same is true of the ecclesiastical usage regarding the term "Church". Like the notion of "sacrament" the term Church refers in ecclesiastical usage directly to the external, visible and legally structured communion of believers . . . It refers only indirectly to men's inner faith and union with Christ by grace' (p. 16).

To be sure, the uses of the word 'Church' are many and varied. Moreover it is only one of these, among a number of others, that K. Rahner represents here as that of 'ecclesiastical usage'. That is not the problem. The theologian's first interest is not in the various uses of the word, but in its signification. Now this is permanent and single. For our part, we do not see any other possible meaning than that which we have set forth in this chapter.

It is doubtless not necessary to understand the word Church, every time it is used in its proper sense, with the full weight of its meaning and with all the characteristics which constitute the definition of Church. But if not, then the theologian must be aware of what he is doing. 'Church' can and does designate not only the visible society of Christians, but also the clergy, or the espiscopate, or the Roman dicasteries round the pope, or the Supreme Pontiff himself. *Each of these usages is legitimate and*

IV. The Conditions for a Complete Definition of the Church

On the basis of our researches hitherto, it may be said that any definition of the Church, to be complete, must take into account the following elements :

1. The Church is at once continuous with the people of God of the old dispensation and sundered from it (dropping of the ethnical constituent; sacramental relationship with the risen and glorious Christ);
2. The Church is on the move towards the complete revelation of the Kingdom of God, which is for it a terminus and an inner attraction;
3. The Church is at once an inner reality (influx of Christ and of the Spirit) and an empirical society;
4. The Church implies the relationship of its members with Christ and with one another.

accurate, but none of them exhausts the connotation of the concept. The Church as such is richer in meaning than any of the contents referred to above. In the examples we have just given, the word 'Church' designates more or less extensive parts of the total reality of the Church. To signify this last, a lot more is needed. As long as the inner reality of the Church is left in the background, we are still in a partial order. In fact, the Church is at once a visible society and an inner community. Where nothing remains of the inner communion (unformed supernatural faith being the absolute minimum), then the Church as such has lost its roots. So much so, that I should say, in opposition to Father Rahner, that Church, taken in the formal, biblical and theological sense of the word, implies the inner reality not only *in obliquo*, but must signify it *in recto*, together with the external reality and in the context of the close relationship that binds the one to the other.

So I find myself equally unable to agree with what follows: 'For this reason, therefore, all those and *only those points which affect the Church as a visible, public and judicial society* are significant and decisive for the question of membership of the Church understood in this precise manner. Since the visibleness and visible unity of the Church are constituted by the sacramental and juridical authority of the Church (. . .), *all and only those belong to the Church as members who are visibly, i.e. in the external forum, subject* to these two powers of the Church' (p. 17, my italics). In short, according to this view of Father Rahner's, sheerly external conformists belong to the Church. Those who, *without believing*, conform with ecclesiastical rites and discipline are to be regarded as authentic members of the Church. I cannot bring myself to accept this conclusion. I do not see what basis there is for it. I am glad to see that I am not alone in rejecting this viewpoint; other authors support my view. (J. Salaverri, in his *De Ecclesia Christi*, 1945 ed., no 1052, has listed those who refuse to consider *undisclosed* heretics as members of the Church.) Further on in the same article, K. Rahner returns to the same viewpoint in another form.

What is to be the starting point, the basic idea of the definition? Perhaps one of the familiar biblical ideas or images: body, people, kingdom, temple, city, bride, communion, fold; or a sociological concept submitted to adequate preliminary criticism: society, institution, community, association, group, assembly, meeting, gathering . . .

I personally have chosen the biblical image of body as the basis of a definition for the various reasons enumerated by the authors of the original *De Ecclesia,* and principally on account of the first.[1] The 'body of Christ' is the most frequent of the New Testament images, and the one which, within the Bible itself, received the most thorough doctrinal elaboration. Again, it has held the attention of theologians and the magisterium more than any other. But every choice involves a sacrifice. Certain of the conditions set out above would fit more easily into a definition founded on another concept or another image. So a definition along the lines of the mystical body is not in any way exclusive of others. We have already stressed this point.[2]

Finally we should observe that the definition of the Church must envisage the present day Church—the Church of which the Bible speaks, in which the faithful live between the resurrection and the *parousia,*—although without cutting it off entirely from the whole economy of salvation.

This having been said, I put forward the following definition: The Church is the mystical body of Christ, that is to say a communion which is at once inward and external, the life of union with Christ, and established (caused) by the economy of Christ's mediation.

This definition has its advantages, but it has its drawbacks too. It embodies as many biblical terms as possible: body, communion, mediation (mediator). It takes into account the requirements stated in the third and fourth conditions set out above. As for the first condition, though the definition indicates adequately what is peculiar to the economy of the New Testament, it does not stress the continuity of the Church. It can be applied both to the Church on earth and to that in heaven. But it does not make absolutely

1. See Chapter I, p. 14.
2. See Chapter II, pp. 63 and 67.

explicit the vitality of the advance towards the Kingdom required by the second condition.[1]

We could restrict our definition in order more directly and clearly to signify the Church militant, as follows : the Church, the mystical body of Christ, is a communion which is at once inward and external, an inner communion of spiritual life (of faith, hope and charity) signified and engendered by an external communion in profession of the faith, discipline and the sacramental life.

The external communion thus specified is that which follows from the exercise of the three offices of Christ, prophet, king and priest, in and through the three powers of the Church—magisterium, jurisdiction and order—on condition that the word magisterium should be understood in the complete sense of the full 'service of the Word'. Our definition must be elucidated by showing the place of the body of bishops and of the successor of Peter in the external communion of the Church. The reader will note how it preserves and gives full value to all that was good in Bellarmine's definition. But from now on it is central to a complete view of the Church.

The two communions are inseparable. The external communion of ecclesiastical life, within its canonical bounds, is not enough to constitute the Church. The inner communion, completely cut off from its generative causes, is not enough either. We are dealing with an economy of incarnation.

Moreover, the expression 'communion' takes fully into account St Paul's doctrine : 'We form one body in Christ, and each acts as the counterpart of the other' (Rom. 12 :5). Because of its union with Christ, the Church is a mystery of interdependence, a network of relationships between persons. We must analyse all the potentialities of this basic fact. We must restore to the term 'communion', with all its aura of tradition and meaning, its rightful importance.

This is to be the object of the remainder of this book. We have

1. The limitations of our definition spring from the fact that we are giving a definition on intrinsic grounds alone. For a definition on extrinsic grounds, see Journet, *L'Eglise du Verbe Incarné*, vol. II, p. 1185. It may be interesting to compare our definition with that of S. Boulgakoff (Orth.), in *Orthodoxie*, Paris, 1932, pp. 1 and 3 (English translation, Bulgakov, *The Orthodox Church*, London, 1935). Despite common elements, the differences will be immediately apparent.

more than once used the word 'communion'. We have employed it to describe, to define, the Church. But hitherto, we have not had occasion clearly to formulate its content.

The second and the third parts of this book will study more closely the form of the Church's social nature to which we have just given a name. This study will of necessity be twofold : communion is one whole, but its components must be analysed. In any social group there is a dialectic of relationships between what gave it birth (and subsistence) and what it permanently is, between its efficient cause and its form. In the reality of things, the immediate generating causes of the communion do not hover above it in a separate universe; they are incorporated into it. Those who in the present-day Church hold the authority of the apostles are on one hand those who establish, unify and move the Christian community, and on the other hand those who provide a structure for it and organize it in a stable fashion, obeying the principles which govern the nature and life of this social group. In the people of God, this is the position of the prophets, the apostles and the priestly hierarchy. They belong simultaneously to the generative side and the formal side.

We shall deal successively with the generative causes of the communion (chapters V to VIII) and with the communion itself (chapters IX to XI, with the appendices). Although, within the communion the priestly hierarchy provides the structure, it should not be forgotten that the communion thus constituted is itself summoned to play an active part, generating growth and vitality in the Church. The entire priestly people is called to 'proclaim the exploits of the God who has called you out of darkness into his marvellous light' (I Peter 2 :9).

PART II

THE MISSION OF THE CHURCH

The Generative Causes of Communion

V

THE ROYAL PRIESTHOOD OF THE PEOPLE OF GOD, BORN OF THE SENDING OF JESUS BY THE FATHER

WE are placing this chapter, together with the three which follow it, under the general heading of 'The Mission of the Church'. We shall be tackling the generative causes of communion, the whole gamut of the Church's ministerial activities, which we have called the 'order of mediation'.[1] We saw, at the end of the last chapter, where this topic fits into our study. Here the word mission is almost synonymous with ministry, work of salvation, messianic work. . . . We have preferred the notion of mission, which seems better to convey the idea of active mediation which we are discussing. The word mission means sending, nothing more. It is the equivalent of the word apostolate. The apostolate is the work of an *apostolos*. The verb *apostellein* means to send. We must always bear in mind this fundamental sense.

I. JESUS CHRIST SENT BY THE FATHER

The mission of the apostolic Church 'proceeds from the holy Trinity and returns to it. It descends from God and from Jesus Christ; through the ministry of the apostles filled with the Spirit it perpetuates the presence of the living Saviour and of his gifts; it leads the elect to the glory of the Father.'[2] These two sentences

1. See Chapter IV, §IV, pp. 91ff.
2. L. M. Dewailly, *Envoyés du Père, Mission et apostolicité*, Paris, 1960, p. 113. For an overall study of the question of the Church's mission, see F. X. Arnold, *Pour une théologie de l'Apostolat*, Tournai and Paris, 1961. This is a translation of *Grundsätzliches und Geschichtliches zur Theologie der Seelsorge*, Freiburg, 1949.

are an admirable expression of what we hope to show. 'The mission comes from God, it relies on God, it reaches its completion in God. Missionary theology is the work of the three divine persons associating themselves with men to save men.'[1]

The sending (*missio*) of Jesus is the starting point of all ecclesiology. The New Testament even applies the word *apostolos* to Christ on one occasion (Heb. 3 : 1). The Father sent his Son.[2] He was sent to become the head of the Church.[3] The Church was thus included in the Father's sending of the Son.[4]

Jesus was sent. With what object? St John gives us his answer: 'When God sent his son into the world, it was not to reject the world, but so that the world might find salvation through him' (John 3 : 17).[5] That sums up the whole motive for the incarnation. But we must go a little further and consider the duties which Christ had to assume in order to fulfil his mission. Sent to bring about the salvation of the world, Christ, we say, was to discharge this responsibility simultaneously as priest, as king and as prophet.

Are there biblical grounds for this threefold division of the functions of Christ? Father Prat says definitely not. The division, 'alien to the messianic speculations of the Jews, practically unknown to the Fathers, was introduced or brought into vogue, after some very odd and tentative investigations, by the reformers of the sixteenth century and does not fit in at all with Pauline theology'.[6] Father Congar, on the other hand, devotes a lot of space to this threefold division. He thinks that 'the idea expressed in this theology may be regarded as traditional'.[7]

1. Dewailly, *Envoyés* . . ., p. 42.
2. Rom. 8:3, Gal. 4:4, John 3:17, 3:34, 5:36, 6:29, 6:58, 7:29, 8:42, 10:36, 11:42, 17:3, 8, 18, 21, 23, 25, 20:21. The reader will note the prominence of this leading theme in St John's gospel.
3. Eph. 1:22, 4:15, 5:23.
4. For a theological analysis of the notion of mission, see *Summa Theol.*, I, q. 43, a. 1.
5. 'Qui propter nos homines et propter nostram salutem descendit de caelis', says the liturgical creed of 'Nicaea-Constantinople'.
6. F. Prat, *La théologie de Saint Paul*, vol. II, fourteenth ed., p. 199 (English translation, from 11th ed., *The Theology of Saint Paul*, 2 vols., London 1926-1927; one vol. edn., 1957). Father P. Dabin takes an exactly contrary view: he talks of 'the somewhat precipitate judgment of his eminent confrère' in *Le Sacerdoce royal des fidèles*, Brussels and Paris, 1950, pp. 30-31. Jean Rivière also is very reserved (*DTC*, vol. 13, col. 914).
7. Y. Congar, *Lay People in the Church*, p. 55. See the *Contents* of this book.

What are the facts? We can agree with Father Prat that the threefold division is not to be found anywhere in the Bible. But we do meet in both Testaments all the elements of the doctrine of threefold function. The first Christian generations had only to put them together. In other words, this doctrine is not revealed by exegesis but it is a fine example of biblical theology.

In the Old Testament, we find a theology of anointing. This was a singling out, a consecration to the service of Jahveh with a view to a special ministry; it conferred a special status on its object: he belonged thenceforward to the sphere of the divine. The ministries in question were kingship, priesthood and prophecy. In the New Testament Jesus is called Christ, that is to say 'Anointed'—in Hebrew, Messiah. This accords with the conviction that the New Testament is the fulfilment of the Old. In a first theological formulation one possibility quite naturally arises: if Christ is called 'Anointed', this was surely in view of those ministries for which anointment was conferred under the old dispensation? Should not the Christ be king, priest and prophet? An investigation of the New Testament provides a threefold affirmative reply to this threefold question.[1]

In the 1559 edition of *The Institutes of the Christian Religion,* John Calvin included a long chapter whose title clearly reveals its contents: 'That in order to know with what object Jesus Christ was sent to us by the Father, and what he brought us, it is necessary chiefly to consider three things in him—viz. his offices of Prophet,

1. References: *The Old Testament* records the anointing of *kings* (I Kings 9:16, 16:3; III Kings 1:34); of the *high priest* (Ex. 29:7; Lev. 8:12; a later addition extends this anointing to ordinary priests: Ex. 28:41); of the *prophet* (III Kings 19:16: there is nowhere any mention of the anointing of a prophet except for Eliseus, and even this solitary text has been questioned. There is nevertheless a spiritual link between anointing and prophecy, cf Is. 61:1). In the *New Testament, the 'anointing' of Jesus* (Matt. 3:13 and parallels; Acts 10:38). Jesus is the anointed one par excellence (Matt. 16:16 and parallels). Jesus is *king* (Matt. 2:2, 21:5, 27:11, John 12:13, 18:37; Luke 23:2; Acts 17:7). Jesus is *prophet* (Luke 4:17-22, where our Lord describes himself as the fulfilment of the prophecy of Isaias); Jesus calls himself a prophet (Matt. 13:57 and parallels, Luke 13:33); he is 'the prophet' (John 6:14), but he is also more than any prophet (Matt. 16:16), for a prophet can play only a preparatory role. Jesus is *priest*; he is high priest of the new covenant (Heb. 2:17, 3:1, 4:14-15, 5:1, 5; 6:20, etc), and on these grounds he is above the Levitical priesthood. Bibliography: I. de la Potterie, 'L'Onction du Christ, Etude de théologie biblique', in *NRT*, 1958, vol. 80, pp. 225-252; J. H. Newman, 'The three offices of Christ' in *Sermons bearing on the Subject of the Day.*

King and Priest' (II :15). Calvin had adopted the threefold division as early as the 1545 edition.[1]

In 1566, the Roman Catechism devoted a long passage to 'Jesus Christ, king, priest and supreme prophet'.[2] What authority has this text? It was not an act of the solemn magisterium. The catechism, which was published by Pius V, had simply been drafted in execution of a resolution of the Council of Trent. It should, however, be considered as a document of the ordinary magisterium of the Church, and it thus enjoys a special authority. Promulgated by Pius V, it has frequently been recommended by other popes and recommended, even imposed, by many local councils. It thus has an authority greater than that of the theologians who prepared it.[3]

In the sixteenth century, the threefold division took its place in a systematic presentation of Christology. But the first Catholic theological treatise to follow the example of the Roman Catechism was Scheeben's in 1882. For all that, the doctrine of the threefold function is a very old one. We find it admirably set out in the work of Eusebius of Caesarea, who died in 339 or 340, which is a model of that reflection of biblical theology which we outlined above.[4] To conclude this historical survey, we should note that St Thomas is aware of the threefold function of Christ. He mentions it more than once. He does not, however, make it a pivot of his theological synthesis.[5]

Just where would the theology of the three functions fit into the plan of the *Summa*? The key here is the theology of anointing by the Spirit, mentioned in Acts 10:38, where we are told that 'God anointed him (Jesus) with the Holy Spirit and with power'. In St Thomas's teaching the plenitude of grace which dwells in the human nature of Christ corresponds to this anointment by the Spirit. St Thomas attributes mediation to this human nature by reason of its

1. Bibliography on the threefold division in the history of theology: There is invaluable historical information in the art. by E. F. Karl Müller, 'Jesu Christi dreifaches Amt', in *Realencyklopädie f. prot. Theol. und Kirche*, vol. 8, pp. 733-741. For St Thomas, see D. Boilot, *La médiation prophétique du Christ*, typewritten thesis, Le Saulchoir, 1951.

2. *Catechismus ex Decreto Concilii Tridentini* (. . .) *editus*, ed. princeps, pp. 20-22.

3. See A. Duval, in encyclopaedia *Catholicisme*, vol. 2, cols. 655-656.

4. *Evang. Dem.*, IV, 15; VII proem; *Hist. Eccles.*, 1, 3.

5. The texts where St Thomas deals with the threefold division, or at least with certain of its elements are: *In Matt.*, 1, 1. *In Rom.*, 1, 1; *In Heb.*, 1, 4; *In Is.*, 61, *init*; *In Ps.*, 44, 5; III, q. 22, a. 1, ad 3; q. 31, a. 2, c.

plenitude of grace and glory, which plenitude is a consequence of the hypostatic union. The theology of anointing is thus linked with the theology of mediation, and this latter doctrine opens the way to the development of the doctrine of the three functions.

The theology of mediation has nothing monolithic about it. It is clear that St Thomas is ready to class priesthood and prophecy in the wider category of mediation.[1] By reason of his plenitude of grace, Christ is at once lawgiver, priest and king.[2] True, the trilogy here is not the same one—unless one identifies 'lawgiver' with 'prophet'—but in the same plenitude of grace we find the basis for a number of complementary functions. Within the framework of St Thomas's thought we can thus regard the triple function as three forms of Christ's mediation.[3] These three functions correspond to needs which arise out of the very nature of things.[4] We conclude these reflections by simply noting that Christ, by surpassing all of them, brings about the fulfilment of the three great functions of the old dispensation.

II. The Priestly People

The priestly, royal and prophetic role of Christ, sent by the Father, is exercised at once by the general ministry of the people of God and by the special ministry of those whom the Lord has singled out. These two ministries are correlatives of each other. It is the whole that must be considered. We will start here with the collective aspect.

A Lutheran theologian advanced the two following theses : 1. The Church is the people of God called by Christ from the world; 2. The Church is the prophetic, priestly and royal people sent by Christ into the world.[5] A specialist in the theology of the laity, Mgr G.

1. III., q. 26, a. l, arg. 1 and ad 1.
2. III, q. 22, a. 1, ad 3.
3. The concept of 'Mediator' is wider than that of *Caput* in St Thomas.
4. Y. Congar, *Lay People in the Church*, p. 55.
5. E. Schlink, in *Kerygma und Dogma*, 1955, no. 3, pp. 208-225. Short bibliography: L. Cerfaux, 'Regale Sacerdotium', in *RSPT*, 1939, vol. 28, pp. 5-39; G. Thils, *L'enseignement de S. Pierre*, Paris 1943; P. Dabin, *Le sacerdoce royal des fidèles dans la tradition ancienne et moderne*, Brussels and Paris, 1950; P. Seidensticker, *Lebendiges Opfer* (*Rom.* 12:1). *Ein Beitrage zur Theologie des Apostels Paulus*, Munster, 1954; E. G. Selwyn (Prot)., *The First Epistle of St Peter*, London 1955; T. F. Torrance,

Philips has pointed out, with good reason, that Catholics and members of the Orthodox Church could subscribe to such a definition.[1] For our part, we should like especially to stress here the royal priesthood, by commenting on the most explicit text on the subject, the second chapter of the first epistle of St Peter. We shall begin by analysis, before drawing our conclusions.

A holy priesthood, to offer up that spiritual sacrifice which God accepts (2 :5). The Church is a spiritual building for a holy priesthood. 'Spiritual building' is the nature of the Church; 'holy priesthood' is its vocation. 'Priesthood' must be understood here in the sense of sacerdotal body and not as sacerdotal act, the exercise of the priesthood.[2] This priesthood is holy, in contrast with the pagan priesthoods of Asia Minor, which were at least spurious, when they were not openly immoral. The Christian Church is a priesthood because it is in the same relation of mediation with regard to the whole of humanity as the official Jewish priesthood was with regard to the whole people of Israel.

The activity of this priestly body is to offer up a spiritual sacrifice. St Peter uses offering up (*anapherein*) in its full meaning, with the definite signification of a priestly act, the ministerial action of the priest. The sacrifice is termed 'spiritual', in contrast with the 'material' sacrifices of the Jews and the pagans. Prophets and psalmists are clearly conscious of this distinction. Sometimes they reject the whole sacrificial mystery, corrupted by the wickedness of men (Is. 1 :11-15); sometimes they stress the superiority of righteousness over sacrifice (Mich. 6 :6-8; Ps. 49 (50) : 13-14); sometimes the spiritual sacrifice appears simply as the condition which renders the ritual sacrifices acceptable (Ps. 50(51) : 19).

In the New Testament we find many examples of sacrificial language which follow the same line of thought. Prayer is described as a

Royal Priesthood, Edinburgh, 1955. This last author, who has a considerable influence in the activities of the World Council of Churches, is a Presbyterian and a professor at Edinburgh. In a recent book, *Le sacerdoce des fidèles*, Bruges and Paris, 1961, Mgr E. J. de Smedt, Bishop of Bruges, has clearly shown the relationship which exists between the priesthood of all believers and the priestly task of the pastors of the Christian people. He stresses the authenticity of the priesthood of believers (p. 15).

1. Cf. G. Philips, *ETL*, 1959, vol. 36, p. 903.

2. Among other reasons, there is the parallel with 2 :9, and through this verse with Ex. 19:6.

sacrifice.[1] 'Righteousness' or 'justice', which are regarded as a sacrifice in the Old Testament, are widened in meaning to include the complete abandonment of the self to God, the oblation of the self (Rom. 12 :1; 1 Peter 2 :5). There are very many particular applications of this general sense. Among sacrifices, we must class faith (Phil. 2 :17), the conversion of the Gentiles (Rom. 15 :16), the priestly duty of preaching the gospel (ibid), the future martyrdom of Paul (II Tim. 4 :6), alms (Phil. 4 :18) and the doing of good to others (Heb. 13 :16). All this may be part of the background of the text on which we are commenting at the moment. Nevertheless certain signs suggest that St Peter has principally in mind the sufferings inherent in the Christian life and the duties of kindness and goodness.[2]

The theology of the prophets and of the New Testament on worship is one long insistence on the conditions that make this worship genuine : respect for the Covenant and for the Word of God, justice, love, and humility before God. It is not an indictment of outward worship, in which the appearances substitute for reality, or at least do not conform to it.

Can we rule out a reference to the eucharist? In 2 :5, St Peter is not thinking of any ritual act nor of the eucharist in any way at all. Such is the opinion of many modern authors (Hort, Windisch and others), who moreover echo as classic a commentator as Estius.[3] But not all authors would agree. E. Lohmeyer, a Protestant exegete, takes another view. He thinks that the whole passage 2 :1-10 hints at a eucharistic framework. Selwyn follows him on this point.[4] Let us sum up the arguments as Selwyn marshals them.

1. The sacrifices offered by the priestly body of the Church are closely linked with the redemptive work of Christ. Jesus is presented as the centre of a new form of worship and of a sacrificial manner of life. The moral philosophy taught in this epistle is an *imitatio Christi*, calling for kindness, patience and sufferings with a view to winning pagans to the faith.The deep and immediate motivation of Christian

1. Apoc. 8:3 -4; Heb. 13:15 links prayer and the confession of faith.

2. Note the insistence on the imitation of Christ (2:21-24) and on the code of social behaviour within the Christian community and towards pagans (2:11-3:12). On all this, see Selwyn, *The First Epistle of St Peter*, London 1955, p. 161.

3. 'Spirituales hostias, id est, opera virtutum . . .; spirituales . . . ad discrimen cultus externi . . . Subest igitur in hac parte exhortatio tacita ad opera bona.'

4. Pp. 295 ff.

behaviour is thus Christlike; it lies in the redeeming act. It does not seek its justification either in any sort of human wisdom or in a general precept of charity.

2. The ethic of the apostolic Church was expressed in a vocabulary linked with worship : temple, priesthood, sacrifice. This language reveals its relationship. The ethic is homogeneous with prayer and with praise.[1] The parallel with Heb. 13:15 is instructive: 'It is through him, then, that we must offer to God a continual sacrifice of praise, the tribute of lips that give thanks to his name.' Here we have the use of the same verb 'to offer' (*anapherein*), a pre-eminently liturgical term, the same reference to the mediation of Christ ('through him'), and the same ethical context (Heb. 13:16; 1 Peter, 2 :11). To be sure, prayers and praise in the primitive Church were not confined to the eucharist. But it is clear that for the New Testament, the eucharist was at once the home and focus of such prayers and their principal occasion. Above all—and this allows us to synthesize Selwyn's two arguments—the eucharistic canon as a whole presents itself as an action of praise and thanksgiving for the redeeming sacrifice of Christ.[2] Consequently we shall not be surprised to find this interpretation in the earliest Christian literature: the *Didache* (XIV:1, 2) applies to the eucharist the 'pure offering' of Mal. 1 :11.

I believe we can conclude with Selwyn :

> 'The "spiritual sacrifices" of which Peter speaks have been correctly interpreted as consisting in righteousness, self-oblation, deeds of kindness and brotherly love, prayer and praise and penitence. But the background against which our author thought of these sacrifices, and out of which they arose, was the worshipping community gathered for the celebration of the Eucharist and in particular, perhaps, for the baptismal Eucharist, of which we have evidence in later days.'[3]

1. It may be worth while to point out here the equivalence between 'spiritual sacrifice' and 'sacrifice of praise'. When the word 'praise' is added to 'sacrifice', it does not limit its significance, as in the case of a specific difference, but rather duplicates its meaning, as with a pleonaxm. If there is no praise or thanksgiving, the sacrifice is not worthy of God and is not accepted by him; it is without content; it does not stand up to its own definition. See however R. de Vaux, *Les instutions de l'Ancien Testament*, vol. II, Paris 1960; p. 294.

2. See I Cor. 11 :26.

3. Selwyn, p. 297.

I think we should take another of Selwyn's assertions into consideration.

> 'The Eucharistic sacrifice consists in the Eucharist taken *as a whole,* the entire Eucharistic service, with its prayers and praises, its almsgiving and social brotherhood no less than its strictly sacramental features, is included in the term.'[1]

What corresponds to the *priesthood* of the Christian people is thus the aggregate of spiritual sacrifices, including the eucharist.[2]

The association of ideas in the expression *royal priesthood* (Peter 2 :9) should not surprise us. The Christian community is born of a mysterious union of the baptized with Christ. Through that very fact, the baptized participate in the priestly dignity and the royal dignity. This theme is present in the New Testament. Christians will exercise the royal function of judges, in particular at the moment of the *parousia* (I Cor. 6 :2). They are already a 'royal race of priests' (Apoc. 1 :6, 5 :10).

The starting point of this doctrine is to be found in the Old Testament, in Ex. 19 :3-6 : 'You shall serve me as a royal priesthood.' A very old reading of the Hebrew gave 'priestly kingdom'; the Septuagint renders it as 'royal priesthood'. 'The fundamental sense, however, is never betrayed : the Hebrew nation, the Hebrew people as such is priestly.'[3]

What is the significance of this expression? The Hebrew people was set apart from the ungodly and the pagans in order to be exclusively consecrated to God by the Covenant. This privilege is priestly, using the term priesthood in an analogous sense. 'Just as the priest is a man chosen out of the midst of the people and consecrated specially to the divinity in order to represent it, so Israel has been chosen out from among the nations to play a role of religious mediation.'[4]

1. Selwyn, p. 297.
2. This does not mean, for all that, that every believer has the ministerial function of celebrating the eucharist. It may be worth while to recall here a passage from *Mentor Dei*: 'That the faithful offer the sacrifice through the priest is clear from the fact that the minister at the altar acts in the person of Christ considered as Head, and as offering in the name of all the members' (C.T.S. translation, p. 40).
3. G. Thils, *L'enseignement . . .*, p. 103.
4. G. Thils, *L'enseignement . . .*, p. 103. See the phrase of Gen. 12 :3: 'in thee all the races of the world shall find a blessing'. In Is. 61 :6, the idea of the priesthood of the Israelites comes up again (cf. L. Cerfaux, 'Regale sacerdotium', pp. 8-9).

The priesthood of every Israelite did not, however, rule out the priesthood of the Aaronic priest. They retained their purpose. Jahveh increased their number (Is. 66:21). The priesthood of the people did not abolish the ministerial priesthood, nor did it identify itself with it: this is a good example of the analogical value of the concept of priesthood.

St Peter applies these biblical texts to the true Israel chosen by God. The baptized form a royal priesthood. Christians are 'mediators among the people who are still groaning in the darkness of ignorance'.[1] Here is a passage from Selwyn on the social implications of the priesthood of the Christian people:

> 'For a priesthood implies a community on behalf of which the priesthood offers sacrifice, the gift being provided by the community; and the Church's task is here set forth as the offering to God and therefore the hallowing of the common life of the communities—village and city, school and factory, nation and world—in which it lives and works.'[2]

Let us pursue the parallel to its conclusion. The worship of the baptized does not in any way rule out a priesthood of office, a ministerial and hierarchical priesthood, based on the power of order. A Protestant theologian makes the following remark:

> 'The expression "priesthood of all believers" is an unfortunate one as it carries with it a ruinous individualism. "Priest" in the singular is never found in the New Testament applied to the believer, any more than "king" in the singular.'[3]

That is true in so far as it means that the believer exercises his priesthood as a member of the people of God. But nevertheless the acts of this priesthood will be personal.[4] Matters must not be carried to extremes.

To proclaim the exploits ... (2:9). Many different renderings have been given of the original *tas aretas* in this verse. Some translate it by 'virtues' (Vulgate, Luther, Bible du Centenaire, Segond), others by 'praises' (Jerusalem, King James), or by 'merits' (H. J.

1. G. Thils, *L'enseignement*..., p. 105.
2. Selwyn, p. 296.
3. Torrance, *Royal Priesthood*, op. cit., p. 35, footnote.
4. Cf. Rom. 12:1.

Schonfield) or again by 'perfections' (Buzy). As Selwyn observes, the word *arete* conjures up excellence in any field of activity whatsoever, and the prestige which such excellence merits. It is not merely a question of the *moral* excellence of virtue. So we must adopt a translation which sees in *tas aretas* the works of God.[1] It is rather a question, as the latest English translation of the New Testament puts it, of the 'triumphs' of God.[2] In the particular case we are considering, the 'exploits' refer specially to the redemption brought about by the death and resurrection of Christ, with the wisdom, the love and the power of God in the background. In what form was this proclamation to be made? What effect could be obtained from it? Had the ministry of the Word, as such, been entrusted to the people of God? Part of the answer is provided by verse 12.

Your life among the Gentiles must be beyond reproach; decried as malefactors, you must let them see from your honourable behaviour what you are; they will praise God for you, when his time comes to have mercy on them (2:12). In the preceding verse (2:11), St Peter had called on the faithful to resist the natural appetites which besiege the soul. He was referring to those impulses which belong to the lowest and most egoistical side of human nature, to the propensities which are characteristic of 'the average sensual man' (Selwyn). The word 'behaviour' (*anastrophe*) signifies above all the moral aspect of conduct. This was a question of the Christian life,[3] of the 'honourable behaviour' spoken of in the second part of the verse, especially the moral duties recalled in this epistle.[4]

This conduct should lead the pagans to praise God. As the apostle sees it, there are three stages: 1. the good works are done; 2. the pagans observe them and reflect on them; 3. as a result they glorify God when his time comes to have mercy on them.

They glorify God. There is an echo here of Matt. 5:16: 'Your light must shine so brightly before men that they can see your good works, and glorify your Father who is in heaven.' There was a time-honoured basis for all this in rabbinical literature: 'My children, if you do what is good, men and angels will bless you; because of you,

1. This fits the context better. Cf. Ps. 111:2: 'the Lord's wondrous doings'.
2. *The New English Bible. New Testament*, Oxford and Cambridge, 1961.
3. *Anastrophe*—'conduct', 'behaviour', occurs 6 times in I Peter; 1:15, 1:18, 2:12, 3:1, 3:2, 3:16.
4. Note the use of 'behaviour' in 3:1.

God will be glorified among the Gentiles; and the demon will flee from you.'[1] This theme must have been familiar to the primitive Church. For its use in the earliest patristic literature we can turn to Ignatius of Antioch, who wrote in his epistle to the Ephesians : 'Pray without ceasing for other men. For there is in them a hope of repentance, so that they can reach God. At least allow them to be your disciples through your works. In face of their tempers, you must be meek, in face of their boastings, you must be humble; in face of their blasphemies, you must show your prayers; in face of their errors, you must be firm in the faith; in face of their violence, you must be peaceful, and never seek to imitate them. Be their brothers through goodness, and try to imitate the Lord.'[2]

In the gospel (Matt. 5 :16), there is a link between good works and the action of glorifying God. But I Peter 2 :12 has more than this. The pagans will praise God *when his time comes to have mercy on* (or *to visit*) *them*. G. Delling gives an explanation which we sum up as follows. We can understand by *hemera* the day when God will grant the pagan slanderers, at the same time as their conversion, true understanding of the quality of the life led by the Christians. By *episcope* is meant the personal experience of mercy through which Christ becomes the Lord of men.[3] Thus we are dealing with a theme of eschatology become fact. Peter's phrase indicates the throes of conversion, not the last judgment. In other words, the conduct of the faithful is the concrete condition of the conversion of the pagans. One day they will acknowledge that God is at work in the life of the baptized.

The author of the epistle goes even further (3 :1) : in circumstances where the preacher has not succeeded in convincing a pagan, the conduct of a wife, by its silent testimony, may succeed in winning him over. The Word of God nevertheless remains indispensable. Nobody can be saved without it. But in this case, it is the wife's personal conduct that gives expression to the Word. The message of

1. *Test. Napth.*, VIII, 4; Selwyn, p. 171.

2. Chap. 10. For the sense of the verb 'to glorify', see Hermas, *Mand.*, 3, 1: 'Love the truth and let nothing but it come out of your mouth, so that the truthfulness of the spirit which God has placed in flesh may shine forth in the eyes of men; thus the Lord who lives in you will be glorified, for the Lord is truthful in all his words, and there is no lie in him.' Glorification of God implies admiration of an act all of whose merit is transferred to God.

3. G. Delling (Protestant), in Kittel, vol. II, p. 956.

the gospel calls for the submission of all mankind. To reject it is fatal. Thus it is clear that St Peter does not mean to say that in certain cases the Word can be dispensed with :[1] far from it.

All this is sanctioned by the liturgy. In the Roman Pontifical, the preface to the consecration of chrism grants the Christian the threefold dignity of king, priest and prophet. 'Confirm then this chrism, your creature, as a sacrament of perfect life and salvation for those whom you will have renewed in the baptism of spiritual ablution . . . , so that, according to the mystery of your pre-established design, impregnated with the *royal, priestly and prophetic dignity,* they may be clothed in the garments of their incorruptible office.'

For our present purposes we shall concentrate on the priestly and prophetic role of the Church. We shall see, moreover, that they are two aspects of the same Christian life, of the same 'conduct'.

1. *The royal priesthood.* What is its object? The whole Christian life, insofar as it is a spiritual sacrifice, a worship offered to God. In other words, it is the life of the Christian insofar as it is lived and directed by the virtue of religion.[2] The idea of priesthood implies the idea of mediation. By his holy life, the Christian is mediator for all men. If the priestly activity is regarded as corporative, it can and must be said that the priestly people is the mediator between God and the rest of mankind.

2. *The 'prophetic' role.* This role is difficult to dissociate from the previous one. I have put the word 'prophetic' in quotation marks. It is a hard term to pin down. In the sense in which we are using it here it evokes the idea of 'testimony'. Its object is to reveal the exploits of God, the great events of the redemption. In the view of certain authors, this role can be called prophetic.[3] 'Prophet' is here used analogically. If we agree that the word 'prophecy' can cover *all active mediation between God and men in the order of knowledge necessary for salvation,* we shall see that the term applies in one way or another to the prophets of the Old Testament, to Christ the Prophet, to the gift of prophecy *in* the Church (hierarchical prophecy and private prophecy), and to the charism of prophecy *in* the Church as a priestly, royal and prophetic people. In this last

1. Unbelievers are the ones who find God's word a stumbling block, 2:8.
2. See II-II, q. 81, a. 1, ad 1; a. 4, ad 1.
3. See Dabin, *Le sacerdoce royal*, pp. 32, 365, 413.

sense, what sort of activity is proper to it? St Peter does not specify any particular form for the oral proclamation of the 'exploits of God'. All that he explicitly depicts is Christian behaviour (*anastrophe*) as an imitation of Christ. It is this behaviour which is destined to play a part in the conversion of the pagans.

III. Supplementary Note on the 'Consecratio Mundi', one of the Three Ways in which the Faithful carry out 'The Work of the World'

In the first part of his speech to the Second World Congress of the Lay Apostolate on 5 October 1957, Pius XII uttered a phrase which set a lot of ink flowing: 'The *consecratio mundi* is in its essence the task of laymen, of men who are intimately involved in economic and social life, who take part in the government and in legislative assemblies.'

It seems to me that this text must be understood in the framework of the royal priesthood of the faithful. It expresses an already traditional idea under a new form.

We find some interesting pointers on the religious and priestly (in the sense of the royal priesthood) character of the works of the active life in St Thomas, when he vindicates the institution of religious orders for active works.[1] One objection was stated as follows: all members of religious orders are supposed to abandon the world. Does not St Gregory say: 'He who leaves the world and does the good he can offers a sacrifice in the desert, as if he had already come out of Egypt'? No form of religious life can thus have as its aim the active life. St Thomas replies by drawing a distinction: there are two manners of being in the world, physical presence and spiritual attachment. The religious who are engaged in active works are in the world only in the first manner.

> 'If they are busy with outward things, this is not because they are looking for something in the world, it is solely for the religious service of God. They make use of the world as if they were not using it at all.'[2]

1. II-II, q. 188, a. 2,
2. Ibid, ad 3.

St Thomas sets parallel with the sacrifice in the desert the possibility of offering a sacrifice in the world. This is completely in line with the main part of the article.

> 'Services rendered to a neighbour, because they ultimately refer to God, are called *sacrifices,* in virtue of the text: Do not forget charity and fellowship; it is by such sacrifices that you become worthy of God. Now it appertains properly speaking to religion to offer sacrifices to God.'[1]

We must not forget that St Thomas, in talking in this way, was thinking not only of the preaching orders but also and especially of the hospital and military orders. It was mainly these last that required physical presence in the world.

Any human activity can be the occasion of a spiritual sacrifice, and on these grounds it can be consecrated. The whole life of the Christian is in itself sacred, not profane. Now the relationships which constitute economic, social, cultural and political life are a network of human activities. As such, through the medium of the royal priesthood of the faithful, they revert to God in the form of a sacrifice of praise.

For the Christian, 'the work of the world' is not only a field for his *priesthood,* it also provides an opportunity for him to be a 'prophet' (a witness) for the exercise of his kingship. We have seen how Christian behaviour can help to 'proclaim the exploits of God'. On these grounds it is 'prophetic'. We must note now how the layman can be the minister of the *kingship* of Christ through his temporal activity. St Paul says in so many words that the magistrate is God's minister.[2] And this is not limited to the administrative sphere; it is true of other fields too. In his economic or cultural activity, the layman can serve as God's instrument and play his part in exercising the kingship of Christ.

Hence the same human activity can have three aspects, related respectively to the priesthood, the kingship and the prophetic character of Christ. When we look at things in this way, we see immediately how the human or natural quality of the work done, and not only its moral repercussions, his importance in God's eyes. The

1. Ibid, in c.
2. *Diakonos,* Rom. 13:4; see St Thomas's commentary on this text, no. 1034.

paschal sacrifice calls for a male yearling lamb, with no blemish on it (Ex. 12 :5). The prophet rails against those who take no pains to find a perfect sacrifice : 'What, no harm done when the victim you offer in sacrifice is blind? No harm done when it is lame or diseased?' (Mal. 1 :8). This is true too of the spiritual sacrifice realized through work in the world, of the testimony and the ministerial exercise of the kingship of Christ.[1]

1. By no means inapposite is a reflection of J. P. Dubois-Dumée: 'The second weakness of the Catholic press is its technical inefficiency . . . There is too great a tendency to believe that theological knowledge, activist enthusiasm or mere determination will suffice. In a domain where craftsmanship and apostolate are one and the same thing, technical efficiency is a means of increasing apostolic efficiency'. *Proceedings of the First World Congress on the Lay Apostolate*, vol. II, Rome, 1952, p. 19.

VI

THE APOSTOLIC FUNCTIONS OF THE HIERARCHICAL MINISTRY

We have been discussing the Christian people in the exercise of its various offices. We must now turn to the 'special' ministries in the Church. These ministries, which we shall define later on, are directly connected with the priestly people. It is important to specify what they are. In the New Testament, the 'special' ministry is never presented as democratically based nor as built up from among the members of the Church. It is not an emanation from the community. It does not rest on a delegation of powers. It represents the head of the body. The ministry is established from the top downwards. It is founded on the gifts of the Lord, who has ascended into heaven (Eph. 4:8). Thus Paul exercises his function in virtue of the commission he has received from God (Col. 1:25). '*God* has given us different positions in the church; apostles first, then prophets and thirdly teachers' (I Cor. 12:28; cf. Eph. 4:11).

But every 'special' ministry is *for* the Church, 'for the common good' (I Cor. 12:7:R.S.V. text), to 'build up the frame of Christ's body (Eph. 4:12). That is true even when the ministry is exercised outside the Christian community, among the pagans. Paul received the grace to be 'a priest of Jesus Christ for the Gentiles, with God's gospel for my priestly charge, to make the Gentiles an offering worthy of acceptance, consecrated by the Holy Spirit' (Rom. 15:16). Paul's priestly office is to put the pagans into a priestly state, to associate them with the royal priesthood of which we have spoken.

It remains for us to examine the nature of the 'special' ministry and how it is linked with Christ. Theologians of a number of Christian confessions would be in broad agreement with what I have been saying. The same is not true when we come to examine more closely the nature of the ministry and how it is transmitted.

I. The Hierarchical Ministry

The hierarchical constitution of the Church is an article of faith. We know that Luther took his stand on the universal priesthood when he wanted to deny the existence of a hierarchical priesthood.

> 'When he consecrates, the bishop does nothing more than if, instead of the assembly as a whole, he chose someone out of the crowd of those who all possess an equal power and ordered him to exercise this power instead of the others, just as, if ten brothers, royal children and all alike heirs, were to choose one of themselves to reign over the inheritance in their place, they would still be kings and equals in power, whereas the responsibility for governing would be entrusted to one alone. And to state the thing more clearly still : if a little flock of pious Christian laymen were made prisoners and deported into a desert place, if they had not with them a priest consecrated by a bishop . . . , they would choose one among themselves . . . and would entrust him with the responsibility of baptizing, of celebrating the mass, of absolving and preaching, and he would be really a priest, as if all the bishops and the popes had consecrated him.'[1]

To this assertion, which is to be found in various forms in the other reformers, the Council of Trent replied with the following declaration : 'If anyone says that in the Catholic Church there is not a hierarchy instituted by a divine disposition, and which is composed of bishops, priest and ministers, let him be anathema.'[2] This canon was preceded by a more explicit chapter where it was stated 'that in addition to the other ecclesiastical orders, the bishops, successors of the apostles, belong above all to the hierarchical order.'[3] The Council did not explicitly formulate a definition of bishops as successors of the apostles; it simply recalled a doctrine already accepted as a matter of faith in the universal Church. We find another assertion of the hierarchical constitution of the Church in

1. *To the Christian nobility of the German nation* (1520). (There are several English versions available: e.g., *Reformation Writings of Martin Luther*, vol. I, London, 1952). The German text appears in the *Weimarer Ausgabe*, vol. 6, pp. 407-408.
2. Denz., 966.
3. Denz., 960.

Pius VI's condemnation of a resolution of the Council of Pistoia.[1] The first Vatican Council declared once more that the bishops are successors of the apostles.[2] We are thus faced with two propositions *de fide*: 1. the Church has a hierarchical constitution; and 2. the bishops are the successors of the apostles.

Our purpose is not to prove an article of faith. We are not in the field of the *preambula fidei,* where rational demonstration is possible. The approach of the *fides quaerens intellectum* is different. We are in the declarative or interpretative field. When the reason applies itself to the dogma of the Trinity, it cannot demonstrate the truth. Its aim is simply to arrive at the best possible harmony or agreement. Although our subject is dealing with very different realities, the same holds true.[3] Our approach is of the contemplative type, within the faith.[4]

The hierarchical constitution of the Church is explained firstly in terms of the economy of sensible mediation proper to the incarnation. This interpretation repeats, as regards the hierarchy, the arguments which St Thomas used to establish 'the necessity of the sacraments for men's salvation'.[5] As C. Journet says,[6] to receive the things of God by the ministry of men is the way most closely adapted to our human condition.

That is the whole intention of the incarnation. It also explains Jesus's preference for action by physical contact: he touches the leper, he goes to the tomb of Lazarus and has the stone taken away, he takes Jairus' daughter by the hand ... at the same time he can also act at a distance and sometimes does so, as with the healing of the centurion's servant.... If Jesus draws attention to action by contact it is because

> 'our nature is wounded, it stands in need of a sensible stimulus to awaken it connaturally to the life of grace.'[7]

1. Denz., 1502.
2. Denz., 1828.
3. 'Rationes quae inducuntur a sanctis ad probandum ea quae sunt fidei, non sunt demonstrativae, sed persuasiones quaedam manifestantes non esse impossibile quod in fide proponitur' (II-II, q. 1, a 5, ad 2).
4. 'Ad fidelium exercitium et solatium' (*C.G.*, 1, 9).
5. III, q. 61. a. 1.
6. C. Journet, *L'Eglise du Verbe Incarné*, vol. I, 1942, p. 9 (English translation, *The Church of the Word Incarnate*, London, 1955, p. 6).
7. Journet, *The Church of the Word Incarnate*, p. 9.

Jesus has gone up into heaven, but the link is not broken.

> 'Before he left us he willed that there should always be among us certain men invested with divine power, by whom the action he initiates from heaven may be sensibly conveyed to each of us and may continue to reach us in the only way connatural to us—through direct contact. These are the powers of the hierarchy.'[1]

The apostolic succession, which is in question here, is one aspect of the mystery of the continuity of the Church. In Catholic theology, it is an issue of capital importance. We often meet with it in a truncated presentation. It frequently calls to mind nothing more than discussions about ordinations. We must be quite clear that the succession is not to be restricted to the question of valid orders, as, for example, it was thought to be at the end of last century when the question of Anglican ordinations was raised.

In contrast with this incomplete view of the apostolic succession, we find in Protestantism a radically different outlook. Karl Barth stresses the apostolic character of the Church very strongly. He even describes it as 'the one and only *nota Ecclesiae*'.[2] But in his eyes, the adjective 'apostolic' means nothing more than

> 'in the discipleship, in the school, under the normative authority, instruction and direction of the apostles, in agreement with them, through listening to them and accepting their message.'[3]

In all this, Karl Barth is a faithful disciple of Calvin. In *The Institutes of the Christian Religion,* Calvin declared that the 'papacy' was not the Church of God and that it appealed in vain to the apostolic succession, for this last was a succession not of *persons* but of doctrine.[4]

The two opinions we have just quoted each contain their particle of truth: sacramental continuity is decisive in the apostolic succession, but this permanence exists with a view to the objects that must

1. Ibid. This whole theme is taken up again by Y. Congar in a stimulating form, in 'Le mystère du Temple de Dieu et l'économie de sa présence dans le monde' in *L'année théologique augustinienne*, 1953, vol. 13, pp. 1-12.

2. K. Barth, *Kirkliche Dogmatik,* vol. IV, 2, p. 797 (English translation, *Church Dogmatics*, ed. T. F. Torrance and G. W. Bromiley, Edinburgh, vol. IV, 1, p. 714)

3. Ibid.

4. IV, 1; see also IV, 3, Part 2.

be passed on. Let me quote a passage from L. Dewailly, which seems to me very illuminating: 'Episcopal consecration is the sacrament of the apostolic succession, that is to say of the mission of the Church in its fidelity and its growth. It is no wonder that when we speak of this succession it is often understood as referring to the sacramental continuity of the hierarchy. The usage can be understood and justified. We are apt to talk both of the baptized and the faithful; we describe as a penitent both the man who confesses and he who repents. The effective sign is taken for its effect because, in point of fact, it is inseparable from it, and only through this sign is the effect perceptible. Thus, provided we never forget this subordination of the sign to the signified, we need not fear the use of this transferred meaning. The sacramental character of Order and especially of the episcopal rank are the sacrament of the authentic handing down of the objects of the Church's life and of the powers which keep watch over these objects, and thus the sacrament of the Church's mission and of its apostolic character.'[1]

Christ's aim, in instituting the apostles, went beyond the men concerned, directly to the heart of the mission. The apostles had been chosen to this end. The powers are relative to it. Beyond the charisms, we must consider the function.[2] 'The function of the apostles in the Church is mission, and thus the apostolicity of the Christian Church is the quality which links it with the mission of the apostles.'[3] As Father Congar clearly shows, apostolicity is the name the unity of the Church takes when it is considered as extending through time and thus necessarily, because of the brevity of human life, through a succession of men. 'What creates the apostolicity of the Church in depth is thus the identity of mission between the Church of today and the apostles, and then, *positis ponendis,* between the apostles and Christ, the first and true "envoy of God".'[4]

Christ's mission is unique. But on analysis we see three aspects in it: Christ is prophet (teacher, master), priest and king. We find the three same aspects again in the mission of the apostles as the New Testament describes it: they preach the gospel, they preside

1. L. M. Dewailly, *Envoyés du Père. Mission et Apostolicité,* op.cit., pp. 100-101.
2. We can say the same of the sending of the Son by the Father: the Incarnation was designed for the mission of salvation. Cf. John 3:17, Gal. 4:4-5, I John 4:9.
3. L. Dewailly, op. cit. p. 59.
4. Y. Congar, in encyclopaedia *Catholicisme,* vol. I, col. 729.

over the eucharist and perform again the sanctifying gestures instituted by Christ, they form communities and administer them. It is to these three aspects of a mission that extends through time that theologians attach the three offices of the Church : the magisterium (or service of the Word), the priesthood (or power of order) and the administration (or power of jurisdiction). 'The ministerial acts of the hierarchy are the very acts of the apostolate of the Twelve and proceed from the acts of the Messiahship of Jesus.'[1]

The whole question of the apostolic succession depends in the last analysis on a correct theological outlook : 'The privilege of the apostles is in no way to be regarded as being for the benefit of those who hold it, it is a twofold service, entirely relative to their mission. Their function counts more than their individuality, and less than the objects and ends which define it. It is the objects, the realities concerned, which here dominate the men.'[2] Everything is at the service of the divine life to be handed on and to be preserved.[3]

II. The Three Great Offices: Magisterium, Priesthood and Administration

These three offices are three forms of the ministry of Christ exercised by the Church. The Church has powers, which are designed to provide a service, just as Christ had all power in heaven and on earth, but in the cause of the redeeming 'service'.[4]

We merely touch on this important point, which we do not plan to go into here. German theology is perhaps more sensitive to such particulars than French theology. The German word for power, *Macht,* is so suggestive of the idea of *constraint* that it immediately becomes necessary to show that what is meant is a very special power,

1. Y. Congar, loc. cit.
2. L. Dewailly, op. cit., 70.
3. Among recent works, see Y. Congar, 'L'apostolicité de l'Eglise selon St Thomas d'Aquin', in *RSPT*, 1960, vol. 45, pp. 209-224. Congar specially stresses the *firmitas fidei*, the continuity of the ministry being at its service.
4. The three offices of Christ and hence the three functions of the Church are indicated by the theme of 'diakonia'. H. Kraemer (Prot.) has something to say on this in Chapter V of *A Theology of the Laity*, London 1958. (Congar for his part stresses the correlation of the three powers and the action of one upon the other.) The three offices bear the stamp of the priesthood of the suffering Servant depicted in Is. 53.

completely committed to *salvation*. German theologians like to repeat that the role of the Church is not that of a '*power*', but rather that of a 'plenipotentiary' (*Vollmacht*) sent by Christ into the world. These clarifications are useful. We shall not lose sight of them in the following pages, in which the word 'power' must always be understood with these shades of meaning.

Here we will confine our inquiries to a very particular point. Are there two powers or three in the Church? In fact the question is limited to this: are the royal hierarchical office—or jurisdiction—and the prophetic hierarchical office—or magisterium—specially distinct?[1]

A great many canonists and some theologians believe that in the circumstances no more than the same single power is involved. The most distinguished of these theologians is undoubtedly Mgr Journet.[2] Among the recent cannonists, we may note the great treatise of Wernz-Vidal, an important Roman commentary on the Code.

We should begin by stressing the features common to magisterium and jurisdiction.[3] In the exercise of these two powers, the Church is the secondary cause, whereas in the priestly power, the Church is a mere instrument of Christ. The Church participates in the priesthood of Christ only in a purely instrumental fashion. And this is true both in the ascending movement of the sacrifice (Christ, the chief priest), and in the descending movement of the sacraments (God, principal cause; humanity of Christ, joint instrument; sacraments, separate instruments). The priestly activities of priests are thus exercised independently of their moral dispositions of holiness and uprightness, independently of their learning too.[4] The situation is different with the magisterium and jurisdiction. The pastoral and teaching roles of the Church are subject to the human qualties of the ministers who exercise them to a greater degree. For this reason they are

1. Does jurisdiction include the magisterium? See on this subject M. J. Nicolas's report on ecclesiology in *RT*, 1946, vol. 46, especially pp. 391ff. See also L. M. Dewailly's review of C. Journet's *L'Eglise du Verbe Incarné*, in *BT*, vol. 6, 1940-1942, pp. 45-53, particularly pp. 49-50.

2. *The Church of the Word Incarnate*, op. cit., p. 21.

3. These common features we, too, accept, but they are arguments equally to hand for those who believe the two powers are one.

4. Still in application of the principle of instrumental causality. See the clearest expression of St Thomas's thinking on this subject in III, q. 62, a. 1. See also footnote 2. p. 120.

not pure transmitters, as instruments are but true principal causes, albeit secondary.[1]

It is just because man is a secondary cause, with his limitations and deficiences, that God has given the hierarchy the charism of infallibility. Indeed, since the depositories of jurisdiction and magisterium are, as secondary causes, sources of initiative and of responsibility, then to the extent that the importance of their role increases, fallibility and error will threaten to enter into the administration of the Church. Hence the special assistance represented by the charism of infallibility. 'I am with you all through the days that are coming, until the consummation of the world' (Matt. 28:20). But we should note again that the charism does not transform the hierarchy into an instrumental cause. We must carefully distinguish this charism from that of inspiration (which transforms the action of the hagiographer into an instrumental cause). *Infallibility is an aid to the principal secondary cause, in its own order.*[2]

1. See on this point Journet's argument from suitability, *The Church of the Word Incarnate*, op. cit., vol. I, p. 12.

2. *Secondary principal cause.* We must explain this scholastic vocabulary. The secondary cause is in contrast with the sole first cause, God. But the secondary cause can be either principal or instrumental. It will be principal when it acts by virtue of what it is (of its form). It will be instrumental when it acts by virtue of an impulse from above received from a higher agent. The professor who gives a lecture is acting as principal cause: he is using his knowledge. The pen which writes down a theological dissertation on paper is a pure instrumental cause. This *tool* is completely at the service of the author whose research and reflection were responsible for the work. *Assistance.* What are we to understand by this? Negative assistance prevents error; positive assistance enlightens the Church so that it knows the truth and teaches the faithful correctly. Infallibility thus implies the action of the subject who receives it. The first Vatican Council was at pains to describe this charism in contrast with that of revelation: 'Neque enim Petri successoribus Spiritus Sanctus promissus est, ut eo revelante novam doctrinam patefacerent, sed ut, eo assistente, . . . fidei depositum sancte custodirent et fideliter exponerent' (Denz., 1836).

The infallible definitions of the Church cannot thus be set on the same plane as the word of God communicated by the Scriptures. 'These holy Books are *the Word of God.* I deliberately said '*are* the Word of God' and not merely *contain* the Word of God, as for example the catechism or a religious manual. They *are* the Word of God, by virtue of this unique charism of inspiration through which God, the eternal Truth, subjects to himself in an unparallelled manner . . . all the faculties of the human writer, and, while leaving him with his own nature, his personal features and his character (Benedict XV, *Enc. Spiritus Paracl.*, *AAS*, 12, 1920, p. 390) makes him express all that which and only that which he, God, wants (Leo XIII, *Enc. Providentissimus*, *AAS*, 26, 1893-1894, p. 289). It is no longer the man who is speaking: it is the Holy Spirit *qui locutus est per* prophetas . . .' (A. Bea, ' Valeur pastorale de la

Both in the exercise of jurisdiction and of magisterium, the Church imparts its message with authority, and is entitled to demand obedience. Nobody doubts that this is true of jurisdiction, but it is equally true of magisterium. The Church does not teach in the same way as philosophers and scholars do.[1] The teaching magisterium is invested with authority. Moreover, jurisdiction and magisterium are acquired and lost in the same manner, that is to say by canonical mission or by its revocation. This is another common feature, in contrast with the power of order, which is acquired by ordination and in an absolutely irrevocable manner.[2]

Why, though, must these powers be regarded as specifically distinct? For a long time, it must be admitted, doctrine distinguished only two powers, order and jurisdiction. That is St Thomas's position,[3] and also that of the catechism of the Council of Trent.[4] There it is stated that the power of order is related '*ad verum corpus Christi*' whereas the power of jurisdiction is related to the mystical body. It was not till the start of the nineteenth century that writers took it into their heads to distinguish a third branch of the powers of the hierarchy, *potestas magisterii*. It was a canonist who opened the way, Ferdinand Walter (1794-1879). He was followed by others.

Parole de Dieu dans la liturgie' in *La Maison-Dieu*, vol. 47-48, pp. 129-148. The passage quoted is on p. 137).

Father Sebastian Tromp has an excellent formula: 'Juridice, non vero physice, locutio Pontificis potest dici verbum Dei, quatenus loquitur ut Dei vicarius (*De S. Scripturae inspiratione*, Rome 1936, third ed., p. 101). See Congar, in *Chalcedon*, III, p. 262.

1. Here is what Wernz-Vidal writes on this subject (vol. II, pp. 52-53): 'Nam magisterium ecclesiasticum non est mere *doctrinale*, sive simplex propositio doctrinae qua nulla imponitur obligatio, sed est *auctoritativum*, quo *vi definitionis* ecclesiasticae oritur obligatio credendi.' A formula to be explained from a Thomist outlook on the faith.

2. See on this subject St Thomas, II-II, q. 39, a. 3. Wernz-Vidal lays much stress on this point, vol. I., p. 53: 'Namagisterium certe non est potestas diversa a jurisdictione . . . si eodem modo acquiritur, augetur, amittitur, atque generatim jurisdictio, scilicet injunctione sive missione canonica vel revocatione competentis Superioris ecclesiastici'. It is understandable that this argument should seem a strong one to a canonist whose attention is necessarily drawn to the manner of conferment of powers. See also Journet, *The Church of the Word Incarnate*, op. cit., p. 21. On the nature of the canonical mission, see the article 'Mission canonique' in the *DDC* (Claeys-Bouuaert), which is interesting, though it extends the notion of canonical mission too far.

3. In II-II, q. 39, a. 3.

4. Pars IIa, c. VII, q. VI.

Thereafter, theologians adopted the same position, among them Cardinal Franzelin.[1] Billot followed in his wake. Today this thesis is spreading more widely and is organizing itself from the theological point of view. What is striking today is the widening of outlook and the placing of this doctrine within the framework of a doctrine of the threefold office of Christ.[2]

What are the arguments in favour of making the distinction? The powers of teaching and of governing in the Church are simply the continuation of and a ministerial participation in the work of Christ as prophet and king. Now these functions are specifically distinct. Analysis of each act is sufficient to elucidate its object. Teaching (that is to say revealing in the case of Christ; preserving and imparting the revelation in the case of the Church) is a thing fundamentally different from ordering. The object of *docere* is specifically different from the object of *praecipere*. On the one hand, it is concerned with the *scientia discipuli* (adherence to the truth); on the other hand it is concerned with an act in terms of its end (adherence to the good). The truth to be communicated, the good to be pursued : these are two formally distinct aims. And in the subject to whom they are addressed, they appeal respectively to an act of the intelligence, teaching being the exemplary cause, and to an act of the will, the precepts given being the moral cause. Once transposed, this is equally true in the fields of magisterium and of jurisdiction.

It is perfectly true that the teaching of the Church is authoritative and thus binding. But the obligation which the magisterium imposes has a basis quite distinct from that which is imposed by the power of jurisdiction. I bow before the magisterium because I am certain that the Church teaches the revealed truth, and that it is sure of what it teaches. I bow before its pastoral power because the Church is responsible for leading me to the common good.

If we identify the magisterium with jurisdiction, we run the risk of stamping adhesion to the faith with a certain volitional character. Faith is essentially an illumination and it is not, above all, an act of obedience. Since its formal object is the primal truth, it is an act

1. See his *De Ecclesia Christi*, Rome, 1887.

2. I have not yet been able to establish when this parallel was first drawn. From this point of view, see J. Fuchs, *Magisterium, Ministerium, Regimen. Vom Ursprung einer ekklesiologischen Trilogie*, Bonn 1940.

of intelligence.[1] I believe because the primal truth has enlightened me. Thus, through faith, I share in a higher knowledge.[2] It is in the sense of sharing in a higher knowledge that we say of faith that it is an illumination.[3]

We have just examined faith from the point of view of the object. Faith, as an act of intelligence, yields to truth. But we must also study it from the point of view of the subject. Here we must leave all necessary room for the dynamism of the will in the act of faith. As St Thomas says, the intelligence is not sufficiently actuated by its proper object. The *assensus* must come to it from elsewhere, that is to say from the will which actuates all the faculties. From this aspect, faith is a kind of obedience. But the act performed under the movement of the will remains essentially an act of the intelligence. The necessary intervention of the will does not go so far as changing the object.[4]

We see in this the pre-eminence of the act of faith, which corresponds to the doctrinal power, over the act of obedience, which corresponds to the pastoral power. Adhesion to the directives and orders of the pastoral power is formally an act of will, an act of obedience in the formal sense of the word.[5] The proper motive of obedience is the *praeceptum superioris,* the order of the superior. Now, the proper motive of the act of faith is the *veritas prima,* that primal truth which is an attribute of God. The difference of level will be seen immediately.

In the act of faith I adhere, through the pronouncement of the

1. II-II, q. 1, a. 1. 'Credere autem est immediate actus intellectu, quia. objectum hujus actus est verum, quod proprie pertinet ad intellectum' (II-II, q. 4, a. 2).

2. 'Qui credit, assensum praebet his quae sibi ab alio proponuntur, quae ipse non videt... Non autem crederet aliquis non visis ab alio propositis nisi aestimaret eum perfectiorem cognitionem habere de propositis quam ipse habeat qui non videt' (*C.G.*, III, c. 40).

3. This is regarded by St Thomas, following tradition, as an effect of baptism: III, q. 69, a. 5, c. For the same reason, St Thomas is able to say: 'Sic sacra doctrina sit velut quaedam impressio divinae scientiae' (I, q. 1, a. 3, ad 2).

4. See Chenu's articles, 'L'amour dans la foi', in *BT*, notes and contributions, 1931-1933, pp. 97-99 and 'La psychologie de la foi dans la théologie du XIIIe siècle', in *Etudes d'histoire littéraire et doctrinale du XIIIe siècle*, second series, Paris and Ottawa, 1932, pp. 163-191.

5. 'Inclinatio quaedam ad implendum mandata secundum quod habent rationem debiti' (II-II, q. 4, a. 7, ad 3).

Church, which is only the condition of my faith, *to a divine utterance* : the real master of my faith is Christ. On the other hand, when I obey the power of jurisdiction there is nothing similar to this immediate action of Christ on my soul. I pursue a good course because the Church tells me to. That is no small thing : the Church is entrusted with leading me to salvation, and it is assured of the assistance of the Holy Spirit in the very special form of the charism of infallibility. But it is, nevertheless, an inferior motive, which reveals by contrast the greatness that belongs to the teaching mission of the Church in putting forward the articles of faith.

VII

THE LAY APOSTOLATE. THE CONFESSION OF FAITH

In the conclusion to the first part of this book (pp. 93-4), outlining the stages of our investigation, we stressed that a complete examination of the generative causes of the Church involved not only a study of the apostolic powers entrusted to the priestly hierarchy, but a consideration of the priestly people. This being established, the question quite naturally arises: what is the position within this people of those who have no hierarchical power, that is to say the laity? This question was tackled in broad general lines in Chapter V: it now remains for us to elaborate the answer on one particular point, that of Christian witness.

Why is such prominence being given to the laity today? Is this an apostolic strategy, because the clergy, overwhelmed with work, can no longer face up to its task alone? Is it because new forces must be tapped at any cost? No, the real reason goes deeper. It lies in the progressive secularization of civil society, of economic, technical and cultural life. Every state in the world, be it composed of Catholics, Anglicans or Calvinists, has been drawn to some degree into the same movement of secularization. It is a complex phenomenon, with varied aspects. 'Pernicious though it may have been in many respects, it would not be just to condemn it outright, allowing no appeal. Let us remember in the first place that Catholic doctrine holds that the State must be secular to a certain degree. The laicist error, in political matters, does not consist in the stress it lays on the right to secularize the State; it consists in the claim of the civil power to carry it to unlimited lengths, to make its own temporal interests the sole standard whereby its action should be determined.'[1]

1. J. Lecler, *L'Eglise et la souveraineté de l'Etat*, Paris, 1946, p. 169 (English translation, *The Two Sovereignties. A Study of the relationship between Church and State*, London, 1952, p. 128).

It has even been said, paradoxically, that : 'The origin of the secularization of the state lies in Christianity itself and in its teaching on the secular power.'[1] In history, the distinction between the temporal and the spiritual emerges as a purely Christian distinction, as an application of 'Give back to Caesar what is Caesar's, and to God what is God's'.

In actual fact, this secularization is a reality as ambiguous as the 'world' itself. But the fact is incontestable. It conditions our existence. It brings out clearly the role and the responsibility of those who are called on by their vocation to live in the 'world'. It emphasizes the urgent need of apostolic action by laymen. *They alone live right in the midst of the world.*

What precise questions must a theology of the laity answer? First and foremost comes the relation of the Word of God to earthly realities. What should be the true attitude of the Christian in the temporal domain : in economic affairs, in politics, in the scientific and technical field, in the work of civilization in general, in his profession or trade . . . ? How and in what conditions can evangelization be carried out by men who are working in the midst of the world and who thereby occupy a particularly important position as missionaries? Finally, how is the layman to be trained to serve Christ, in the world and starting from the world, how is he to be equipped from the doctrinal and spiritual point of view?[2]

The people of God are called on to 'proclaim the exploits' of God.

1. Ibid.

2. Short bibliography: G. Philips, 'L'état actuel des pensées théologiques au sujet de l'apostolat des laïcs', in *Eph. theol. lov.*, 1959, vol. 35, pp. 877-903. This article is very comprehensive: it also appeared in a booklet by the same author, *Etudes sur l'apostolat des laïcs*, Brussels, 1960. There is a good bibliography in the German Protestant encyclopaedia, *Weltkirchenlexikon*, art. 'Laien', by H. H. Walz, Stuttgart 1960. The outstanding work is still that of Y. Congar, *Jalons pour une théologie du laicat*, Paris, 1953, (English translation, *Lay People in the Church*, London 1958); G. Philips, *Le rôle du laicat dans l'Eglise*, Tournai and Paris 1954, is also worth reading (English translation, *The Role of the Laity in Church*, Cork, 1956), while one of the latest books out is J. Comblin, *Echec de l'Action catholique ?*, Brussels 1961. A Protestant view, though one receptive to oecumenism. is provided by H. Kraemer (Calv.), *A Theology of the Laity*, London 1958, while N. Afanassieff, professor at the St Sergius Inst. of theology gives an Orthodox view in 'The Ministry of the Laity in the Church', in *Oecumenical Review*, 1958, vol. 10, pp. 30-38. For an appraisal of recent writings, see J. Hamer, 'Bulletins d'ecclésiologie', particularly in *RSPT*, 1957, vol. 41, pp. 552-556; 1959, vol. 43, pp. 340-347. Y. Congar's article, 'Laienstand' (I-III), in *LTK*, vol. 6, cols. 733-740, is followed by an up-to-date bibliography; vol. 6 appeared at the end of 1961.

The Christian behaviour of the faithful, who try to imitate Christ, may contribute to the conversion of pagans. It is solely in relation to the Word of God that this Christian conduct enters into the process of conversion; this is because it leads directly or indirectly to the revealing of faith in Christ. We shall study this *disclosure* of adherence to Jesus Christ in the *homologia,* or confession of faith, as expounded by St Paul in the epistle to the Romans (10 :9-10).

I. 'Homologia' and 'Kerygma' in Rom. 10

Faith and the confession of faith, that is where salvation lies: 'Thou canst find salvation, if thou wilt use thy lips to confess that Jesus is the Lord, and thy heart to believe that God has raised him up from the dead. The heart has only to believe, if we are to be justified; the lips have only to make confession, if we are to be saved' (Rom. 10 :9-10).

Let us try to define the relationships between faith and the confession of faith according to this text. At first sight, they seem to be two different acts, existing side by side, with two objects and two ends which are apparently different. But in fact these two objects and these two ends overlap: the Lordship of Christ and his resurrection from the dead are one and the same mystery. In the same way justification, the recompense of faith, and the salvation which is won by the confession of faith are two closely allied realities. The oneness of the concrete act of faith cannot be questioned. In the same way as the human organs, the heart and the mouth, form a single human being, faith and the confession of faith must be considered in the same perspective.

As a matter of fact, faith quite naturally expresses itself in confession. A passage from the second epistle to the Corinthians stresses this link: 'I spoke my mind, says the scripture, with full confidence, and we too speak our minds with full confidence, sharing that same spirit of faith' (II Cor. 4 :13). If in this passage St Paul reverses the normal order and speaks of confession before the act of faith, it is on account of the text he is interpreting: 'This message of mine is close to thy side; it rises to thy lips, it is printed on thy memory; thou hast only to fulfil it' (Deut. 30 :14).

We, too, in talking of the confession of faith, must not forget the context in which it takes place either. It is much more than the statement of a formula: it is part of a complete Christian way of life.[1] It has a pronounced liturgical connection: it is not only the outward assertion of conviction, but also an act of praise. According to St Paul, the confession of faith culminates in prayer (II Cor. 4:15). Perhaps we should see in the prayer the rough equivalent of the confession. There is a parallel in Heb. 13:15: 'It is through him, then, that we must offer to God a continual sacrifice of praise, the tribute of lips that give thanks to his name.' The name of God cannot be pronounced like any other name, but only in prayer and praise.

These brief observations should suffice to show the importance of the confession of faith in the process of salvation. The confession of faith is so bound up with faith that it is an integral part of it. Everything that has been said of faith applies also to the confession of faith. It is no more an optional act, a step that can be taken or omitted, than faith is. Just like faith, it is the condition of salvation. 'He who believes and is baptized will be saved; he who refuses belief will be condemned' (Mark 16:16). The inward adhesion of the heart must be accompanied by an outward profession of faith expressed in the step of baptism. Both are necessary to salvation.

But alongside the confession of faith (*homologia*) St Paul discusses another form of testimony which is anterior to it and which he calls *kerygma* or preaching. The two are linked, for the confession is dependent on the preaching: 'How are they to call upon him until they have learned to believe in him? And how are they to believe in him until they listen to him? And how can they listen, without a preacher to listen to?' And St Paul adds, quoting Is. 52:7: 'And how can there be preachers, unless preachers are sent on their errand? So we read in scripture, How welcome is the coming of those who tell of peace, who tell of good news' (Rom. 10:14-15). For St Paul, indeed, there can be no preaching unless there is an assignment or a mission. The clear statement on this point in Rom. 10:15 is confirmed by the association of the two verbs *apostellein* and *kerussein*, very frequent in the New Testament. Thus St Mark records that Christ appointed twelve apostles to be his companions and 'to go out preaching at his command' (Mark 3:14). Luke employs the same expression when he reports the mission of the twelve: 'And he called the twelve apostles to him ... sending them out to proclaim

1. Titus 1:16.

the kingdom of God' (Luke 9:1-2). Christ himself, quoting Isaias, acknowledges himself as one sent by the Father: 'The Spirit of the Lord is upon me... He has *sent me out* to preach the gospel to the poor; to *bid* the prisoners go free... to *proclaim* a year when men may find acceptance with the Lord' (Luke 4:18). A little further on, he defines his mission even more clearly: 'I must preach the gospel of God's kingdom to the other cities too; it is for this that I was sent' (Luke 4:43-44). Following Christ's example, St Paul was to define himself as a preacher and envoy: 'Of that wisdom I am the chosen herald, sent as an apostle' (I Tim. 2:7; cf. II Tim. 1:11).

The obvious conclusion from these texts is that not just any Christian is charged with this office of preacher. During Christ's life on earth, it was the twelve who enjoyed this privilege.[1] 'So he called his twelve disciples to him, and gave them authority to cast out unclean spirits.... These are the names of the twelve apostles (envoys) ... These twelve Jesus sent out; but first gave them their instructions ... Preach as you go, telling them, The kingdom of heaven is at hand' (Matt. 10:1-7). This first mission was to the people of Israel only. It was renewed after the resurrection of Christ, with universal application. Christ appeared to the eleven and told them: 'Go out all over the world and preach the gospel to the whole of creation' (Mark 16:15). The apostles did indeed go out and 'preached everywhere' (Mark 16:20). Every people without exception must henceforth hear the message. Before Christ returned, 'the Gospel must be preached to all nations' (Mark 13:10) and St Paul also testifies that the Gospel 'has been preached to all creation under heaven' (Col. 1:23).

The preacher is thus defined first and foremost by his mission: he is an envoy. He who sends him gives him the necessary authority, gives him as it were a 'power of attorney'. The mission confers on the preacher the power of preaching. But it must be added that at the same time it restricts his freedom. The preacher does not preach what he wants to, nor his own experiences, his own conceptions or anything that comes into his mind. He preaches what he has heard and received orders to pass on. As the plenipotentiary of a higher power, the preacher is constrained to a complete fidelity. 'What I

1. We must also take into account the mission of the seventy-two disciples, of which only Luke speaks (10:1-2). These disciples were charged with the proclamation that the kingdom of God was at hand.

have told you under cover of darkness, you are to utter in the light of day; what has been whispered in your ears, you are to proclaim on the house-tops' (Matt. 10:27). If there is no call or mission, preaching is an absurdity and a lie, but if there is no fidelity to the message, it is a betrayal.

It will be understood that in the same way the value and effectiveness of preaching do not in the last resort depend on the merits of the preacher or of his personal life. Even preaching inspired by impure motives may proclaim Christ. 'What matter', says St Paul, 'so long as either way, for private ends or in all honesty, Christ is proclaimed?' (Phil. 1:18). All the same, the preacher's way of living is far from being of no account. There may be a discrepancy between his message and his private life. It is precisely this inconsistency that St Paul holds against the Jewish missionaries: 'Tell me, then, thou who teachest others, hast thou no lesson for thyself? Is it a thief that preaches against stealing?' (Rom. 2:21). He, on the contrary, tries to remain in harmony with the gospel he is proclaiming: 'I buffet my own body and make it my slave; or I, who have preached to others, may myself be rejected as worthless' (I Cor. 9:27).

This brief analysis of these two concepts—preaching and the confession of faith—should enable us to grasp their difference and their relationship.

To confess the faith is openly to manifest one's belief. To believe and to confess are one and the same thing: whoever has faith confesses his faith. To preach is a testimony of another order: it is to transmit the Christian message with authority and fidelity.

To confess one's faith is a universal obligation, as universal as faith. Preaching on the other hand is incumbent only on those who have been the object of a choice and in consequence of this choice have received a mission.

To confess the faith is the condition of salvation. It is impossible for a man to be saved unless he is bound to Christ by faith and thus manifests his faith by confessing it. Preaching, on the other hand, is not a condition of salvation, except for those who have expressly been sent. Whereas all Christians are bound to believe and to confess the faith, all Christians are not bound to preach in order to be saved.

But though preaching and confessing the faith are two distinct acts, for all that they are not completely unrelated: preaching is a pre-requisite for confessing. We have only to refer to the succession of actions enumerated by St Paul in Rom. 10:14-15 to understand that this is so. These actions are linked in the following order: sending, *preaching,* listening, believing and *calling upon the Lord* (or confessing). Faith, and thus the confession of faith, springs from the preaching which has been heard (v. 17).

II. Preaching in the Teaching of St Thomas Aquinas

In his commentary on the epistle to the Romans, St Thomas asks the following question: Why must the preacher be sent? His answer is that the mission would be superfluous if the preacher could, like the philosopher, draw the content of his message from his own store of ideas. But he may not, for 'the preacher does not derive the things that concern the faith from himself, but from God'.[1] St Paul speaks of 'the tradition which I received from the Lord, and handed on to you' (I Cor. 11:23).

The preacher's mission can be of two kinds. It can either be received directly from God through an inner inspiration, as was the case with the Old Testament prophets and with St John the Baptist, or it can be received from God indirectly, through the medium of those who occupy Christ's place. St Paul was speaking of this second form of mission in II Cor. 8:18, and we shall now turn to it.

The status of the missionary has been fixed, since the beginnings of Christianity, by Christ's words: 'I came upon an errand from my Father, and now I am sending you out in my turn.' When, in his commentary on St Matthew's gospel, St Thomas writes of the Mission of the apostles: 'Misit eos, sicut ipse missus est, scilicet ad praedicandum,'[2] he is simply explaining St John's formula. Just as the mission entrusted to the apostles was no more than an extension of that which Jesus had received from the Father, the preacher's mission is no more than an extension of the apostles'. Through it, the preacher is linked with the historic Christ and through him with the Father. Every mission entrusted to a member of the Church today depends, through an uninterrupted succession, on the mission

1. St Thomas, *In. Rom.*, cap. 10, lect. 2, Marietti ed., no. 837: 'Ea vero quae fidei sunt, praedicatores a semetipsis non habent sed a Deo.'
2. *In Matt*, cap. 10, lect. 1, Marietti ed, no. 817.

which the apostles received from Christ.[1] Through this chain, it depends on the first mission, the prototype of all the rest : that which Christ received from the Father.

The basis of the right to preach is therefore not personal qualities, knowledge or holiness,[2] but that one is given, by God or the prelate, a mission. Since for St Thomas, preaching is a 'public activity which concerns the whole Church',[3] it requires a *public* authority, which only this mission can give it. In an article of the *Summa Theologica,* St Thomas, in connection with the texts of I Cor. 14 :34 and I Tim. 2 :12, asks whether women have the right to preach. He then distinguishes between two kinds of address : *private* address is delivered to one or a few people, in an intimate setting (*privatim ad unum vel paucos, familiariter colloquendo*), and there is no objection to this sort of speech being made by a woman. *Public* address, on the other hand, is made before the whole ecclesiastical community (*publice alloquendo totam Ecclesiam*). This form of address is reserved to members of the hierarchy, for teaching and proselytising publicly in the assembly is not a matter for ordinary believers, but for prelates.[4]

From these formulae we may readily grasp what was in St Thomas's mind, and discern what was, in his view, the decisive

1. *Contra impugnantes . . .*, cap. 4, Mandonnet ed., p. 49: 'Ad id quod postea objicitur, quod non debent praedicare nisi . . . dicendum quod etiam illi missi a Domino, possunt alios mittere, sicut Paulus qui misit Timotheum ad praedicandum.'

2. This does not mean that a preacher's personality plays no part in his job. St Thomas considers that the qualities required of a preacher concern his life as well as his knowledge. He must understand the divine mysteries, 'plenitudo cognitionis divinorum' (I-II, q. 111. a. 4, c.), but he must above all possess Christian perfection, charity: 'Nullus autem debet assumere praedicationis officium, nisi prius fuerit purgatus et in virtute perfectus' (III, q. 41, a. 3, ad 1). The synthesis of these two qualities is to be found in the contemplative life (II-II, q. 180, a. 1, c.). It will immediately be seen how much intensity of love can contribute to the act of knowledge. The more a man loves God, the more he will want to know him, and the more capable he will be of making him known in preaching and teaching. This is why the 'propositio credendorum', which is the effect proper to preaching, will be the more perfect according as the preacher's personal life conforms with Christ. If the preaching of Christ is to be fully grasped, it must not be isolated from his person. It is *Christ preaching* rather than an independent message, which could be taken down in writing or recorded. Thus, the more the preacher conforms with the holiness of Christ and his knowledge of the mystery, the more fitted he will be to pass the message on *perfectly*. But it is still true that the mission remains indispensable: without it, the message cannot be transmitted with apostolic authority.

3. *Quodl.*, 12, a. 27: 'Publica respiciens totam Ecclesiam'.

4. II-II, q. 177, a. 2, c.

element that distinguished public address from private address. This was not the greater or lesser extent of the 'publicity' given to the speech in question, nor even the size of the audience, though this might be a sign which would allow the two to be distinguished. A private address, however, does not become a public address because the number of the audience increases. Public address is basically different from private address, for it is delivered, not to isolated individuals, but to the people of God as such, to the Church as such. It is address which presupposes authority, and hence mission. The parish priest who at his Sunday mass speaks to his parishioners, even though they be few, is publicly addressing the Church as such. On the other hand, the superior of a nunnery who talks to her sisters, even though they be many, is giving a private address. Since she does not form part of the hierarchy, she has neither mission nor public authority: she cannot address the Church as such. Canon Law confirms this distinction, taken in this sense, when it forbids the faithful, even religious, to preach in churches.[1] All those who preach in the Church must have a delegation of power. They share in the public authority invested in the prelate, who delegates this, and become the coadjutors of the bishop.[2]

A few parallel texts from St Thomas furnish useful complements to this important question. In a question in the *Summa* on Christ's appearances after the resurrection, he writes: 'A woman is not allowed to teach publicly in the Church. But she is allowed to teach privately, in the form of a private exhortation. That is why, as St Ambrose says, we send women to those who are in the house, but we do not depute them to bear witness of the resurrection *to the people*.'[3] In this case, the message entrusted to women is not, strictly speaking, preaching. This emerges again from St Thomas's commentary on I Cor. 14:34: the apostle forbids women to speak in the churches, but does not this go against the practice of God who often, in the New Testament as well as in the Old, uses women to impart his word? This is the case, for example, of the Samaritan woman

1. *Codex Juris Canonici*, can. 1342, §2: 'Concionari in ecclesia vetantur laici omnes, etsi religiosi'.

2. *Contra impugnantes* . . . cap. 4, Mandonnet ed., pp. 49-50: 'Ex commisione Episcoporum et presbyterorum, possunt etiam alii multi ad praedicta mitti . . . et omnes illi sic missi a praelatis Ecclesiarum . . . inter opitulares computantur, quia ipsi majoribus open ferunt'.

3. III, q. 55, a. 1, ad 3.

(John 4), of Anna (Luke 2), of Deborah (Judges 4) and of many others as well. St Thomas resolves this difficulty by distinguishing between public communication and private communication. Women are barred from the former, but they can very well be used for the latter, for then what they are doing is not preaching, but *communicating*.[1] And with reference to Deborah, who taught the people of Israel, St Thomas states that this was not public preaching, but *advice* given under the inspiration of the Holy Spirit.[2] We have not the least intention of discussing here the ministry of women in the Church. What little we have said on the subject was intended simply to show how inseparable the ecclesiastical mission is from preaching in the strict sense of the word.

III. The Confession of Faith according to St Thomas Aquinas

In his commentary on the epistle to the Romans, St Thomas distinguishes three sorts of confession : 1. the confession of sins or confession of the penitent; 2. the confession of God's goodness on account of his blessings, the confession of the Christian who gives thanks; 3. the confession of the divine truth or confession of the believer.[3] St Thomas adds that in this text St Paul is talking of this last type of confession.[4] In fact, as we have seen, the concept of *homologia* in St Paul seems to cover both the confession of faith and praise, that is to say the last two forms of confession which St Thomas distinguishes. But this discrepancy between the results of exegesis and those of theological analysis does not in the least affect the value of St Thomas's conclusions.

St Thomas, like the Bible, sees the *confessio fidei* as simply the outward act of faith; it is at once the sign and the expression of faith. St Thomas does not dwell on this relation.[5] On the other hand, he shows himself much more concerned to define the relationship

1. *In I Cor.*, cap. 14, lect. 7, Marietti ed., no. 879.
2. *In I Tim.*, cap. 2, lect. 3, Marietti ed., no. 80.
3. For a wider view on this last point, see W. Dürig, 'Die Salbung der Märtyrer. Ein Beitrag zur Märtyrertheologie der Liturgie' in *Sacris Erudiri*, 1954, vol. 6, pp. 14-47.
4. *In Rom.*, cap 10, lect. 2, Marietti ed., no. 832, Cf. II-II, q. 3, a. 1, ad 1.
5. II-II, q. 3, a. 1, c.

between the confession of faith and salvation, a relationship expressed by St Paul himself when he asserted : 'Thou canst find salvation, if thou wilt use thy lips to confess that Jesus is the Lord' (Rom. 10:9). St Thomas resolves the problem in the following manner. Confession is something positive and affirmative. Hence it can only come under an affirmative precept, that is to say a precept which obliges us to do something. Such precepts are obligatory *semper sed non ad semper*: they are permanently binding, but do not compel us to perform the act at any particular moment. They exist as an obligation of principle, but concrete circumstances alone turn them into an actual obligation. The duty of almsgiving, for example, is an affirmative precept : the Christian must alleviate the poverty of others, but that does not mean to say that he must give alms at every turn, devote his life, his whole time and all his goods to this single duty. The affirmative precepts are thus obligatory in particular circumstances only. What are these circumstances with regard to the confession of faith? St Thomas replies, every time that rendering of honour to God or the service of one's neighbour require it.[1] The problem has now been narrowed down to the appreciation of these concrete circumstances.

It should be noted that the mediaeval attitude towards this problem was very different from our own. St Thomas lived in a country that formed part of Christendom and overflowed with clergy. It was easy to be convinced that the Christian faith was diffused over almost the whole of the habitable world. In such circumstances the confession of faith did not assume the least urgency. Such urgency could only be foreseen in exceptional circumstances, when, for example, the Christian was subject to persecution. In the *Summa Theologica* St Thomas does indeed distinguish between ordinary times and cases of necessity.[2] As a rule, to instruct others in the matter of faith was not for the faithful as a whole : Christian society shouldered the responsibility. But when the faith was in danger, every believer was bound to proclaim it, either for the instruction of others or for their confirmation in this faith or to hold in check the attacks of the infidels.

This reply shows that the place of what today we call the lay apostolate is, in St Thomas, the doctrine of the confession of faith.

1. II-II, q. 3, a. 2, c. et ad 1.
2. Ibid., ad 2.

The argument urged by him: 'Where the faith is in danger, every Christian is bound to proclaim his faith' is practically the same as Pius XI utilized to justify the laity's taking a share in the apostolate. St Thomas stated the principle, but because of the privileged circumstances in which he lived, he did not see it applied in his time.[1]

We find an assertion of the same principle, and the same practical attitude, when St Thomas discusses the duties of godparents.[2] 'Whoever agrees to be the godfather of a newly baptized child accepts the responsibility of a teacher,' and hence the obligation to teach if necessity requires it. But the rest of the passage showed that in ordinary circumstances this role would not have to be assumed. That was why men with little education could be granted this trust. The Christian environment would make up for their deficiencies, 'for everything that concerns the Christian life and faith is *publicly* known to all'. On the other hand, if there were any sort of danger for the faith, the godfather should be chosen from among knowledgeable Christians.[3]

The same attitude and the same pastoral appreciation are to be found in the commentary on the Books of Sentences. The role of the godfather is to translate, to adapt to a particular child, according to its needs, the common Christian doctrine taught by the prelates.[4] But in fact, St Thomas adds, this teaching role is not a very formidable one, and people must not be afraid of accepting the obligations of a godfather, for 'as far as our modern times are concerned', since the parents are Christians, the role of godfather is not encumbered with heavy responsibilities; but things were not the same in the primitive Church. 'And even now the responsibility of the godfather might again become heavy if the child's parents were suspected of unbelief, or if the child was going to be brought up among unbelievers.'[5]

The whole of tradition tells us that the confession of faith is bound up with the sacrament of confirmation. Through this sacrament, Christians are 'made confessors of the faith'. 'Confirmation is the

1. See also *Quodl.* 9, a. 14: Peter sinned gravely in denying Christ 'quia negavit fidem in loco ubi periclitabatur, et ejus confessio requirebatur'.
2. III, q. 67, a. 8.
3. Ibid. ad 1.
4. *IV Sent.*, d. 6, q. 2, a. 2, sol. 2,
5. Ibid. sol. 3, ad 3.

sacrament of the confession of the faith.'[1] When he wrote these formulae, St Thomas was accepting a traditional datum which he does not discuss but for which, in accordance with his usual practice, he gives a theological explanation. Following the first gift of the Spirit, conferred in baptism, confirmation gives the plenitude of the Spirit. And since St Thomas orders all his sacramental teaching on the analogy of the development of human life, he is able quite reasonably to regard this plenitude as the age of discretion, the adult age of spiritual life in relation to which baptism is no more than a birth. Developing the same analogy, he goes on to explain the link between the confession of faith and confirmation. 'Whereas up till then he had lived individually and for himself alone, the man who has reached the age of adulthood begins to enter through his activity into communion with others.'[2] The sacrament of confirmation gives him the inner strength necessary to give spiritual battle to the enemies of the faith. This battle is one every Christian fights against invisible enemies, against the devils. But it belongs to adults in the faith, to the confirmed, when it must be fought against visible enemies, that is to say persecutors of the faith. It is by the 'public' confession of faith that they fight the battle. And St Thomas sums up his ideas by asserting that the confirmed Christian receives, through confirmation, a sort of special function : the power of publicly confessing in words his faith in Christ.[3]

The importance which we have attributed here to the confession of faith leads us to raise a question which has often been discussed in Catholic Action circles.

What is the point of the mandate in Catholic Action? It is not a delegation of hierarchical power, still less a sort of supplementary sacramental reality, from which the Christian's apostolic obligation

1. *IV Sent.* d. 7, q. 1, a. 2, sol. 2; q. 2, a. 1, qc. 2, arg. 3; q. 3, a. 2, qc. 3, arg. 3; a. 3, qc. 2, arg. 2.

2. III, q. 72, a. 2; see also q. 72, a. 5, c. et ad 1.

3. Ibid, q. 72, a. 5, ad 2: 'Confirmatus accipit potestatem *publice* fidem Christi verbis profitendi, *quasi ex officio*.' The fact that we describe confirmation as the sacrament of the confession of the faith does not necessarily mean that the unconfirmed are never bound to confess their faith. There are cases when they too must do so. How can we accept both these apparently irreconcilable points of view? St Thomas deals with the difficulty by holding to the view that confirmation is the sacrament of the confession of the faith, but stressing that the effect of a sacrament can sometimes exist without the reception of this sacrament, through the mere desire (*votum*) for it. III, q. 72, a. 6, ad 1.

stems.[1] A declaration of the Assembly of French Cardinals and Archbishops draws attention to this point. 'The word mandate, which has been employed in a number of the pronouncements of the Holy See and of the French episcopate, seemed to provide an appropriate definition of the relationship between the hierarchy and the organized laity.... Through his mandate, the Bishop closely associates the Catholic Action movement, not with his heirarchical functions, but with his pastoral cares and apostolic activity (Pius XII). Far from derogating from the dignity of their peculiar mission as laymen or modifying its nature, the mandate confers on this organized lay apostolate an official value and a public character in the Church, while leaving it entirely within the sphere of an apostolate of laymen.'[2]

So we can grasp the relationship between Catholic Action and the apostolic duty incumbent on every believer. Membership of Catholic action 'turns a spontaneous personal resolution into a state acknowledged by the Church'.[3] The mandate does not create the duty of apostolate: we have seen that according to tradition, confirmation is the basis of this duty. But the mandate makes official, organizes, coordinates and stimulates, along many different lines and in diverse movements, the apostolic duty common to all Christians. 'We may interpret Catholic Action,' Y. Congar writes, 'as the form of Christian or apostolic activity which has become a legally recognized reality in the Church.' And to make his meaning clearer, the author draws a parallel between Catholic Action and the religious life. A religious life can be led by an individual, following the spirit of the evangelical counsels, without belonging to any religious order of congregation. But usually the religious life is sanctioned by public vows and lived in accordance with an approved rule. 'The public vows are neither virtuousness nor the call to perfection; but they ratify and provide for them in a publicly recognized state of life.'[4] In the same way, Catholic Action does not create the duty of apostolate, which existed before the commission. Catholic Action merely organizes a spontaneous and personal apostolate which thereby becomes official and public.

1. Cf. Y. Congar, *Lay People in the Church*, p. 352.
2. *Documentation catholique*, 13 March 1946, vol. 43., cols. 743-744.
3. Y. Congar, *Lay People in the Church*, p. 353.
4. Ibid., p. 354.

The definition most often given by Pius XI was: 'Catholic Action is a participation of the laity in the hierarchical apostolate.'[1] How are we to understand the term 'participation'? Certain theologians have not hesitated to give it its strongest sense—the philosophical sense.[2] In this sense, Catholic Action is instituted through a *partial conferment* of the hierarchical apostolate; the faithful become participants in the powers of the hierarchy. P. Dabin writes, for example: 'The word participation is the only one that is obligatorily and exclusively called for, because between the Catholic activity of laymen as such and of laymen insofar as they are united with the hierarchy, there is not a difference of degree, but of kind. Catholic Action does not exist side by side with the hierarchy, it is one with it.'[3] And in another work: 'The hierarchy is indeed the formal cause in Catholic Action. . . . The choice of the word participation is strictly accurate. The word collaboration is much less suitable, because it expresses no more than a mere juxtaposition of forces . . . thus leaving an irreducible heterogeneity between them, having nothing in common but the end in view, that is to say the final cause. It is principally through the fact of the formal cause, the hierarchy, that the Catholic Action of laymen, insofar as they act as members of this Catholic Action, ceases to be in all respects a purely lay activity. It is not a purely lay activity but an almost hierarchical activity exercised by laymen.'[4] V. Pellet goes even further and presents the lay apostolate as a completely new reality in the Church. He speaks of 'the single and identical commission which was first received by the apostles, was passed on by divine right to the hierarchy and was retained by the latter as its exclusive property until the Supreme Pontiff, inspired by the Spirit, took the initiative of transmitting it to laymen in the form of a communication or delegation of power'.[5] Much the same line is followed by K. Rahner, who defended his position in

1. See references in Y. Congar, *Lay People in the Church*, p. 346.

2. In the philosophical sense applicable here, participation should be understood of what L. B. Geiger calls 'participation by similarity with the formal hierarchy'. 'Participation stands for the diminished, particularized and in this sense shared state of an essence whenever it is not realized in the absolute plenitude of its formal content' *La participation*, first ed., Paris 1942, p. 29.

3. P. Dabin, *L'Action catholique. Essai de synthèse*, eighth ed., Paris 1937, p. 83.

4. P. Dabin, *L'apostolat laïque*, Paris 1931, pp. 82-83.

5. V. Pollet, *L'Action catholique à la lumière de la théologie thomiste*, Brussels, 1937, p. 32. See also *De actione catholica principiis theologiae thomisticae dilucidata*, in *Angelicum*, 1936, vol. 13, p. 455, n.1.

an article which created a considerable stir and would require a fairly lengthy discussion.[1] We have had occasion to deal with it elsewhere,[2] and we will not revert to it here. The problem seems to us to have been adequately dealt with by what has gone before.

To my mind, the opinions we have just been discussing have numerous drawbacks:

1. They overestimate the scope of the mandate given to Catholic Action. They make of this a sort of endowing with mission such as that which is the basis of the hierarchy. In consequence, the apostolate of the layman in the ranks of Catholic Action is seen as a new event in the Church, not only in fact, but also in principle.

2. On the other hand, they deprive confirmation of a great deal of its significance and minimize its traditional importance as the sacrament of Christian testimony.

3. Consequently, they reserve the exercise of the apostolate to a selected group of Christians, whereas it is in reality an obligation common to all who have been confirmed.

4. They take little note of the proper status of the believer within the Church, since the exercise of a spiritual apostolate would more or less translate him from the position of a layman to that of a member of the hierarchy.

That is why it seems to us a mistake to interpret Pius XI's formulae in too strict and philosophical a sense.[3] When he defined Catholic Action as a 'participation of the laity in the apostolate of the hierarchy', he certainly did not mean to transform the faithful into clergy. It often suffices to refer to the context to see his real meaning. Moreover, it is to be noted that later statements, by Pius XII, replace the word 'participation' with 'cooperation' or 'collaboration', which avoid any misunderstanding. In the speech he made to the Second World Congress of the Lay Apostolate, Pius XII clarified this point. He said:

1. K. Rahner, 'Über das Laienapostolat' in *Schriften zur Theologie*, 2 (English translation, 'Notes on the Lay Apostolate', *Theological Investigations*, vol. II, London, 1963).

2. See *RSPT*, vol. 41, pp. 552-556.

3. At the First World Congress of the Lay Apostolate, Cardinal Antonio Caggiano, Bishop of Rosario de Santafé, also contested the philosophical interpretation of the word 'participation' in the definition of Catholic Action. See his speech in *Proceedings of the First World Congress on the Lay Apostolate*, vol. 1, Rome, 1952.

'The acceptance by the layman of a particular mission, of a mandate of the hierarchy, though it associates him more closely with the spiritual conquest of the world undertaken by the Church under the direction of its pastors, does not suffice to make him a member of the hierarchy.'[1]

The doctrine of the confession of faith seems to us to account for all the elements of the problem better than these views which have been analysed here. In addition to its scriptural and traditional bases, which give it straight away a certain advantage, it does explain, as we have shown, how ordinary believers can exercise an apostolate which covers the same field as the apostolate of the hierarchy without, for all that, becoming members of the hierarchy. So it is possible to preserve both the autonomy proper to the laity in their order and the organic connection of their apostolate with that of the hierarchy.

1. C.T.S. translation, pp. 5-6.

VIII

THE LAY APOSTOLATE AS A STATE OF LIFE

To confess the faith is the act of every *believer*. At the moment, we are discussing the *lay* apostolate. This involves us in a study of the lay condition, the state of life in which the witness of the confession of faith is lived. In the first place, in order to locate the problem, we shall set down a few preliminary observations concerning three terms.

The Faithful

The faithful may be distinguished from one another by three things: their state (*status*), their function (*officium*) and their rank (*gradus*).[1] Rank does not concern us here; our present concern is with state. We have just been dealing with the function of Christians. Functions are distinguished by their acts.[2] This being so, we may say that the function of the baptized believer and of the confirmed believer is purely and simply a Christian life, that is to say a way of living that is in complete harmony with the faith.[3] In such a manner of life, and in order to express its real meaning before God and before men, the confession of faith plays an important part. Whenever this meaning needs to be elucidated and asserted, as time, place and circumstances may require, public confession of faith becomes a necessity.[4] This shows us that the *proper function of the Christian* in the Church is Christian 'behaviour', with all that that implies.

What is more, since this is a life which all baptized or confirmed

1. II-II, q. 183, a. 2 and 3.
2. Acts concerning one's neighbour: a. 3, ad 2.
3. This life also concerns one's neighbour, since it is entirely informed by the virtue of charity.
4. II-II, q. 3, a. 2.

Christians ought to live, whatever their state or rank, we must ask ourselves whether it would not be less ambiguous, on many occasions when the apostolate of the people of God is concerned, to talk of the apostolate of *believers* rather than of the *lay* apostolate.[1]

Apostolate

We have found ourselves using this word several times. Now we must define its meaning more clearly. The strict sense of apostolate is sending, or mission. That is its fundamental meaning. The aim of this sending is to pass on and to preserve divine life, salvation. This is achieved through the threefold function of which this single apostolate is composed: the ministry of the Word, the priesthood (power of order) and the administration (power of jurisdiction). But, as we have seen in the New Testament, one of these functions is more directly and explicitly bound up with the apostolate: that is the preaching of the Word. This proclamation in pursuance of a mission is carried out on various planes, according to whether it involves Christ himself, the Twelve, the bishops who are the successors of the apostles, or ordinary believers. But even on this lowest plane, the analogy of the apostolate still holds good without equivocation: *in his own way, the ordinary believer is called to the orderly diffusion of the message of the faith by reason of a definite mission.* This diffusion is not grounded in any hierarchical power; it carries with it no priestly power. It is based on the sacraments of baptism and of confirmation. It is thus founded on the mission of the whole Christian people, which is called on to 'proclaim the exploits' of God.[2]

Layman

The words 'believer', 'Christian' and 'baptized person' suggest membership of the people of God, but the word layman suggests a distinction within this people. This last point has been well brought out in an article of first-rate importance.[3] It is often said today that

1. In addition to the function which falls to him as a believer, the preacher has a special function which assigns him to a *precise* activity, the hierarchical ministry of the Word, by virtue of his mission.

2. This general mission is in certain cases complemented by the sanction of the hierarchical authority's 'mandate'. See also p. 14b, note 1.

3. I. de la Potterie, 'L'origine et le sens primitif du mot "laïc"', in *Nouvelle revue théologique*, 1958, vol. 80, pp. 840-853.

in the primitive Church, layman meant 'member of the *laos,* of the people of God'.[1] As a result of a detailed analysis of the texts, Father de la Potterie has shown that this is simply not true : the word always means 'a special category of Christians, those who have not been ordained for the service of God'.[2] 'If the word "laymen" really meant all the members of the people of God taken as a whole, it would be hard to understand why priests too should not be "laymen", since they are Christians. On the contrary, the texts always contrast the latter with the former. There could hardly be a better proof that the word layman is a specific term, implying a classification within the Christian people.'[3]

I. Laity as a State of Life

If the state of life is the stable and abiding condition of life, it must be admitted that laity is a state. But to what does it owe its stability? Chiefly from the layman's exemption from any obligation to the hierarchical functions. That is the negative aspect of this state. Whereas a cleric is incorporated into a state of life through the obligations attaching to the performance of the sacred functions (celebration of the mysteries and preaching in its strict sense), the layman belongs to a state because he is free from all obligations of this order. He is free of the hierarchical functions.

We know that in St Thomas's view, 'state' signified a certain position in accordance with which a reality is ordered in a befitting manner, with some stability.[4] Two elements thus come in : 1. a connatural disposition; 2. stability, fixity, permanence and a guarantee of continuance. For example, a business is 'in a fit state' when it has got its articles of association, and is properly organized internally and in relation to its social and economic environment : staff, customers, competitors, creditors and supplies. As soon as a business has established its internal equilibrium and has adjusted itself to its environment, it is 'in a fit state', that is to say in good running condition.

This guarantee of continuance is determined in relation to an

1. Ibid., p. 851.
2. Ibid., p. 853.
3. Ibid., p. 853.
4. II-II, q. 183, a. 1.

obligation. It should be noted that stability does not necessarily call for an obligation, but that it is judged in relation to an obligation.[1] The obligation affects both the man who is subject to it and the man who is exempt. That is why the free man and the slave are typical examples of states, or conditions, from the mediaeval viewpoint. When he receives the priesthood, not only is the priest entitled to perform the duties of this order, he is obliged to do so. His hierarchical function, which has become an obligation for him, by that very fact involves his life in a state, and in a corresponding condition. The sign of the clerical state is thus the hierarchical functions. The layman is simply the man who is exempt from these functions. He does not preach, nor does he confer the sacraments (except for baptism, in exceptional circumstances), nor does he celebrate mass. This permanent exemption puts him in a situation of freedom in relation to this obligation. It involves him in the state of a layman.

Can we give a positive definition of laity as a state of life? This question is less difficult to answer if the laity is considered *collectively*. In fact, on the laity reposes almost the entire weight of temporal activities. To the laity taken as a whole belongs the task of doing the work of the world, building the earthly city.

> 'It is not fitting for the priest to take over secular affairs; that is the laity's business. Nor is this an arbitrary judgment; it is founded both on facts and on rights.
>
> 'The fact is that only the laity are truly present in the temporal order, since they live in it, and are in continuous and immediate touch with factories, homes, and districts. But their irreplaceable role comes neither solely nor mainly from this reason—it comes from their *vocation*. Placed by God at the head of a family, or of a firm, or in some profession, it is the *duty of their state* to direct these institutions to their proper end. It means an eminently constructive work which falls to their special lot. . . .'[2]

In other words, it is to the laity that temporal affairs (the world) are entrusted.

Returning now from the collective to the individual plane, all

1. See q. 183, a. 1, in corpore: 'Quod respicit obligationem personae hominis'.
2. Cardinal Suhard, '*The Priest in the Modern World*', in *Cardinal Suhard Pastoral Letters*, London 1955, p. 158; *DC*, 1949, vol. 46, col. 782.

we need say is simply that *most* laymen are professionally engaged in temporal jobs which constitute their principal and permanent occupation. This stable calling provides them with a basis for their state of life. These laymen thus enjoy a condition of existence which is characteristic of the laity as such, insofar as it is specifically distinct from the clerical state. This condition commits them to the world.

But yet there are also a certan number of laymen who do not share in this commitment, or do so to a very slight extent. Some may find their principal and permanent occupation in the work of the Church. There are Christians who devote their whole lives to evangelization. In certain countries, teachers of religion in secondary schools are laymen. These laymen, who are by profession assistants to the clergy, constitute a special problem. One may add that they often try to group themselves within the framework of a canonical institute. When they remain within the category of the ordinary layman, they cannot avoid feeling a psychological solidarity with the laity who are committed to what are strictly speaking temporal jobs. There is a certain osmosis due to social relationships and environment.[1]

1. These laymen who are professionally and permanently engaged in the work of the Church deserve special consideration. Where do they stand in the Church's apostolate? An Austrian canonist, H. Heimerl, recently studied one aspect of this question. The Church entrusts the responsibility for teaching to these lay catechists. In the circumstances, does this amount to a canonical mission? Opinions are divided. After a detailed inquiry into Canon Law, the concordats and other documents of the Holy See, H. Heimerl answers in the affirmative. The 'juridically public' character of religious teaching is formally bound up with the canonical mission (*Laien im Dienst der Verkündigung. Laienmitwirkung an der Lehraufgabe der Kirche*, Vienna, 1958, pp. 100-101). The author does consider that these laymen hold a special position. Their status as members of the Church is complemented by that of *envoys of the magisterial power*.

We will confine ourselves to two remarks on this point. 1. The canonical mission of the lay catechist is different from that which involves jurisdiction. The latter carries with it, to a greater or less degree, a certain participation in the *administration* of the faithful and, to the same degree, confers a certain authority of head or judge. According to most authors, jurisdiction can be conferred on clerics only. The lay catechist remains a layman, even after he has been entrusted with responsibility by the ecclesiastical authority. 2. Likewise, this canonical mission differs from the mandate of Catholic Action. The latter only renders official, by endorsing it, a duty which is incumbent on every Christian by virtue of the sacraments he has received. In the catechist's canonical mission there is something more, a real participation, though one which it is difficult to determine, in the ministry of the Word entrusted by Christ *to the Twelve*. With these clarifications we accept Heimerl's formula: the lay catechist is an envoy of the magisterial power.

The layman who is completely committed to the service of the world is psychologically at home in the whole temporal field. Such a layman, who because of his state of life is a man of his own particular age, has his own individual way of doing things; he is habitually concerned with a certain type of problem. His state of life produces habits of mind, creates psychological attitudes and forms a

But in that case, how is the transmission of the Word to be shared out between the priestly hierarchy and the laymen? Winding up a discussion in the review *Parole et Mission*, P. A. Liégé advanced certain 'provisional answers' which seem to shed light on the dispute and to point the way for research.: 'Episcopal and priestly teaching is to a greater extent *a form of teaching which gathers, founds or regroups the Church with authority* . . . Episcopal and priestly teaching is *a form of teaching more expressive of transcendence and of objectivity*, and for that very reason it supervises orthodoxy . . . Episcopal and priestly teaching will *be more explicitly related to the eucharistic act.* It will lead much more directly to the prayer of intercession which is already an expression of worship . . . On the plane of evangelization, *the priest already anticipates in his teaching the eucharistic celebration* which will bring the full meaning of the Church to the community of believers which the laymen and he have created together' ('Sacerdoce, Laïcat, Parole. Conclusions de notre troisième colloque,' in *Parole et Mission*, 1960, vol. 3, no. 11, pp. 592-602. The passages quoted appear on pp. 601-602). In short, the teaching of the priestly hierarchy is always *immediately related to* the three powers of the Church. It is the teaching of a head, it supervises doctrine, its most immediate aim is eucharistic. Here again we meet with the power of jurisdiction, the magisterium in its twofold function of transmitting the message and checking on its authenticity, and the power of order. We for our part should incline to say: by virtue of his canonical mission, the lay catechist takes part only in the function of passing on the message.

But the discussion is still open. The problem was recently the subject of an able study in an important doctoral thesis: Sauvage, *Catéchèse et laïcat. Participation des laïcs au ministère de la Parole et mission du frère-enseignant dans l'Eglise*, Paris, 1962.

We will not tackle here the problem of the lay *religious* (the monk who is not a priest, the teaching or nursing brother, the lay brother or coadjutor in the clerical orders, the nun, etc.). There are not just two states in the Church, but three. Pius XII made a number of pronouncements on this point which refer back to Canon Law.

'The public state of perfection was numbered among the three principal ecclesiastical states and (. . .) the Church took from it alone the second order and canonical degree of persons (can. 107). One thing is well worth careful consideration: the two other canonical orders of persons, that of clerics and that of laymen, by divine right (which is complemented by ecclesiastical prescription, can. 107 and 108, §3) are based on the Church as a hierarchically constituted society; the category of religious, placed between clerics and laymen, and which may be common to both, is derived completely from its close and special relationship with the end of the Church, that is to say with the sanctification to be sought efficaciously by adequate means' (*Provida Mater*, 2 Feb. 1947; *DC*, 1947, col. 579). We find the same teaching in *Discours aux membres du Congrès des états de perfection*, 8 Dec. 1950; *DC*, 1950, col. 1670. The theological problem of the lay religious is an important one and should be studied, it seems, along the lines suggested by St Thomas in II-II, q. 188, a. 2, ad 3.

mentality. We intend all this in a positive sense. The business executive, the engineer, the tradesman, the official, the sailor and the workman necessarily have a way of approaching every problem which is conditioned by their principal occupation. Each of them, of course, has his own manner of assessing a situation, because his own field is different from his neighbour's. But all the same there are features common to the psychology of those who are assigned to temporal occupations, features which distinguish them as a whole from those who are immersed in hierarchical work, who also have their own common features. The bishop, the assistant parish priest, the chaplain, the radio preacher and the professor of theology may well each bear the imprint of their particular activity; all the same the fundamental unity of all the hierarchical functions gives them the air of belonging to the same family.

All this is perfectly natural. We perfect ourselves, in accordance with our own personality, through what we do. The fact that the mind is concentrated on a certain number of problems cannot blind it to the universality of the real but should create spheres of connaturality and increased sensibility which ultimately enrich the society of the faithful in the Church. It is in vocabulary above all that this familiarity will come out. The layman is better qualified than the cleric to hit on the word that will make sense in the contemporary world and obtain the widest hearing there. He finds it easier to avoid the 'tongue of Canaan'.[1]

II. The Layman in the Temporal Field

The layman is on his own ground in the temporal field, in the service of the world, in the earthly city : he feels at home there. He is the specialist in secular matters. The cleric, whose speciality is in the spiritual field, always feels a little foreign and self-conscious there. What are the consequences of all this?

The Christian laity is under an obligation to pursue the callings of the world. These callings are legitimate and necessary, and they must be done. There can be no question of running away from them on the grounds of some dubious ideology. Since they have their place in the divine harmony of the universe, it is to laymen that they fall.

1. Hence the importance of the presence of laymen in Bible translation commissions. See that of the Bible de Jerusalem.

The cleric, as we have seen, is exempt from secular activities. The Church expects clerics 'to abstain in the ordinary course from occupations which may nevertheless be necessary and excellent, whether they be of a professional character: medicine and surgery, the profession of notary, jurisprudence, management of property and trade;[1] or of a political character: secular administrative and jurisdictional functions and membership of parliament;[2] or of a military character: voluntary enrolment in military service and participation in revolutions and civil wars.[3] It claims on their behalf privileges of which the most important is that of personal immunity, which exempts clerics from military service and from secular administrative offices and duties, which are alien to the clerical state.[4] The intention of the Church in all these measures is plain: it wants clerics to work as much as possible on the spiritual or ecclesiastical plane and as little as possible on the temporal or secular plane.'[5] Temporal responsibilities should be assumed by Christian laymen.

Through his temporal activity, the Christian layman is the instrument of Christ's Lordship over the universe. The work of the world is performed in obedience to God and his commandments. It enables man to participate, in a limited sector, in the divine government of the universe, in the single providential economy of which Christ is the architect and the king.[6] When today men are associated, in their modest niche, in the execution of the divine government of the world, they become by that very fact agents of the universal kingship of Christ, God and man.[7] Government is, indeed, the royal act *par excellence*.[8]

1. Can. 139, §1 and 2; 142 (this reference, like the three following ones, is quoted by C. Journet).
2. Can. 139, §2 and 4.
3. Can. 141, §1.
4. Can. 121.
5. C. Journet, *L'Eglise du Verbe Incarné*, vol. II, pp. 1014-1015.
6. Cf. I, q. 103, a. 6.
7. Cf. enc. *Quas Primas*, Pius XI, 1925: Christ 'is king, not only in his divinity, but also in his humanity'. 'By sole virtue of the hypostatic union he possesses supreme power over every creature.' 'Christ is our king not only by natural right, but by acquired right.' 'He received from his Father an absolute dominion which extends to every creature. But during his earthly life, he did not wish to exercise this temporal kingship.' Further on, Pius XI quotes this passage from the enc. *Annum Sacrum*, of Leo XIII, 25 May 1899: 'The kingdom of Christ is really and precisely as wide as the world and as humanity'.
8. See 'Kingship over the world' in Y. Congar, *Lay People in the Church*, pp.224-230.

By acting in such a way that the temporal sphere shall be faithful to itself, that is to say completely directed towards its proper end, the Christian layman brings it healing and salvation. He restores it to its place in the divine economy. 'First, comes the professional and human vocation; the improvement of hygiene, security, conditions of work and housing; a better distribution of goods and of employment; the promotion of the arts and of culture and scientific research, none of these can be secondary and optional activities for them. The attainment of such human goals cannot be a matter of indifference. The true Christian will give himself entirely, and without any ulterior motives of proselytizing, to these human tasks, and to fraternal collaboration.'[1]

What is more, by this simple faithfulness to the special nature of the temporal, the layman is preparing an environment and a breathable atmosphere which will predispose souls to receive and to live the Christian message. For between the temporal and the spiritual there are the same relationships as between the mystery of the creation and the mystery of the redemption, or the new covenant. As C. Journet rightly observes:

> 'Whereas spiritual activities depend on the mystery of the redemption . . . temporal activities depend on the anterior mystery of the creation, of this nature which God gave us from the beginning by placing us between the angels and the animals.'[2]

We can profit here from the reflections of Father Bouillard, who brings out some cogent lines of thought in Karl Barth's treatise on creation. 'The creature', Barth says, 'has its end not in itself, but in what the creator wants for it. Now God propounds a different one than it does itself, not out of caprice or need, but in order to show this being the love he has felt for it from all eternity, to achieve the loving intention which constitutes the eternal decree of the covenant'.[3] According to Barth, the first biblical narrative 'describes the creation, so to say, from the outside, *as a methodical preparation, comparable to the building of a temple, whose plan is determined as*

1. Cardinal Suhard, 'The Priest in the Modern World', op. cit., p. 159; *DC*, 1949, vol. 46, col. 782.
2. *L'Eglise du Verbe Incarné*, vol. II, pp.1002 and 1201.
3. H. Boillard, *Karl Barth*, Paris 1957, vol. 2, p. 188.

a whole and in detail by the liturgy for which it is going to be used. What constitutes at once the end of the work of creation and the beginning of the history of the covenant is the rest on the seventh day, the joyful sabbath when God invites man to enter into communion with him.'[1] And here is how Father Bouillard reacts to Barth's position : 'We can admit . . . that the creation is the necessary basis of the covenant, in the sense that it *establishes the field in which the history of the covenant is to unfold, the subject who is to be the partner of God and the nature to whom grace is to be addressed. . . .* We are inclined to believe that the idea of creation does not assume its real meaning and is not lasting except in a consciousness which feels itself integrated in a process of salvation.'[2]

Through their temporal activities, Christian laymen effect the *consecratio mundi,* the offering of the universe to God as a spiritual sacrifice. In the work of the world, as we have seen, the Christian can exercise his 'royal priesthood'.[3] A man's whole life becomes a spiritual sacrifice to the extent that it is ruled by the virtue of religion. Through this spiritual sacrifice, the whole network of relationships which constitute the world and are the result of human activities—culture, politics and economics—return to God. The report of the Second Assembly of the World Council of Churches, held at Evanston in 1954 expresses this very happily in the following passage :

> Work is an offering to God, a way of bringing back creation after the fall to its original place in God's plan, by the labour of our hands. At the same time it offers our minds and our bodies as a living sacrifice to God through the instrumentality of the discipline of work. (This conception) links man's work with the worship which the Church renders to God, and in particular to the adoration of God explicitly defined by the term eucharist. What we have here is the sanctification of all work on earth.'[4]

The only surprising thing is a comment appended to this passage :

> 'We have here a Catholic and Orthodox conception in the widest sense of these terms.'

1. H. Bouillard, p. 188; my italics.
2. H. Bouillard, p. 195; my italics.
3. See Chapter V, III, pp. 110ff.
4. *L'espérance chrétienne dans le monde d'aujourd'hui*, Neuchâtel and Paris 1955, p. 444.

I myself believe that this is the biblical conception.[1]

In what conditions can earthly work be a witness to Christ for men's salvation? Considered either as a spiritual sacrifice or as the exercise of Christ's kingship in the world, temporal work is only indirectly apostolic, though this in no way compromises its effectiveness. Prayer has apostolic repercussions. Sound human institutions provide an environment favourable to the spread of the gospel, and such developments in themselves advance civilization. They do not *per se* proclaim the gospel. They become 'prophetic'; they bear witness to Christ before men when, breaking free from prevailing conventionality, they make men wonder, and pose a question to which the only cogent answer is a confession of faith. Thus 'in many cases the work of civilization and of evangelization are advanced by one and the same activity'.[2]

Refusing to obey Hitler's racial laws was an act of evangelization. To defy the racial segregation regulations in South Africa, be it in political or in professional life, inevitably leads to proclaiming the lordship of Christ and his love for all men. The same is true of the lay Christian's commitment to the collective advancement of the working class world. 'It is through this commitment that the working class activist can most easily fulfil his role of witness to and apostle of Christ.'[3] In certain cases, verbal witness, when it gives voice to the witness of life, can bring out the deepest realities of Christian living. 'Thus, a Christian worker, who wanted to explain to his comrades why he had refused a move up for himself talked to them of Christ, of the poverty and suffering of Christ, and above all of Christ's love for all men.'[4]

And so on. It is easy to see how important a missionary laity is.[5] 'No doubt the Church as such is not directly entrusted with raising living standards, winning independence or preserving works of art.

1. A brief presentation of the Orthodox position is given by C. Lialine in one chapter ,'L'action de l'Orthodoxie', of the collective work in which he collaborated with P. Dumont and F. Mercenier, *Qu-est-ce que l'Orthodoxie? Vues catholiques*, Brussels, 1945; see pp. 209-210.

2. *Civilisation et évangelisation. Note doctrinale du Comité théologique de Lyon*, Lyons 1957, p. 409; see also p. 429.

3. Commission épiscopale du monde ouvrier, *L'engagement temporel*, Paris, undated, p. 61.

4. *L'engagement temporel*, p. 48.

5. See on this point Dr L. P. Aujoulat, 'Les laïcs au service des missions,' in *Histoire universelle des missions catholiques*, Paris 1959, vol. 4, pp. 141-152.

But Christians, on the contrary, have a direct responsibility for serving the community and implanting everywhere the living ferment of the gospel principles and of brotherly love. Even more in the new Christian countries than in Europe, the technical capacity of Christians, their disinterestedness and the human value of their services constitute the indispensable *substratum* of their testimony in favour of the truth of Christianity. This is what makes the testimony of a *carefully trained Christian laity* even more indispensable in missionary countries than in Europe, and even more imperative today than formerly.'[1] In this context, the medical, cultural, educational and social work undertaken by the laymen of *Ad Lucem* are worthy of note.[2]

It will be seen that in all this we have simply commented in a new way on the teaching of I Peter, which is rounded off by Rom. 10; we can win unbelievers to the gospel simply by living as Christians, by letting it be seen through out confession of the faith, that the whole thing is an imitation of Christ. For this is one way of 'proclaiming the exploits of the God who has called us out of darkness into his marvellous light' (I Peter 2:9).

III. The Layman in the Spiritual Field

By his confirmation the Christian layman is equipped to participate, by means of the confession of faith, in the whole area covered by the Christian message. *A priori,* no domain is closed to him. No section of the material object of faith is withdrawn from him and reserved exclusively for clerics. Nevertheless, insofar as he is working in the world, he is familiar in a professional way only with the temporal domain. Thus, in the ordinary way, the layman will not be entrusted with a work of theological investigation, but rather with the establishment of close and lively links between the world and the spiritual domain.[3]

1. Aujoulat, op. cit., p. 149.
2. Dr Aujoulat's contribution includes a brief account of the various achievements of the missionary laity.
3. On all this, see Y. Congar's *Lay People in the Church*, pp. 294-298, and H. Heimerl, *Laien im Dienst der Verkündigung* . . . Heimerl devoted a first 'special part' to the religious instruction of children: parents, their substitutes, lay catechists; the second part deals with the participation of laymen in the spread of the faith

Is theology ordinarily the province of laymen? The Church's first theologians were laymen: Justin, Clement and Origen, who became a priest later.... It was as a result of the barbarian invasions that higher education became a privilege of the clergy. Bishops and monks saved culture. The reason why the tradition of lay theologians is still preserved today in the eastern Orthodox Church is that the east did not experience the same historical vicissitudes.[1] The humanist movement brought laymen back into the stream of religious thinking. A layman, Contarini, wrote a *De officio episcopi.* Pascal in the seventeenth century, Chateaubriand, de Maistre and L. Veuillot in the nineteenth, played an incontestable role in this field. Gilson, Maritain, Vignaux and many others hold an honourable place in the Catholic doctrinal work of this century.

Is the layman as qualified as the cleric for theological activities in the strict sense? What is necessary for the study of theology? Faith and a sound hold on the historical and philosophical tools. It must be admitted that some laymen do very well at it. There is nothing *per se* even to prevent laymen teaching in ecclesiastical faculties. Canon Law does indeed require that the teachers in seminaries shall be priests.[2] But the Constitution *Deus scientiarum Dominus,* which lays down standards for universities, does not insist on holy orders as a prerequisite for the teaching of the ecclesiastical sciences.[3]

But it must be acknowledged that such a vocation is exceptional. The layman is not in a state of life which familiarizes him *professionally* with the mystery with which theology deals. It is not just a question of that inner harmony with the mystery, which every Christian possesses through the theological virtues and the exercise of the virtue of religion, but of that quite special familiarity that comes with the exercise of a *function* which has become a regular profession.

generally; godparents, catechists in missionary countries, preaching by laymen, lay theologians, the press and the wireless, the lay apostolate and Catholic Action. Pius XII's address (31 May 1954) to the cardinals and bishops on the Magisterium of the Church on the occasion of the canonization of Pius X, should be read. An English version of this is published in *Catholic Documents,* vol. XVI, pp. 28ff.

1. Laymen form the majority on the theological faculty at Athens. It should be noted that Orthodoxy has not produced the theory for this practice. See on this subject C. J. Dumont, 'Le sacerdoce dans l'Orient chrétien,' in *Etudes sur le sacrement de l'Ordre, Lex orandi,* 22, pp. 391-411, particularly p. 403.

2. Can. 1360, §1.

3. Art. 21. See Heimerl, p. 129. So, in himself, a layman could receive the canonical mission enabling him to practise this form of teaching.

The cleric celebrates the mystery; he thus is in living and habitual contact with the very realities with which theology is concerned.

The layman is at the junction of the Church and the world. The experience and the opinion of the world are at his finger-tips. Thus the vast field of contacts between the dogmatic tradition of the Church and contemporary problems is primarily his affair. Attempts to interpret the fundamental Christian ideas and apply them to mundane questions, the presentation of Catholicism as an attitude or an atmosphere, new cultural initiatives, successful apologetics, all this provides scope for an enormous field of work to which the layman can consecrate the best of himself, his experience and his ingenuity, while remaining completely faithful to his proper state in life. Journalism and strictly literary activities, the radio, the cinema and the arts, are his domain. Even on the spiritual plane, the lay apostolate is carried out *with the world as the starting-point.* For the same reason, the layman will feel more at home in catechetics than in scientific theology. Catechetics, especially with adults, is pre-eminently a field of give and take which calls for at least as much familiarity with the contemporary mentality as it does for knowledge of the deposit of the faith. The cleric also can profitably appeal to the experience of laymen in his strictly theological work, in every question which implies joining issue with the world; and they, without going beyond their role, can bring him news of the seekings and the struggles of the world in which they live.

[illegible]

[illegible] He [illegible] the [illegible] of the Church and the world [illegible] the [illegible] field of change between the [illegible] of the Church [illegible] to interpret the [illegible] of [illegible] [illegible]

PART III

COMMUNION IN ITSELF AND IN ITS VARIOUS MODES OF EXPRESSION

IX

DOES THE TERM 'COMMUNION' APPLY TO THE CHURCH?

Now that we have considered its generative causes, we can tackle the actual nature of communion.[1] This brings us to the question posed in the title of this chapter. If we can answer it in the affirmative then in what sense are we to understand the word 'communion'? The definitions provided by the best reference works are very vague. André Lalande's *Vocabulaire de la Philosophie* gives two meanings of this word : 'A. Similarity of feelings, ideas or beliefs between two or more people who are conscious of this similarity. B. Mutual attraction or grouping together founded on this similarity.' The Church is more than a similarity, more even than a group founded on this similarity. To answer the two questions we have raised we shall have to study Scripture, the history of institutions, and the history of theological thinking.

I. THE NEW TESTAMENT

Does the word *koinonia* tell us anything about the Church? 'Nowhere in the writings of St Paul does the word *koinonia* suggest 'community ' in the sense of a society or association (*Genossenschaft*)', writes Seesemann.[2] 'We therefore have no justification for

1. To see where this part fits into the whole, see the summary of the first part, pp. 93-4 above.

2. Seesemann, *Der Begriff Koinonia in Neuen Testament* (Beihefte zur Zeitschrift für die neutestamentliche Wissenschaft, 14) Giessen, 1933, p. 99. On *koinonia*, reference may also be made to A. R. George, *Communion with God in the New Testament*, London, 1953; S. Muñoz Iglesias, 'Concepto biblico de koinonia' an extract from the *XIII Semana Biblica Española*, Madrid, 1953 and J. G. Davies, *Members of one another*, London, 1958. The number of non-catholic studies on the concept—all these quoted here except Muñoz Iglesias—stresses the importance in the oecumenical dialogue of any study on *koinonia*.

drawing a parallel between the concept of *koinonia* and that of *ekklesia*. The word *koinonia* tells us nothing of the idea Paul formed of the Church, despite numerous attempts in this direction. The use of *koinonia* in the rest of the New Testament also debars us from establishing any sort of relationship between this concept and that of the community of the Church (*Gemeinde*).' We shall return later to this extremely categorical assertion.

We know that the word occurs on nineteen occasions in the New Testament, fourteen of which are in the Pauline writings. In these, Seesemann thinks the word bears three senses, according to whether it suggests 1. the action of giving a part of or contributing (*Mitteilsamkeit*); 2. that of having a part in or of participating (*Anteilhaben*); 3. the community (*Gemeinschaft*).[1] I do not think Seesemann means to say that we are faced with three different concepts which have nothing in common but their name. We are concerned with the same single concept whose implications are only partly used each time.

Seesemann ranges two texts from the great epistles in the first category. Reminding the Corinthians of the blessings which result from the collection of offerings for the believers, St Paul wrote to them: 'This administration—of the collection—makes men praise God for the spirit of obedience which you shew in confessing the gospel of Christ, and the generosity which you shew in sharing (*koinonia*) your goods with these and with all men' (II Cor. 9:13). The epilogue of the epistle to the Romans carries the same sense: 'Macedonia and Achaia have thought fit to give those saints at Jerusalem who are in need some share (koinonia) of their wealth' (Rom. 15:26). In the same category we must also place a recommendation of the epistle to the Hebrews: 'Do not neglect to do good and share what you have, for such sacrifices are pleasing to God' (Heb. 13:16, R.S.V. text).

A more numerous set of texts uses the word in the sense of participation. In the first place, the chief passage on the eucharist: 'We have a cup that we bless; is not this cup we bless a participation (*koinonia*) in Christ's blood? Is not the bread we break a participation (*koinonia*) in Christ's body?' (I Cor. 10:16). It is in the same sense that we must understand: 'The God who has called you

1. H. Seesemann, ibid.

into the fellowship (*koinonia*) of his Son, Jesus Christ, is faithful to his promise' (I Cor. 1 :9). 'Common fellowship (*koinonia*) in the spirit' (Phil. 2 :1) and the 'imparting (*koinonia*) of the Holy Spirit' (II Cor. 13 :13) must also be taken in the sense of participation. Talking of the extreme generosity of the churches of Macedonia, Paul wrote : 'Begging us earnestly for the favour of taking part in the relief of the saints' (II Cor. 8 :4, R.S.V. text). 'So full a part have you taken in the work of Christ's gospel,' Paul wrote to the Philippians, who had contributed not only by monetary help, but by their sufferings (Phil. 1 :5). To these texts, we must add two more : 'to share (*koinonia*) in Christ's sufferings' (Phil. 3 :10) and 'thy generosity in the faith' (Philem. 6).

According to Seesemann only one Pauline passage is to be placed in the third category. St Paul, speaking of his discussions in Jerusalem with James, Cephas and John, wrote : 'And so, recognizing the grace God has given me, they joined their right hands in fellowship (*koinonia*) with Barnabas and myself; the Gentiles were to be our province, the circumcised theirs. Only we were to remember the poor; which was the very thing I had set myself to do' (Gal. 2 :9-10). The word *koinonia,* which is employed here absolutely, must be understood in the sense of community of views, solidarity and a practical understanding. The second part of the passage in any case indicates clearly the significance of *koinonia* here : it implied the sharing out of apostolic duties and help to the poor of Jerusalem.

One final passage, which we have not yet considered, is difficult to relate to any of the senses so far distinguished : 'What is there in common between light and darkness?' (II Cor. 6 :14). The passage is, however, secondary, and the word is not employed there in a specifically religious sense.

In the other New Testament writings, the term *koinonia* occurs only in the sense of community. This is equally true of Acts (2 :42) : 'These (converts) occupied themselves continually with the apostles' teaching, their fellowship in the breaking of bread' and of the first epistle to St John, where the author says : 'This message about what we have seen and heard we pass on to you, so that you too may share in our fellowship. What is it, this fellowship of ours? Fellowship with the Father, and with his Son, Jesus Christ. . . . If we claim fellowship with him, when all the while we live and move in darkness, it is a lie; our whole life is an untruth. God dwells in light; if we too live and move in light, there is fellowship between us' (1:3, 6-7).

There is, then, good reason to group the different texts round these three components of the concept of *koinonia*. To be sure, in more than one case, exegetes will take a different view, and will place this or that passage in another category than that assigned to it by Seesemann. But that does not affect the validity of the categories themselves to which they are allocated.

Underlying these three senses is the fundamental meaning of the word. *Koinonoi* are people who own something in common, who share in a common interest. Such were the fishermen of Galilee, who were joint owners of a small fishing fleet (Luke 5:10). *Koinonia* is thus in the first place joint ownership. The solidarity which it implies remains, even when there is no longer any question of property in the strict sense. It is easy to see how this fundamental meaning is present in each of the usages we have noted.

When we consider the New Testament use of the word, we must beware of reducing *koinonia* to mere friendly relationships between man and man. The vertical dimension is the primary one : *koinonia* is founded wholly on Christ and on the Spirit. It is by no means accidental that some of the principal texts are found in the category of participation. We participate in the blood of Christ, in his body, in the Son himself, in his sufferings and in the Spirit. In the first epistle of John, it is the message concerning the 'Word who is life' that is the starting point of communion. The horizontal dimension in *koinonia* must thus be regarded as resulting from a vertical relationship, and can only be explained through this.

The Protestant exegete Dodd is thus on sure ground in establishing a parallel between *koinonia* and the two images, that of the tree and that of the body.[1] 'I am the vine, you are its branches ... ; separated from me, you have no power to do anything,' Christ says (John 15:5). Explaining the mystery of Israel to the Romans, St Paul says : 'The branches have been thinned out and thou, a wild olive, hast been grafted in among them; sharest, with them, the root and the richness of the true olive. That is no reason why thou shouldst boast thyself better than the branches' (Rom. 11:17-18). The image of the body, which St Paul uses to explain the Church

1. C. H. Dodd, *The Johannine Epistles*, London, 1946 (third imp. 1953), pp. 6-9.

in the passages which we studied earlier, with the Christian community's dependence on Christ and the interdependence of its members one upon the other, is even closer to our reading of the idea of *koinonia*. 'These metaphors make it clear that the "partnership" of Christians is not a mere pooling of their own individual resources, whether material or spiritual; for neither tree nor body is constituted by an association of separately living parts; the life that is shared exists only as shared; and in the application of the metaphors it is made clear that the life of the Church is the divine life disclosed . . . in the incarnate Christ and communicated through his spirit.'[1] In short, the implications in all these terms and images are the same. *Koinonia,* vine, olive tree, body—all reflect the same profound reality.

We are now able to reconsider Seesemann's somewhat sweeping assertion. When he talks of 'numerous attempts' to elucidate the concept of Church with the aid of the concept of *koinonia,* he is thinking principally of C. A. Anderson Scott. In various works, Scott tried to show that the *koinonia* of the New Testament, more particularly that of Acts 2 :42, was the equivalent of the *chaburah* of rabbinical literature. The *koinonia* that resulted from Pentecost was a new name for a new thing. It was not a nondescript sort of fellowship, but fellowship in the highest sense of the word. The group of disciples gathered round Jesus undoubtedly took or was given a name, and this was probably that of the '*chaburah* of Jesus', of which the *koinonia* of the Acts was no more than the Greek translation. This would show that *chaburah* had transmitted to *koinonia* the sense of religious society.

Seesemann has no difficulty in showing that these conjectures lack any serious basis. It is impossible to prove that the word *koinonia* in the New Testament designates the *Church as a social group,* in the sense in which we speak of a local community (village or ward) or of a religious community. But Seesemann goes beyond his premises when he concludes that *koinonia* can throw no light on the concept of the Church. This seems to me to lose sight of the fact that *koinonia* in the New Testament denotes *a way of living* (being and acting), a relation with God and with men characteristic of the Christian community. Thus, even though the word *koinonia* is not

1. Dodd, op. cit., pp.7-8.

synonymous with Church in the sense of a social group, it nevertheless signifies the mutual relations of Christians among themselves in their common dependence on Christ and the Spirit. We are at the very heart of the mystery of the Church. The parallel between *koinonia* and 'body of Christ' reveals the light this concept sheds on the nature of the Church.

In succeeding generations, the word *koinonia* was not limited to the Church as a new order of life, but came to include the elements which make a social group of the Church. Moreover, the institutional element is already perceptible in the way of living which *koinonia* conjures up in the New Testament. When 'those who were reputed to be the main support of the Church' held out their hands to Paul and Barnabas 'in fellowship', this was a good deal more than a gesture concluding a difficult bit of negotiation and setting the seal on an acceptable agreement. It involved the unity of God's people which was to show itself in practical terms through the collection in aid of the poor of the Church in Jerusalem.

II. The Primitive Church: Institution Forms

Father Louis Hertling has devoted a well-documented study to the concept of communion in the early Church.[1] We shall try to profit from his researches. For St Augustine, the *communio* is nothing other

1. L. Hertling, 'Communio und Primat', in *Miscellanea Historiae Pontificiae*, vol. VII, Rome, 1943, pp. 1-48: this study has just appeared in Italian translation in a separate booklet, *Commvnio. Chiesa e papato nell'antichita cristianà*, Rome 1961., The subject has also been investigated by a Lutheran theologian, W. Elert, *Abendmahl und Kirchengemeinschaft in der alten Kirche hauptsächlich des Ostens*, Berlin 1954. It is astonishing to note that this author is absolutely unaware of L. Hertling's work. W. Elert returned to this question in a posthumous contribution to a collective work, 'Abendmahl und Kirchengemeinschaft in der alten Kirche', which appeared in *Koinonia. Arbeiten des Oekumenischen Ausschusses der Vereinigten Evangelisch-Lutherischen Kirche Deutschlands zur Frage der Kirche und Abendmahlsgemeinschaft*, Berlin, 1957, pp. 57-78. M. J. Le Guillou made the idea of communion the centre of a work devoted to the oecumenical problem, *Mission et Unité. Les exigences de la communion*, two vols., Paris 1960. Two important studies by Y. Congar tackle the problem as a whole, 'Note sur les mots "Confession", "Eglise" et "Communion"', in *Irenikon*, 1950, vol. 23, pp. 3-36, and 'Peut-on définir l'Eglise. Destin et valeur de quatre notions qui s'offrent à le faire', in *Jacques Leclercq, L'homme, l'oeuvre et ses amis*, Tournai and Paris 1961, pp. 233-254.

than the Church.[1] In the Fathers, the *communio sanctorum* frequently means the visible Church. Though, to start with, the word *communio* signified on the whole an attitude or a kind of behaviour, in the usage of the primitive Church it became an exact term denoting the link which forms the social unity of the Christian community all over the world. A similar evolution of the vocabulary can be observed with other words. 'Peace' became an equivalent of 'communion', with the same meaning. In a letter to St Jerome, St Augustine writes: 'There has just come to me a pious young man, *catholica pace frater*'.[2] The *pax catholica* has the precise meaning of membership of the Catholic Church. In a number of passages, the words *concordia, eirene* and *agape* have the same meaning: the community of the Church.

Eucharistic communion furnishes the sign of this community in the Church. In the middle of the second century, Polycarp of Smyrna and Pope Anicetus could not reach agreement on the date of Easter. But they did not therefore sever the ecclesiastical communion. On the contrary, 'they communicated one with the other', writes Eusebius.[3] We must not understand from this that each gave the other communion, but that Anicetus let Polycarp celebrate the eucharist in the Rome assembly. The link between ecclesiastical communion and participation in the eucharist was so strong that the patriarch Macedonius of Constantinople wanted to oblige the believers who resisted him to receive *his* communion. He had their mouths opened by force. Catholics who travelled in heretical areas carried their own eucharist with them. The heretics, it must be added, did the same, to avoid entering into communion with Catholics.

A Christian who left for abroad provided himself with a sort of passport issued by the bishop, which was known under various names: letters of communion (*litterae communicatoriae*), canonical letters, letters of introduction (*commendatitiae*), or again letters of

1. 'Nullo interprete indigent canonicarum scripturarum testimonia quae commendant *Ecclesiam in totius orbis communione consistere*' (*De unit. Eccl. contra Donat.*, 20, 56, *PL*, vol. 43, col. 434). 'Ego in Ecclesia sum, cujus membra sunt omnes illae ecclesiae, quas ex laboribus Apostolorum natas atque firmatas simul in litteris canonicis novimus; earum communionem, quantum me adjuvet Dominus, sive in Africa, sive ubicumque, non deseram' (*Contra Crescon.*, III, 35, 39, *PL*, vol. 43, col. 517).

2. *Epist. 131*, 2, *PL*, vol. 22, col. 1125.

3. *Hist. eccles.*, V, 24.

peace (*pacificae, litterae pacis*). These documents guaranteed considerable advantages. Their holders were received everywhere as brothers; bishops offered them free hospitality. According to Father Hertling : 'Every bishop, or at least every Church of any importance, later on chiefly the metropolitans, drew up a list of the principal Churches of the world with which they were in communion. Such lists served as directories when it became necessary to issue passports. Then again, the documents of travellers were checked with the aid of the same lists. A passport was accepted when it came from a bishop mentioned in the list. Outside Africa, the Donatist bishop with whom Augustine was at loggerheads did not of course appear on any list. Augustine was thus able to tell him : "Make out a passport for Alexandria or Antioch, then, and we shall soon see whether you are on the list of orthodox bishops there".'[1]

The counterpart of communion was then excommunication, which was not yet, or at least not exclusively, the *poena vindicativa* and *medicinalis* of later ecclesiatical law, but merely the severing of communion, the breaking off of relations. Excommunication could come about between a bishop and the members of his church, clergy or laymen, and between a bishop and another bishop, on the grounds of suspected heresy, for example. But it could also occur between a layman, of the Christian community, and their own bishop, in the sense that the body of believers could, under certain circumstances, sever relations with their spiritual head. According to St Cyprian, the body of believers would be bound to withdraw from the communion of a bishop whose faith was corrupted.[2] On Christmas day, the emperor Arcadius refused to 'communicate with' St John Chrysostom as long as the latter had not cleared himself from the accusations that hung over him.[3]

In this severing of relations, the reference to the eucharist naturally played the principal and essential role. The excommunicated sinner was first of all excluded from eucharistic communion. On the other hand, his reinstatement into the community of the Church was expressed by his admission to the eucharist. This did not prevent the severing of relations from being expressed in varying degrees. For example, exclusion from the eucharist did not necessarily mean

1. L. Hertling, *Communio* . . ., p. 12.
2. Cypr., Epist. 67, 3, *CSEL*, vol. III, 2, p. 737.
3. Socrates, *Hist. eccles.*, VI, 18.

exclusion from the prayer meeting. The same was true, the other way round, of readmission. As early as the third century, the penitentiary practice of the East allowed for various degrees of penance: the sinner who repented approached the altar progressively.

How was any given bishop's membership of the communion to be established? The test could lie either in his links with the episcopate as a whole or in his relationships with the oldest Churches. Now Rome held the first place in the list of Churches. A Church which was in communion with Rome was, by that very fact, in communion with the whole Church. The idea that Rome was the head of the communion was one of long standing. We find characteristic expression of it in a letter from St Ambrose in 381, in which he asked the Emperors Gratian and Valentinian to 'see to it that the Roman Church, head of the whole Roman world, is not destroyed, for from it there spreads to all the other Churches the rights of communion that must be reverenced'.[1] The pope, the unifying principle of the Church, is not forced to furnish proof of his role by issuing juridical decisions. These do not establish his authority, but flow from it. 'The pope is never more a pope than when the whole Church, all the bishops and all the faithful are in complete agreement with him. A father's authority over his family is never stronger than when it is unnecessary to appeal to it, when in some way or other his wife and children "feel" it.'[2] There are, nevertheless, some early texts which show this authority in action, as it were regulating the communion.

The word communion does not therefore mean merely *similarity in faith*. The sinner, excluded from the society of brothers, might very well share the same faith. That could equally be true of entire communities. The Novatians had the same creed as the Catholics, but all the same they were excommunicated. The *sacramental element* is to the fore in the concept of communion. Excommunication debarred a man from participating in the eucharist. The principal object of letters of communion was to allow Christians travelling outside their own country access to the eucharist.

Moreover the normal functioning of the Communion implied the presence of a *factor of authority*. Whoever held the office of head of the community issued the letters of communion and admitted believers to the eucharist or debarred them from it. It was through

1. Ambrose, *Epist.*, 11, 4, *PL*, vol. 16, col. 946.
2. L. Hertling, *Communio* . . ., p. 45.

the action of the bishops that the links between one local Church and another were established and maintained. It was at the heart and highest point of this communion of bishops that the privileged position of the Roman Church—*Ecclesia principalis,* in St Cyprian's words—emerged.[1]

Thus communion could be expressed as a whole in terms of faith and of sacramental life, and also in terms of institutional and juridical structures which were still in the making. But the primitive Church had evolved no theory of the *communio.* History presents it to us as being above all a reality lived from day to day in the constant give and take of a universal and ordered brotherhood.

III. Theological Thinking in the Middle Ages

In the primitive Church, excommunication was the severing of communion or communication. Now, in writers of great repute, the word 'communion' was used directly of the Church. The relationship between these three terms, excommunication, communion and Church, called for definition. Theological thought came progressively to clarify these terms, which was of benefit to ecclesiology. The introduction of a fourth element, sin, sparked off a more profound study of all the components of the problem, which was not a simple one.

Today we draw a clear distinction between the effects of sin and the effect of the sentence of excommunication. This distinction was seldom made in primitive Christianity. 'The two types of effect were confused. Essentially, these effects lay in exclusion from the Church. Nobody thought of distinguishing between the "major" or "ontological" effect of sin and the "minor" and principally external effect of excommunication. This differentiation was only gradually established and the canonical, essentially disciplinary notion which we find in present Canon Law was only gradually arrived at.'[2]

1. Cyprian, *Epist.*, 59, 14, *CSEL*, vol. III, 2, p. 683: 'Ad hanc enim ecclesiam propter potiorem principalitatem necesse est omnem convenire ecclesiam' (Irenaeus, *Haer.*, III, 3, 2, *PG*, vol. 7, col. 849). It is not for us here to go into the many arguments to which this text has given rise. On all this, see L. Hertling, *Communio* . . ., p. 24.

2. F. Russo. 'Pénitence et excommunication. Etude historique sur les rapports entre la théologie et le droit canon dans le domaine pénitentiel du IXe au XIIIe siècle', in *Recherches de science religieuse*, 1946, vol. 33, pp. 257-279, 431-461; the pas-

In the early Middle Ages, writers had no hesitation in stating that excommunication hands the sinner over to Satan.[1] There was a fairly general tendency to attribute too great a significance to sentences of excommunication. But as Russo very properly observes: 'Though there may be mistakes to rectify in these conceptions, we should note that they possess the great merit of presenting the problem of the offence and its reparation in a really ecclesiological and social setting. Today when we are trying to rediscover a deeper sense of the Church, it is perhaps not without interest to resume contact with this theology, which was still a little immature but which so rightly assigned a central place to the Church.'[2]

The way to this necessary differentiation was paved by a closer study of the effects of sin. Is there any need of an external sentence to separate the sinner from God? By the single fact of his transgression, the sinner severs certain links and wilfully sets himself at a distance. When this truth was clearly recognized, men came to see in the sentence of excommunication no more than its purely external effects. The distinction between anathema and excommunication which we find in Gratian can doubtless be regarded as a stage in this evolution. Anathema, of course, designates an extreme measure which separated a man from Christ, whereas excommunication denoted a sentence whose effects were principally external.[3] Though the vocabulary remained imprecise, it is interesting to note that the idea of excommunication, regarded as separation from the visible society of the faithful, was beginning to emerge.

We owe a considerable advance in vocabulary and in ideas to William of Auvergne, who died in 1249 and was one of the most

sage quoted here is on p. 264. On the use of *Communio* in the middle ages, abundant material will be found in H. de Lubac, *Corpus Mysticum*, second ed., 1949, pp. 27-34.

1. 'Omnis Christianus, dilectissimi, qui a sacerdotibus excommunicatur, sathanae traditur; quomodo? Scilicet quia extra ecclesiam est diabolus, sicut in ecclesia Christus, ac per hoc quasi diabolo traditur, qui ab ecclesiastica communione removetur. Unde illos, quod tunc Apostolus sathanae esse traditos predicat, excommunicatos a se esse demonstrat' (Gratian, *Decret.*, C, XI, q. 3, 32; Friedberg, col. 653).
2. F. Russo, *Pénitence* . . ., pp. 267-268.
3. 'Hengiltrudam uxorem Bosonis noveris non solum excommunicatione, quae a fraterna societate separat, sed etiam anathemate, quod ab ipso corpore Christi (quod est ecclesia) recidit, crebro percussam' (Gratian, *Decret.*, C. III, q. 4, c. 12; Friedberg, col. 514).

representative theologians of the secular clergy of the period. He drew a clear distinction between the effects of sin and the effects of the sentence of excommunication, and in this context the distinction between inner communion and external communion—so valuable in ecclesiology—was to emerge. William of Auvergne was contending with an error which may be summed up in the following formula: *Peccatum excommunicat hominem, non sententia.*[1] In other words, the ecclesiastical judge can exclude only the sinner from communion, not the righteous man; for strictly speaking, it is the sin and not the sentence that excommunicates. The first question our theologian puts to those who profess this error is: 'What do they understand by excommunication? Separation from the external communion of the sacraments and the faithful, or separation from the inner communion of the same realities? If they add that the intention of excommunication is to separate the accused from the inner communion of the sacraments and the faithful, we will ask them another question: what do they mean by inner communion? It obviously means the communion and the society of the saints and the righteous. There is no doubt at all that only sin separates and excludes a man from that. Nobody in the Church of God has ever imagined that an ecclesiastical judge could possess this power over it. This, indeed, would lead to its destruction. According to this view, excommunicating would be tantamount to hacking the mystical body to pieces and tearing off its limbs, this mystical body which is composed and constructed of saints and of righteous believers.'[2]

Having made this point, William attacks the other alternative. If, as his antagonists believe, sin alone excommunicates, must the word excommunication be understood as loss of the external communion? After recalling that a judge may be led to excommunicate a man who, in other respects, is righteous, the author puts the following reply in his opponents' mouth. It could be asserted that the righteous man, despite his expulsion from the Church (*ejectus foris ab ecclesia, a sacris et a sacramentis, ejectus inquam ejectione exteriori et litterali*), nevertheless continues to remain in communion with the saints and the sacraments, and that he is thus still on the inside. 'It is indeed one and the same thing to be in communion with the

1. *De sacramento ordinis*, chap. 8, Venice, 1591, p. 511 D.
2. Ibid., chap. 12, p. 518, H and F.

saints and with the sacraments and to be within or to be inside the Church' (*Idem est communicare sanctis et sacramentis, quod intus esse, sive intra ecclesiam esse*). This position is contradictory. It is untenable.

There is thus no other explanation but the following : the excommunicated righteous man 'no longer possesses, through himself, anything but the inner communion. The latter is without any doubt the fruit and the advantage (*utilitas*) procured by the external communion and its *res*. The external communion is the *signum* of this. (Our opponents) will thus come to acknowledge the truth : the righteous man who is excommunicated has only the fruit or the *rest* of the external communion, he does not possess it in itself.'[1]

At the heart of the reality of the Church, William of Auvergne draws a sharp distinction between an inner communion, from which we are excluded only by sin, and an external communion, from which a sentence of excommunication can expel us. The two communions are closely linked. The reason why the inner communion is not only the *res,* but the *fructus* and the *utilitas* of the external communion is that the latter is not only the *signum* of the inner communion but also its principle and its cause, though these two last terms are not employed by the author. The external communion exists for the sake of the inner communion. This general assertion is confirmed—though in a paradoxical manner—by the case of excommunication. 'It is from the external communion alone that the Church means to exclude a man,' William of Auvergne continues. 'She excludes him from the external communion with a view to bringing him back to the inner communion. The only reason she strikes with the sword of excommunication is to heal through the remedy of spiritual communion. . . . It should nevertheless be realized that contempt for excommunication and also contumacy constitute one of the sins which do more than others to destroy spiritual communion. . . . (On the other hand) the man who is excluded from the external communion sometimes progresses more through the virtue of patience and of humility, and endures excommunication in a more meritorious manner than that in which he had previously made use of the external communion. . . . For many people, indeed,

1. Ibid., Chap. 12, p. 519 D, for the passage we have just quoted and that in the preceding paragraph.

the burden of excommunication is no less difficult to bear, and no less formidable, than martyrdom.'[1]

William of Auvergne thus saw two levels of communion. St Bonaventure was to distinguish three. He was led to do so by a consideration of the double form of excommunication : minor excommunication, which debars a man only from receiving the sacraments and major excommunication which also cuts him off from the society of the faithful. This distinction may date from the beginnings of the thirteenth century. We find it formulated in legal terms in a decretal of Gregory IX.[2] For the rest, St Bonaventure adds nothing to the more exhaustive theology of William of Auvergne.

In a passage in which he is dealing with the legitimacy of excommunication, St Bonaventure raises the following objection against himself : '*Excommunication is separation from the communion.* But the communion exists through charity. Therefore nobody can excommunicate. . . .' The first, italicized, sentence of this objection is taken from Gratian's decree. St Bonaventure replies by giving a schematic view of the theology of communion, based on the following distinction : 'Communion is threefold : the first form is purely spiritual (*spiritualis omnino*)—this is the communion of inner charity : the second is corporal—this is the communion of outward relations (*quantum ad exteriorem conversationem*); the third is between the two (*medio modo*)—this is the communion of the reception of the sacraments and more particularly of the sacrament of the altar. I say therefore that nobody can nor should be excluded from the first communion as long as he is on earth; what is more, excommunication does not debar him from this communion. As to sacramental communion, anyone who is under a major or a minor excommunication is excluded from it. Finally, major excommunication concerns outward relations. In virtue of it, there is a prohibition of communion in the form of the following four legitimate acts : the kiss (*osculum*), conversation (*colloquium*), the meal (*convivium*) and prayer (*oratorium* : prayer and the sacraments). This is what is meant by the line : *Os, orare, vale, communio, mensa negatur*. There

1. Chap. 12, p. 519, A-C.

2. 'Si quem sub hac forma verborum: "Illum excommunico", vel simili, a judice suo excommunicare contingat, dicendum est, eum non tantum minori, quae a perceptione sacramentorum, sed etiam majori excommunicatione, quae a communione fidelium separat, esse ligatum' (*Decret. Gregor IX*, lib. V, tit. 39, c. 59; Friedberg, col. 912).

is thus, then, a threefold communion: spiritual, sacramental and corporal.'[1]

The new element introduced by St Bonaventure is also to be found in St Thomas. 'The man who is made part of the Church through baptism is intended at once to live in the community of the faithful (*ad coetum fidelium*) and to participate in the sacraments (*ad participationem sacramentorum*). This second object presupposes the first: the social communion of the faithful extends to participation in the sacraments. Consequently there are two different ways in which excommunication can put someone out of the Church (*extra Ecclesiam fieri*).... But it must be borne in mind that the communion of the faithful (*communicatio fidelium*) takes two forms: the first is practised in the spiritual domain (*in spiritualibus*), for example in prayers for one another and in meetings (of worship) to receive the sacred things; the second is of the order of legitimate corporal acts (*in corporalibus actibus legitimis*).'[2]

We must note certain variations in the vocabulary of St Thomas and that of his contemporaries. A limited search has not led me to discover a single passage where St Thomas uses *communio* or *communicatio, in an ecclesiological context,* to designate the internal links created by charity. In his work, therefore, the word 'communion' is not an *all-embracing* term which will allow us to grasp in a single glance all the richness and complexity of the reality of the Church. *In its ecclesiological context,* this term is used principally to designate the outward and visible links in the domains of sacramental life and of brotherly society.[3] But this remark holds good of the vocabulary only. We have seen above, in Chapter III, how St Thomas's ecclesiology grasps all the ecclesiological implications of the expression *corpus mysticum.*

To conclude, the word 'communion' can be applied to the complex reality of the Church, but only on condition that it is not shorn

1. *IV Sent.*, dist. 18, pars 2, art. 1, q. 1, contra 1; Quaracchi, p. 485.
2. *Suppl.*, q. 21, a. 1, c. (=*IV Sent.*, d. 18, q. 2, a. 1, qc. 1, c.).
3. We know the prominence given to *communicatio* in another connection in the treatise on charity.; see L. B. Gillon, 'A propos de la théorie thomiste de l'amitié. "Fundatur super aliqua communicatione" (II-II, q. 23, a.1)', in *Angelicum*, 1948, vol. 25, pp. 3-17; also P. Philippe, *Le rôle de l'amitié dans la vie chrétienne selon Saint Thomas d'Aquin*, Rome, 1938. There is an excellant note on *koinonia* in Aristotle in R. A. Gauthier and J. Y. Jolif, *Aristote. L'Ethique à Nicomaque. Introduction, traduction et commentaire*, Louvain and Paris, vol. II, 1959, pp. 696-697.

of any of the components it has acquired during its long history.

1. At the start, this term designated a way of being in the Church: it fell within the province of the order of life. There was a progressive evolution from within towards institutional structures, its origin being none other than the requirements of the communion as a form of sociability. But it would be a pity to retain only the final outcome of this process. A similar evolution is going on in contemporary language. The word 'brotherhood', which has for a long time been used in the Church of a type of behaviour, is being used more and more to designate certain religious associations.[1] It is the term which Voillaume has chosen for his foundations (The Brotherhood of Charles de Foucauld). But if brotherhood, in the sense of an association, is to retain all its meaning, it must be scupulously faithful to its origins, to brotherhood as a manner of living. In the same way communion as an institution must lose none of the connotations of communion as behaviour.

2. Over the centuries, the word 'communion' has acquired a distinctly relational sense. In the primitive Church it designated the relations between Church and Church, Christian and Christian. The

1. An interesting study enables us to follow a similar evolution in the case of the brotherhood, or *confraternitas*: J. Duhr, 'La confrérie dans la vie de l'Eglise', in *Revue d'histoire ecclésiastique*, 1939, vol. 35, pp. 436-478. In his introductory remarks, the author shows how realities which may refer to sociability and behaviour must accede at a given moment to the institutional plane. 'By *his* great commandment, Christ enjoined his disciples to love God as their Father and to treat each other as brothers. Immediately the old word 'brotherhood' became irradiated with charity . . . The Church loves to hear herself called *ecclesia fratrum*, *fraternitas*, or *adelphotes*. Tertullian left us a touching picture of the devotion and brotherly mutual aid of the Christians of his time . . . With the growing number of believers, charity too expanded and became specialized. *Brotherhood gave birth to brotherhood*, but the unity of spirit was not affected, for all that. (Our italics in the last sentence). The Roman *collegia* were then at the height of their prosperity. To diversify its activities, the Church adopted their framework.' (pp. 440-441). I have to thank Father André Duval, of Le Saulchoir, for the following details of the use of the word *fraternitas* in the institutional sense. In the second rule of St Francis (1223), we read: 'Universi fratres unum de fratribus istius religionis teneantur semper habere generalem ministrum et servum totius *fraterhitatis*' (VIII, 1). 'Nullus fratrum (. . .) audeat praedicare, nisi a ministro generali hujus *fraternitatis* fuerit examinatus et approbatus.' (IX, 2) One must ask the pope for a cardinal 'qui sit gubernator, protector et corrector istius *fraternitatis* (XII, 3).

The word *fraternitas* in the institutional sense appears in the first lines of the oldest document known concerning the *Ordo de poenitentia*, 1221. The same word *fraternitas*, still in the institutional sense, occurs four times in the very first chapter of the Rule given by Munio de Zamora to the 'fraternities' of the *Ordo de poenitentia* under Dominican obedience.

communion was an aggregate of connections, the fruit of manifold reciprocal relationships. I am somewhat surprised to learn that the only deep-seated substratum of meaning for communion that the sociologist G. Gurvitch could find was *fusion,* that is to say unity psychologically experienced within a 'We'.[1] The elimination or freezing of the category of relationships seems to me impossible here. In current usage, the word 'communion' is still permeated with its entire history, stamped with the experience of the primitive Church. Even in its secular uses, it suggests the idea of a network of relational interchanges. The psychological experience of communion is secondary by contrast with this basic component.

3. As applied to the Church, communion has two aspects, one directed towards God, the other towards the links that unite men to each other. As we said earlier with regard to the New Testament, *koinonia* covers a reality in which the relation to God is primary in comparison with the relations of men with each other. The position of Christians with regard to each other is the result of their complete dependence upon Christ. It is also conditioned by their relationship to those who have the mission in the Church of bringing them Christ through the Word and through the sacraments.

4. Communion is stratified into different levels. If we proceed from its external aspects to the deeper-lying components, we are confronted successively with Christian social life, its sacramental life (which is its kernel) and its inner life of charity. Some mediaeval authors distinguished three forms of communion within the Church. These can be reduced to two : external communion, of which we should say today that it is constituted by the totality of the means of grace, and inner communion, which consists in the life of grace. These two communions are not merely juxtaposed : together they constitute the Church. William of Auvergne gave an excellent definition of the relationship which exists between them. The external communion is *signum* in the strongest sense; the inner communion is *res*. In the context of the providential economy, these two communions cannot be dissociated : they form a whole.

5. The external communion is not flat or horizontal, but organized hierarchically. Its normal functioning, as we have seen, requires

1. Gurvitch proposes a threefold division of the forms of sociability: the crowd, the community and the communion (*La vocation actuelle de la sociologie*, Paris 1950, p. 153). See appendix III below.

the presence of a factor of authority. It was on the bishop's initiative that relationships were established between Church and Church. Furthermore, a governing principle of communion asserted itself as central to these inter-relations. From the very first centuries, the Roman Church occupied a pre-eminent position within the universal communion. This position was gradually clarified, as the whole history of the Church testifies. The role of the papacy in the communion was happily expressed by Pius IX. As head of the Church and seal of its unity, the successor of Peter is 'entrusted with confirming the brotherhood that is in the world'.[1]

The Church is a communion. We now know the full richness of this expression. Subsequent theology has not subjected the term to theological analysis. But we should note right away, before returning to it in the following chapter, the importance and the interest of a penetrating analysis of the underlying *reality* carried out at the beginning of the sixteenth century by that experienced theologian Cardinal Cajetan, around the question: Just what constitutes that unity of the Church to which schism is opposed?

1. An extract from the encyclical *Etsi multa*, of November 21 1873. Here it is in context: 'Nobody can be considered a lawful bishop, unless he is united through the communion of faith and of charity with the stone on which the Church of Jesus Christ is built, unless he is faithful to the supreme Pastor to whom all the sheep are confided so that he may feed them, and unless he is linked with him who is entrusted with confirming the brotherhood that is in the world' (cf. I Peter 5:9). In this part of his encyclical, Pius IX was dealing with the ecclesiastical problem raised by the 'Old Catholics'.

X

THE COMMUNION OF THE SPIRIT

'THE grace of our Lord Jesus Christ, and the love of God, and the imparting (*koinonia,* communion) of the Holy Spirit be with you all' (II Cor. 13 : 13). Does this mean the communion between Christians *effected* by the Spirit, or the communion of Christians who rediscover each other in the Spirit which they *possess* in common? Is St Paul talking of a work of the Spirit or of a participation in the Spirit? Exegetes are still debating the question. But its very ambiguity makes this formula a perfect introduction to the twofold theological theme which is the subject of the present chapter. When we consider theology's approach to the relations between the Spirit and the Church we discover two major themes : the Spirit makes the Church and the Spirit inhabits the Church.

I. THE UNITY BROUGHT ABOUT BY THE SPIRIT: CAJETAN'S ANALYSIS

We shall be concerned here solely with this analysis. We shall summarize it with the strictest faithfulness. It is severe in its style. It may appear dry. The use of the Aristotelian categories of relation, action and passion will not make it easy reading for everyone. Nevertheless it deserves to be tackled as it stands. In this way, it will reveal all its richness. Its ecclesiological content will make up for its difficulty.[1]

Schism is a sin which opposes the unity brought about by charity,

1. It occupies three complete columns of the Leonine edition of the works of St Thomas, heading the commentary on the question of schism as a sin against charity, in the *Summa theologica*, II-II, q. 39, a. 1 (Nos. I-IV).

or more precisely that *unitas Spiritus* which is the binding link of the whole Church. Now this unity comprises two aspects : the mutual relationship of the members or *communion* (*communicatio*), and the relationship of all the members to the same head, Christ, whose place is occupied in the Church by the Supreme Pontiff. That is why, St Thomas concludes : 'We shall call schismatics those who refuse to submit to the Supreme Pontiff, and who refuse to communicate (that is to say, to be in communion) with the members of the Church who are submissive to him.'[1] This text gives us a better understanding of St Thomas's conception of the unity of the Church.

What constitutes this unity of the Church to which schism is opposed? Cajetan clarifies St Thomas's position on this point. He starts by stating the difficulty. Schism intends to remove unity. Now unity is a property of being. Schism must thus remove a certain 'being', a certain *esse*. Now though we can easily see that schism does indeed remove a certain *esse relativum* of the members to the head, we do not see what other common *esse* can be removed by the disruption of schism. The *esse* of faith, of hope, of the sacraments and of worship are still there in schism. The *esse* of charity is indirectly affected by any mortal sin and directly by contempt for this virtue. But that is not schism. The man who does not want charity to exist either in himself or in anyone else is not for that reason a schismatic. The implied conclusion of this weighty objection is that it is useless to resort to *communicatio* or to the *connexio membrorum ad invicem* to define the Church.

Before looking at Cajetan's reply to this difficulty, it will be well to stress a certain tendancy to lapse into the superficiality of reducing schism to disobedience, to rupture of the hierarchical links. In the *Summa theologica* attributed to Alexander of Hales we find a definition of this kind.[2] The same is true today of certain contemporary manuals, including some of the best.[3]

1. II-II, q. 39, a. 1.
2. 'Illa discessio dicitur schisma, cum aliqui vim et potestatem Romanae Ecclesiae adnullant, praecepta ejus et instituta pertinaciter contemnendo, nec caput eam reputando' (*Summa theologica*, Secunda pars, secundi libri, Inquisitio 3a, Tractus 8us, Tit. 4, c. 1, sol. 2a; Quaracchi, vol. IV, p. 753).
3. 'Schisma (. . .) consistit in subtractione pertinaci ab oboedientia Summo Pontifici debita' (D. Prummer, *Manuale theol. moralis.*, Freib.-im-Br., 1935, vol. I, p. 361).

Cajetan's reply is illuminating. The Church is a congregation of all the faithful and is a *numerical* unity.[1] Whence do this *esse* and this numerical unity come? Not from an *esse* which constitutes the thing in itself, but from an *esse* which establishes this thing as being ordered to another thing (*ad aliud*). Alone among the Aristotelian categories, those of relation and of action and passion unite separate beings. As it happens, the aim of the Church is to establish a unity among believers who are all separate beings, insofar as they are persons. So we must necessarily look in these two categories for what constitutes the Church. Let us therefore consider the supernatural gifts that dwell in the faithful.

(a) *The unity of the theological virtues and of the sacraments.* 'If believers had no other unity than this, the Church would not, strictly speaking, be one, but the believers would merely be alike.'

(b) *The unity of the head* : in heaven, Christ; on earth, his vicar. Through this unity, there is in every believer an *esse relativum* of order to a single head (numerically one) : what is more there is in each of them another link belonging to the category of action and passion, that is to say a relation that depends on precept and submission. The Holy Spirit inspires the faithful not only to believe and to hope . . . , but also to submit to the vicar of Christ. All the same, this double hierarchical relation is not enough. 'If there were no other unity among the faithful, we could not say that the Church is one, but that it is subordinated to a head.'[2] Several kingdoms, each enjoying their internal autonomy, can be governed at the top by a single prince. It would be the same with the Church.[3]

(c) *The collective unity of all believers* (*unitas collectionis universorum fidelium*). *This is the unity of communion.* This unity implies the existence in each believer of an *esse relativum,* that of the part to the numerically single whole.[4] Through this *esse* there is in each of us a dependence with respect to the whole. The whole is the standard and rule for the parts, their point of reference. It is the same with *actio* and *passio* under divine impulsion. Believers are impelled by the Spirit to all the works of spiritual life : faith, love,

1. There are thus two elements to consider: not merely any sort of congregation, but a congregation which has a numerical unity; nor, in addition, any sort of numerical unity but a numerical unity of congregation.

2. Non diceretur una sed *sub uno*.

3. Numerical unity to be sure, but not a unity of congregation.

4. 'Scilicet esse partem unius numero populi'.

sanctification and obedience. But this impulsion affects not only the 'substance' of the action, but also the manner of its performance. Each of these acts must be performed by a subject who is part of a whole. *Each of the faithful believes that he is a member of the Church, but it is also as a member of the Church that he believes, that he administers the sacraments, that he teaches and that he listens to the word.* It is indeed in, for and according to the Church that he does all this.

What is the final basis of this behaviour of the faithful, which implies an *esse relativum?* The sovereign disposition of the Holy Spirit, who placed among the articles of faith: *unam sanctam Ecclesiam*; who was determined that the Catholic (that is to say universal) Church should be strictly one and that there should not be a number of Churches. Cajetan compares this fact with I Cor. 12:11: 'All this is the work of one and the same Spirit, who distributes his gifts as he will to each severally.'

Cajetan draws the inference from this: 'It follows that between Churches which appear to be completely separate, such as those of Spain and Scotland, there is not only a conformity (*convenientia*) of faith, hope, charity, the sacraments and submission to the same head, but a genuine link between one part and the other (*colligatio*) in a numerically single union (*in una numero congregatione*) directed primarily and principally by the Holy Spirit.'

There we have the unity of the Church which schism destroys, the unity of which the outward sign is the general council. This unity is the supreme good among the blessings which concern our neighbour: it is the spiritual good of the world. Schism is in the last resort simply a determination to break this unity, a refusal to act as part of the Church, whatever the motives that prompt this refusal. These reasons may be diverse, of an affective order or of an intellectual order. Schismatics are all those who deviate from the path of the Church, to the extent of no longer wishing to behave as parts of it, and who mean to act as autonomous wholes, for the purpose of teaching or being taught, governing or obeying, sanctifying or being sanctified.[1]

1. It would be well to bring out now the psychological and spiritual implications of this analysis. On this point see Y. Congar, 'Rythmes de l'Eglise et du monde,' in *Vie Intellectuelle*, April 1946, pp. 6-22, and his article 'Schisme' in the *DTC*. We will return to this point later.

There is even more to be said. The difficulty has not been completely cleared up. How can the unity of the Church be the work of charity, since schism removes and seeks to destroy a unity which can be possessed without charity? Even so, by no means every sinner is a schismatic. To this question (*secundum dubium*) Cajetan replies that the unity of the Church is a spiritual unity brought about in us by charity. So it is an effect of charity. 'Through charity, the Spirit impels all believers to want to be parts of a single Catholic *collectio* quickened by him; he impels them to form the single Catholic Church.'

Nevertheless we must distinguish among the effects of charity between those that are 'formed' (that is to say those which are inseparable from the actual possession of the virtue of charity) and those which may be 'unformed'. Among the former we must put contrition, among the latter certain supernatural works of mercy, such as alms given *propter Christum.* Now the unity of the Church, which in its proper state (*simpliciter,* as Cajetan puts it) is 'formed' —the Church, of course, is always in a state of grace—may be unformed in this or that individual believer. Whence the conclusion that the link of unity with the Church may be retained by some people who are in a state of mortal sin.[1] A man becomes schismatic only through the wilful act of withdrawing himself from the unity of the Church, which is a definite effect of charity.

This would seem to be the place for a somewhat deeper study of the comparison suggested by Cajetan. The unformed virtue of mercy still remains in the sinner who gives alms because of Christ. It is a *supernatural gift.* But its act is still really not perfect because it is cut off from its end, the 'divine good' which is present through charity.[2] In the same way, the unity of the Church, which in the sinner is unformed and hence imperfect, is nevertheless still a gift of the Spirit. The sense in which we must regard the unity of the Church as an effect of charity will be seen.

Mgr Journet comments on this text as follows :

> 'The unity of the Church is obtained *formally* by its righteous members who are in charity and *materially* by its sinful members

1. A man can continue to perform actions and maintain a habitual type of behaviour corresponding with a higher state than that which he has lost.
2. Cf. II-II, q. 4, a. 3.

who are bereft of charity. Charity . . . remains in the strictest sense the proper and *formal* cause of the natural and normal unity of the Church. It may be however that a particular Christian who has lost love will nevertheless remain sufficiently united to the Church to perform, doubtless in a *material* and handicapped manner, deprived of its crown, the acts which are required of him to remain part of Church unity.'[1] But Journet thinks we must go further: 'The charity of the Church exercises its formative influence even on its sinful members.'[2]

The charity of the righteous members exerts a sort of indirect, inspiring and elevating effect on the sinful members.

'It is to the impetus of the collective charity of the Church that (the sinful members) are yielding when they take their children to be baptized, accept the new definitions of dogma which the Holy Spirit suggests to the Church and participate through almsgiving in its missionary work.'[3]

A final difficulty still remains to be tackled. How can schism separate the Church from one of its properties? One can no more separate the Church from its unity than deprive it of its being. The unity of the Church is a dogma of the faith, likewise its indefectibility. Why then define schism by its opposition to unity? Cajetan here introduces a very illuminating twofold distinction. The schismatic intends to destroy the unity *secundum affectum* but he does not succeed in doing so *secundum effectum*. In reality, he merely destroys this unity in himself, in his own person: he separates himself from this unity.

This summary should lead readers to study this important text for themselves. Cajetan's treatment is not a word analysis. All the same what he has written is indeed a masterly analysis of *communio*. Communion is not merely resemblance in the same Christian faith, nor even obedience to the same head. It is these things, but with something extra, which explains and includes everything. Cajetan has discerned with admirable clarity that Christian existence in the Church is, of its own nature, *relational*. In each of us there is

1. *L'Eglise du Verbe Incarné*, vol. II, pp. 699-700.
2. Ibid., p. 700.
3. Ibid.

a dependence with respect to the 'whole' in the very thing that makes us Christians and members of the Church. The 'whole', the Church of the risen Christ, consequently conditions our being and our behaviour. Our activities will always be those of members of the Church, whatever the importance of the function we fulfil in the Christian community.

II. The Unity Brought About by the Presence of the Spirit in the Church. The Church as the Temple of the Spirit

We are not going to discuss the Spirit in Scripture.[1] Let us for the moment take it for granted that the Spirit is given to the Church as such; that he firmly establishes its existence *qua* body of Christ; that he performs in it all the acts of life, and that he is the fundamental principle of its unity.[2] The Bible's concern to bring the Church into close relation with the Spirit is well expressed in St Irenaeus' maxim: 'Where the Church is, there the Spirit of God is too, and where the Spirit of God is, there is the Church and all its grace.'[3]

The idea of the Holy Spirit as the soul of the Church is dear to St Augustine.[4] The encyclical *Mystici Corporis* deals with it

1. Short bibliography: E. Bardy, *Le Saint-Esprit en nous et dans L'Eglise d'après le Nouveau Testament*, Albi, 1950; S. Tromp, *De Spiritu Sancto anima corporis mystici*, vol. I, *Testimonia selecta e patribus graecis*; vol. II, *E patribus latinis*, Rome, 1932—another work by the same author, *Corpus Christi quod est Ecclesia*, was referred to earlier; E. Vauthier, 'Le Saint Esprit principe d'unité de l'Eglise d'après S. Thomas d'Aquin', in *Mélanges de science religieuse*, 1948, vol. 5, pp. 175-196 and 1949, vol. 6., pp. 57-80; A. Liégé, 'Ame de l'Eglise', in *Catholicisme*, vol. I, cols. 434-436; Y. Congar, 'Le Saint-Esprit et le Corps Apostolique, réalisateurs de l'oeuvre du Christ', in *RSPT*, 1952 and 1953, reprinted in the second ed. of *Esquisses* . . . Paris 1953, pp. 129-179, and 'L'Esprit-Saint dans l'Eglise,' in *Lumière et vie*, 1953, no. 10, pp. 51-74; P. Bonnard (Prot.) 'L'Esprit-Saint et L'Eglise selon le Nouveau Testament' (report presented to an oecumenical conference at Chevetogne, Sept. 1956) in *RHPR*, 1957, vol. 37, pp. 81-90; C. Journet, *L'Eglise de Verbe incarné*, vol. II, Paris, 1951, pp. 522-580; Dom. A. Vonier, 'The Spirit and the Bride', in vol. II, *Collected Works of Abbot Vonier*, London, 1952; L. M. Dewailly, 'L'Esprit et les chrétiens dans l'Eglise du Christ', in *Le Saint-Esprit, auteur de la vie spirituelle* (Cahiers de la vie spirituelle, Paris and Lyons 1944, pp. 67-83).
2. Cf. Y. Congar, *L'Esprit-Saint dans l'Eglise*, p. 51.
3. *Adv. Haereses*, III, 24, 1; *PG*, vol. 7, col. 966.
4. See the texts in S. Tromp, *Corpus Christi quod est Ecclesia*, quoted above.

explicitly.[1] The theme of the Spirit, soul of the Church, is a very rich one. It has two principal aspects: the soul vivifies, sanctifies and animates the body, and the soul is the principle of unity of the different parts of the body. In our present discussion, it is this second aspect that interests us most. We will study it briefly following St Thomas.[2]

According to St Thomas, the Spirit contributes to unity in three ways:

1. He is for all believers the object of an identical faith and love;
2. He is present simultaneously in all the members of the mystical body;
3. He exercises a unifying activity in the Church.

What is the relative value of these three explanations? According to E. Vauthier, the last is not characteristic of the theology of the mystical body.[3] It is seldom cited in this context.[4] It is not in the foreground. The first explanation only appears once, at the beginning of St Thomas's career, in the *Commentary on the Books of Sentences*. Why did he abandon it?[5] In any case, it is indisputable that the second explanation bulks largest in the work of St Thomas.

E. Vauthier has summarized St Thomas's position on this point very accurately. 'The Holy Spirit unifies the Church by being present *unus et idem numero* in all the members of the mystical body. Two elements contribute to make the unity thus brought about extremely strong and profound. On one hand, the Holy Spirit is the principle of *numerical* unity among the faithful. On the other, he is the *immanent* principle of unity, for he is the guest of their souls

1. *Mystici corporis, AAS*, p. 210 (C.T.S., pp. 34-35) which should be compared with the passage on the *Inhabitatio Spiritus Sancti, AAS*, p. 231 (C.T.S., p. 47).

2. See the texts: III *Sent.*, d. 13, q. 2; a. 2, sol. 2; ibid., sol. 2, ad 1; *De ver.*, q. 29, a. 4, c.; *In I Cor.*, 12, 12-14 (no.734); *In Eph.*, 1, 13-14 (no. 42); *In Col.*, 1, 18 (no. 46); *In Rom.* 8, 9 (no. 627); 12, 5 (no. 974); II-II, q. 183, a. 3, ad 2; *In Jo.*, 1, 16 (no. 202); *Expositio in Symbolum, ad verba*, 'Sanctam Ecclesiam' (Mandonnet ed., p. 378). A study of the texts is somewhat disappointing: many of them contribute very little. The three first are the most important. Father Malmberg gives a fuller list which is not confined, as is ours, to texts which concern the Spirit as the *principle of unity* (cf. *Een lichaam en een geest*, pp. 281-284).

3. E. Vauthier, *Le Saint-Esprit principe . . .*, p. 60.

4. It is this one, however, which Cajetan selects in commenting on II-II, q. 39, a. 1., in complete conformity with the biblical sources.

5. It is a fact that Cajetan, in the text we have been considering, does not regard this explanation as sufficient to constitute the peculiar unity of the Church.

(*inhabitat est*), he is possessed by them (*habent*), he fills them (*replet omnes sanctos*) and he thus fills all the Church (*replet et unit totam Ecclesiam*).'

The indwelling of the Holy Spirit gives the Church its supernatural social nature, in its numerical unity. Its members are gathered together in unity by the presence of the Spirit. The numerical unity involved here is that of the person of the Spirit. The Church profits by this unity to the extent that it is united with the Holy Spirit in the closest possible union. Now the indwelling is nothing other than this union, which is the most perfect possible, this side of the hypostatic union. The immanence of indwelling makes every soul present to the same, single person. This necessity of immanence explains for our benefit why St Thomas did not retain his first proposition, on the unifying role of the Spirit. The indwelling presence implies the imminence of the presence of immensity, and actual union through the loving will. In these conditions alone can the indwelling presence be realized as an intimate union with the person of the Spirit by means of the experiential knowledge of the gift of wisdom.[1]

We must nevertheless beware of the error which consists in establishing a sort of compound union between the Spirit and the Church. Paul never said, 'as others have said, or have seemed to say, that the Spirit is now united with holy souls and with the Church in much the same way as the Word was united with the human nature of Christ'.[2] Take as an example the Amauricians. who claimed that the Holy Spirit had become incarnate in them.[3] It is not even advisable to use the mystery of the incarnation to explain by analogy the indwelling of the Spirit. The comparison is more ambiguous than illuminating. From this point of view, the form of words used by Cardinal Manning in a memorandum preceding the first Vatican Council does not appear a happy one.[4] Father Congar has very

1. Classical explanation of the presence of indwelling according to John of St Thomas. A detailed account of this view is given by H. Dondaire in the appendix to vol. II of his commentary on the *Trinity*, in the *Summa* of the *Rev. des Jeunes*.
2. E. Mersch, *Le Corps mystique* . . ., 2nd ed., vol. I, p. 200.
3. E. Mersch, *Le Corps mystique* . . ., 2nd ed., vol. II, p. 147.
4. 'Spiritum Sanctum inter et Ecclesiam *nexum individuum, juxta incarnationis analogiam*, seclusa tamen unione hypostatica intercedere'. Letter of 15 Nov. 1865; Mansi, vol. 49, col. 171.

clearly marked out the distinctions that need to be drawn in this domain : 'The union of men with the divinity, which is brought about in the Church, is not *per esse, secundum esse* : it is merely *per operationem, in operatione*.'[1] The consequences of this are considerable. The hypostatic union makes the humanity of Christ unequivocally impeccable and adorable. The coming of the Spirit into the Church leaves the members of the mystical body with their human personalities, does not free them from their condition as sinners, that is to say from the possibility of sinning, and does not of itself confer on them the charism of infallibility, which is connected with a particular aid, a special gift of the Spirit, quite distinct from the indwelling presence in the souls of the just.

Must we distinguish between a created and an uncreated soul of the Church? Controversy on this point has arisen between two specialists in the theology of the mystical body, E. Mura[2] and C. Journet. Mura considers that the Spirit alone can be called the soul of the Church. Journet, on the contrary, thinks that the term soul of the Church applies to created grace, and is thus led to talk of the created soul and the uncreated soul of the Church.[3]

Without exaggerating the importance of the dispute we still feel that it amounts to more than a mere difference over vocabulary. We can grant Journet that some excellent theologians have regarded created grace as the soul of the Church. We can also admit—as is obvious—that it is through created grace that men receive within themselves the Holy Spirit. But this being said, I think that we must firmly opt for the first view against the second. As we have seen, the Spirit is called the soul of the Church because *unus et idem numero totam Ecclesiam replet et unit*.[4] Grace does not provide this unifying function in the same way. Grace is numerically distinct in different subjects. Only uncreated grace, which is identical with the Spirit, is numerically one. To be sure, St Thomas does say that

1. 'Dogme christologique et Ecclésiologie', in *Das Konzil von Chalkedon*, vol. III, Wurzburg, 1954, p. 251. (Reprinted in *Sainte Eglise. Etudes et approches ecclesiologiques*, Paris 1963.)

2. *Le corps mystique du Christ, sa nature et sa vie divine*, Paris, 1936, p. 214. Information on the various phases of and participations in the discussions will be found in a note by L. M. Dewailly to his review of vol. I of C. Journet's *L'Eglise du Verbe Incarné*, *BT*, vol. 6, 1940-1942, p. 48, note 1.

3. *L'Eglise du Verbe Incarné*, vol. II, pp. 566-569.

4. *De ver.*, q. 29, a. 4.

charity is formally the life of the soul, as the soul is the life of the body.[1] But then he is not talking of the Church and of its unity. Created grace can be called the formal cause of our individual sanctification. But we cannot 'extend the thing from the individual domain to the ecclesiological domain, and talk of created grace as the soul of the Church'.[2] Grace does not play directly the role which Journet has attributed to it. But that in no way prevents grace from constituting, strictly speaking, the inner *communion* of the Church.[3]

Without doubt, one of the most important future tasks of ecclesiology lies in working out more clearly and fully the relations between the Spirit and the Church. Contemporary ecclesiology is principally concerned with questions of Christology. It is consequently in danger of not attaching enough importance to the complete equilibrium of the doctrine of the Church as we find it in the New Testament. Again, there is still a lot to be drawn from mediaeval theology, a complete survey of which on this question has not yet been attempted. A big job remains to be done, from which doctrinal theology will profit.[4]

The context of the present Œcumenical Council encourages research in this field. The Spirit is, indeed, the creator of unanimity. Newman called him the conscience of the Church.[5] In this capacity

1. II-II, q. 23, a. 2, ad 2.
2. E. Vauthier, *Le Saint-Esprit, principe* . . ., p. 74.
3. A few supplementary remarks:

a. In tradition the theme of the soul of the mystical body has been drawn upon in other ways still: for Origen, it is the *Logos*, for Leo XIII it is the eucharist. See references in S. Tromp, *Pius Papa XII. De mystico Jesu Christi corpore deque nostra in eo cum Christo conjunctione. 'Mystici Corporis Christi'*, third ed., Rome, 1958, pp. 130-131.

b. In tradition, the term *inhabitatio* is not confined solely to that which comes about through grace. In early writings, we find many texts where indwelling is linked with gifts and with charisms; cf. S. Tromp, commentary on *Mystici Corporis*, p. 141.

c. In III, q. 8, a. 1. ad 3, we read: 'The *heart* has been used as a comparison for the Holy Spirit, who invisibly vivifies and unifies the Church.' The simile is different, but the reality signified is the same.

4. On this subject, see E. Mersch, *Le corps mystique du Christ*, vol. II, p. 164 (with regard to St Bonaventure and St Thomas). The reader will also find, on p. 163, a French translation of a fine text from the second book of the *De Sacramentis* of Hugo of Saint Victor. See particularly Father Tromp's recent book on the Holy Spirit, referred to in Chapter I, p. 18, note 2.

5. 'I will cite Newman for whom the Holy Spirit is the conscience of the Church. That is to say the Holy Spirit is to the Church what the conscience is to the individual in the order of nature' (H. F. Davis, in the summary of the dis-

the Spirit is at once the principle of unification in the whole of the Church's activity and the principle of its continuity in time. But in addition to that, as we have seen, he is the creator of that particular form of unity which is communion. It belongs to him 'to bring about the eschatological inwardness, to surmount the externals and divisions which space and time try to impose on us, and which impede his presence; to surmount even the division between persons, which hinders communication between different mentalities and hence hinders communion.'[1] Such is the nature of the Spirit's activity, as attributed to him by appropriation, on the basis of what God has told us, as Scripture testifies.

Œcumenical Councils are 'lawfully convened in the Holy Spirit'. This is not a mere stylistic mannerism but a profound conviction of our faith. The Spirit *fulfils* the purpose of the Council. 'He makes it possible, not only for the life of the Church spread over space, but for its communion of faith right down the centuries to be made instantly present. Through him, the faith of St Paul or St Athanasius is present and personal to me.'[2] The oneness of the Church lived in communion depends primarily not on the prudence of its leaders, the shrewdness of its theologians, the capacity of its organizers, the vigour with which its message is disseminated or the strict application of a universally accepted discipline. It depends on the Spirit. Without him any human effort is void. Through him, man becomes fruitful. 'Wherever the advent of the Holy Spirit is needed, his coming should be implored.... In the biblical and Christian tradition, this invocation of the Spirit in prayer is accompanied by fasting: prayer and fasting combined—and, naturally, combined with love!—are the classical means, divinely appointed and sanctioned by Christian existence, of the fight against the devil, and of

cussions which concluded the volume containing the proceedings of a colloquy organized by the faculty of Catholic theology of Strasbourg in Nov. 1959: *L'Ecclésiologie au XIXe siècle* (Unam Sanctam, 34), Paris 1960, p. 378.

1. Y. Congar in *Le concile et les conciles. Contributions à l'histoire de la vie conciliaire de l'Eglise*, Paris and Chevetogne 1960, p. 312. This volume contains the proceedings of the œcumenical discussions at the Chevetogne monastery in autumn 1959. Father Congar contributed two papers, 'La primauté des quatre premiers conciles oecuméniques. Origine, destin, sens et portée d'un thème traditionnel' (pp. 75-110) and 'Conclusion' (pp. 285-334).

2. Y. Congar, *Le concile* . . ., p. 312.

the sovereign coming of the Paraclete.'[1] Reflection in communion, and its implementation, can only validly take place in the framework of invocation of the Spirit.

1. Y. Congar, *Le concile . . .*, pp. 313-314. The same author devotes several pages to communion in his study, 'Peut-on définir l'Eglise? Destin et valeur de quatre notions qui s'offrent à le faire', in *Jaques Leclercq. L'homme, l'oeuvre et ses amis*, Paris and Tournai 1961, pp. 233-254.

XI

PSYCHOLOGICAL AND SOCIAL IMPLICATIONS OF COMMUNION

WE have seen that *koinonia* is not a purely interior reality. It should therefore find expression in communal forms of behaviour. In the primitive Church, as we saw in Chapter IX, there was a whole network of services within Christendom. There were letters of communion, collections made, help given, journeys undertaken and, in particular, journeys to Rome. All this expressed the concern the different parts of Christendom felt for each other and the mutual aid between them. A great deal remains to be said on the implications of the idea of communion. It would be necessary to investigate the various characteristics of communion and show the infinite variety of ways in which these various aspects are fulfilled in the Church. The present chapter will deal only with a relatively limited area. Readers can refer to the two appendices in which we consider two major consequences among others : the relations between the pontifical magisterium and the Church, and the role and authority of the body of bishops.

Here we would like merely to present in outline a theology of the communion at work on a limited scale. There is interesting work to be done on the theology of the group : the meeting or the community as distinct from the sect. In order to set up the problem we shall start by studying the way in which one aspect of Protestantism and one trend within Orthodoxy envisage the relations between Church and community.

I. Church and Community. The Congregationalist Position[1]

We can find the whole Congregationalist position in embryonic form in the text of a petition to Queen Elizabeth I by a group of prisoners,

'According to the saying of the Almighty our God (Matt. 18:20), "Wherever two or three are gathered together in my name there am I", so we, a poor congregation whom God hath separated from the Churches of England and from the mingled and false worshipping therein used, out of the which assembled the Lord our only Saviour hath called us, and still calleth, saying, Come out from among them and separate yourselves from them and touch no unclean thing, then will I receive you and I will be your God, and you shall be my sons and daughters, saith the Lord (II Cor. 6: 17-18). So as God giveth strength at this day, we do serve the Lord every Sabbath day in houses, and on the fourth day in the week we meet and come together weekly to use prayer and exercise discipline on them which do deserve it, by the strength and sure warrant of the Lord's good work, as in Matt. 18:15-18 (I Cor. 5).'[2]

There is a twofold tendency in Congregationalism, particularly in its more radical forms: firstly towards strict separation and next towards concentration on the community for worship and discipline. These major features were clearly formulated and defended in the writings of Brown and Barrow, the theoreticians of Congregationalism. But the text of the petition enables us also to discern the biblical basis of Congregationalism, principally in the passages from St Matthew's gospel on the presence of the Lord in the Assembly (18:20) and on brotherly chastisement (18:15-18).

Congregationalism confronts us with a conception of ecclesiastical

1. Short bibliography; A full list of references will be found at the end of Y. Congar's excellent article 'Congrégationalistes', in *Catholicisme*, vol. 3, cols. 10-12. See also W. B. Selbie (Prot.), 'The religious principle of Congregationalism', in *Mansfield College Essays*, London, 1909, pp. 21-42; 'The Congregationalists' in *The Nature of the Church*, papers . . . edited by R. Newton Flew (Prot.), London, 1952, pp. 169-185; M. Schmidt, 'Kongregationalismus', in *RGG*, third ed.

2. W. B. Selbie, 'The religious principle . . .' p. 28.

organization entirely based *on the living presence of Christ,* to the exclusion of any organization founded on holy orders or on a tradition of the episcopate, on synods or on the secular authority. Within the current of the Reformation, Congregationalism seems to be the logical outcome of the Protestant position, in its refusal of any intermediary between the soul and God. We find a marked sympathy for the Congregationalist principles in contemporary Protestantism, thinkers as different as Harnack, Karl Barth and Emil Brunner. But what interests these authors is not the radicalism of this breakaway position. They are concerned more with the principles of the presence of Christ and of a community, particularly a community of worship.

In Karl Barth's view, everything that stands between the local community and the Lord of the community must be pitilessly rejected. The Catholic Church and the Episcopalian and Presbyterian Churches with their synods have all the same failing, that of introducing an alien element between Christ and his members. But is it not necessary for the pastor to lend his assistance to the meeting between Christ and his members? No, for in the community there are services (*Dienste*), but there are no offices (*Amter*), still less authorities or dignitaries. To be sure the service of the Word is an important community service; but it remains on the same plane as the other services, such as the 'elders' or the 'bell-ringers'. It does not constitute a grade in a hierarchy.[1] At the first meeting of the World Council of Churches in Amsterdam in 1948, Karl Barth gave a talk on 'The Church, the living congregation of Jesus Christ, the living Lord'. In reading this text, we must bear in mind the sense in which Barth understands the word *congregation*: it is the worshipping community, meeting regularly in a fixed place, entirely under the influence of an always new action of the Lord. The Congregationalist explanation lays exclusive emphasis on the immediate character of the Church, the famous 'actualism' of Barth. The Church came into existence through the act of Jesus glorified. 'This act . . . is performed once and for all.'[2]

According to the New Testament, the Church is not an institution; it is a brotherhood (*Bruderschaft*) in the Spirit; it is 'a *community* of persons (*Personengemeinschaft*) and nothing else'. That is Emil

1. Cf. J. Hamer, *Karl Barth*, The Newman Press, Westminster, Maryland, 1962.
2. Karl Barth, *Credo, A presentation of the chief problems of dogmatics with reference to the Apostle's Creed*, London, 1936, p. 110.

Brunner's position in his book on what he terms The Misunderstanding of the Church.[1] The historical 'Churches' are realities very different from the *Ekklesia* of Scripture. 'The most palpable sign of the characteristic difference lies in the matter of organization and polity.... The fundamental thesis of Rudolph Sohm, that the essential nature of the Church (he means the *Ekklesia*) stands in antithesis to all law, is irrefutable.'[2] A veritable transformation has occurred with the passage of time. Two elements laid the foundation of institutionalization: the sacrament and the priestly office. The Lord's Supper became the centre of salvation. From its beginnings as a *communal* meal it developed into a thing administered by the priests. The people 'now *receive* the Body of Christ instead of *being* the Body of Christ'.[3] The sacrament postulates the priest, minister of the sacrament; and, in its turn, the priesthood strengthens sacramentalism.

For all that, E. Brunner does not fall into an ecclesiological spiritualism. The *Personengemeinschaft* is not the invisible Church. The centuries-old distinction between visible Church and invisible Church is a false solution. Neither one nor the other of these Churches is a *community*. How, then, are we to visualize the present-day problem of the Church? What solution does E. Brunner propose? No Church can revert to the *Ekklesia*. All the Churches must consider themselves elements of the Church in the making. The recognized Churches have fallen behind. New forms of community are forging on ahead of them, for instance the Y.M.C.A. and Moral Rearmament.[4] For a time, the Churches were 'vessels' containing the *Ekklesia*. Today, they must stand aside. God wants new 'vessels'. Œcumenism is necessary today, but it would be taking the wrong road if it reunited the historical Churches: that would be to support institutionalism. To be sure, Brunner is not a Congregationalist. But he is obviously in profound agreement with the major tenets of Congregationalism. In Barth and in Brunner, as in classical Congregationalism, we touch on one of its limitations: the difficulty of accounting for the permanence of the Church and its universality. This is the major problem of contemporary Protestantism.

1. E. Brunner, *Das Missverständnis der Kirche*, Zurich, 1951.
2. E. Brunner, *Das Missverständnis* . . ., p. 122.
3. E. Brunner, *Das Missverständnis* . . ., p. 87.
4. E. Brunner, *Das Missverständnis* . . ., pp. 127-128.

II. Church and Community. An Orthodox Position[1]

The position of Nicolas Afanassieff is characteristic of a contemporary trend in Orthodox ecclesiology. According to this author, the Church must be defined in the framework of a eucharistic ecclesiology. 'The Church is manifest in its fullness and in its unity *at the eucharistic assembly* of each local Church.'[2] The Catholic Church is constituted 'by each local Church, gathered *in a eucharistic assembly* under the presidency of the bishop.'[3] 'For the Christians of the first centuries, the fundamental principle of Church life consisted in being always together . . ., gathered for the same thing (*epi to auto*). This principle formed part of the concept of the Church.'[4]

'So far as it is the sacrament of the assembly, the eucharist is *musterion tes ekklesias*.[5] But very soon a transformation came about. Instead of being the sacrament of the Church, the eucharist became a sacrament *in* the Church. This process must have begun when *the fundamental principle of eucharistic ecclesiology* was infringed. According to this principle, in a local Church there can be only one eucharistic assembly. For various reasons, 'there came to be several eucharistic assemblies in the local Church instead of a single one. *Epi to auto* ceased to be the principle of the local Church's unity; it was the bishop who became this principle.'[6]

1. Short bibliography: B. Schultze, S. J., 'Eucharistie und Kirche in der russischen Theologie der Gegenwart', in *ZTK*, 1955, vol. 77, pp. 257-300; N. Afanassieff (Orth.), 'L'apôtre Pierre et l'évêque de Rome', in *Theologia* (Greek review, but article written in French), 1955, pp. 465-475, 620-642, and 'Le sacrement de l'assemblée', in *Internationale kirchliche Zeitschrift*, 1956, vol. 46, pp. 200-213; Prof. Afanassieff recently returned to some of these themes in 'L'Eglise qui préside dans l'amour', included in a book written in collaboration with N. Koulomzine, J. Meyendorff and A. Schmemann—the first a colleague of the author at the St Sergius Institute in Paris and the latter two teachers at the St Vladimir seminary in New York—*Le primauté de Pierre dans l'Eglise Orthodoxe*, Neuchâtel and Paris, 1960; pp. 9-64; J. Meyendorff (Orth.), 'Sacrements et hiérarchie dans l'Eglise', in *Dieu vivant*, no. 26, 1954, pp. 73-91; P. Evdokimov (Orth.), *L'orthodoxie*, Neuchâtel and Paris, 1959, pp. 128-135.
2. N. Afanassieff, *L'apôtre Pierre* . . ., p. 474.
3. Ibid. Our italics in this passage and the preceding one.
4. N. Afanassieff, *Le sacrement* . . ., p. 201. On *epi to auto*, see p. 195, note 3.
5. N. Afanassieff, *Le sacrement* . . ., p. 206.
6. N. Afanassieff, *Le sacrement* . . ., p. 207.

Then began the individualization of Church life. Justifications were brought forward. One such justification 'consisted in dropping the realistic conception of the idea of assembly and transposing it to the mystical field'.[1] According to this interpretation, the eucharist is still an act of the Church 'when it is celebrated in an empty building by a priest who is completely alone, because the saints and the dead members of the Church take part in it'.[2] This idea leads to an unwarranted spiritualization of the eucharist and a fragmentation of the concept of the people of God and of the Church.[3]

In Afanassieff's view, the eucharist is the Church. But we must be clear what he means by this. His ecclesiology is based on the *celebration* of the eucharist and not on the *effect* of the eucharist. The distinction is a vital one. In his view, the Church is *the assembly united for the celebration* of the eucharist. He does not define the Church as resulting from the eucharist (*res eucharistiae*). Here then is a point where the ecclesiology of Barth and of Afanassieff concur : the identity of the Church with the assembly of worship. This point is fundamental if we are to grasp the implications of this common outlook.

The two theses we have just been considering encourage us to concentrate our attention on the presence of Christ in the assembly according to Matt. 18:20 and on the assembly in the framework of eucharistic symbolism.

III. The Presence of Christ in the Assembly: Exegesis of Matt. 18:20[4]

If we are really to arrive at the meaning of this difficult passage, a page or two of philological analyses would seem indispensable.

1. N. Afanassieff, *Le sacrement* . . ., p. 208.
2. Ibid.
3. The expression *epi to auto* is frequently used by Prof. Afanassieff. It is an allusion to Acts 2:47. The expression suggests both a meeting in a single place and internal unity between the members of the community. The literal translation might be 'for the same thing'.
4. Here we are using the word 'assembly' in its active sense, designating the actual meeting of a number of people. Bibliography: commentaries on Matthew by J. Knabenbauer (*Corpus Scripturae Sacrae*, 1893), by M. J. Lagrange (*Etudes bibliques*, 1927), by J. Schmidt (*Regensburger Neues Testament*, 1956), by J. Schniewind

Two or three. In 18:19-20, St Matthew is starting a new theme; the preposition *palin* indicates the change clearly. It is interesting to note the similarity between our passage and a text of rabbinical literature: 'When two are seated, occupied with the Torah, the Glory is in the midst of them.'[1] Doubtless this conviction was already widespread in Our Lord's time. Comparison with this assertion will be most valuable in the exegesis of the verse from Matthew. 'Two or three' indicates the most elementary form of group or community, the smallest of assemblies.[2]

Gathered together in my name. Exegetes have shown some embarrassment when it comes to defining the sense of the expression 'in my name'. Some fail to give any explanation. Others put forward various hypotheses. Knabenbauer provided a whole gamut of opinions. Lagrange says nothing. Of the authors we have consulted, only Schniewind and Bietenhard draw attention to the grammatical structure of the expression with a view to determining its sense.

In the Greek, we have an accusative, *eis to onoma,* and not the dative, *en to onomati.* The accusative gives the formula a very clear, final sense, of which we are not always sufficiently conscious. This shade of meaning does not come over in the Vulgate, which has toned down the text by translating it 'In nomine meo'. The accusative formula is relatively infrequent. It appears about fifteen times in the New Testament, whereas the formula with the dative is to be found more often.

A rapid comparison with a few uses of *en onomati* will allow us to grasp the difference. 'Blessed is he who comes in the name of the Lord' (Matt. 21:9) means he who comes on behalf of the Lord, sent by him. 'All that I do in my Father's name' (John 10:25) refers to the works performed through the power and under the authority of the Father. 'No-one who does a miracle in my name' (Mark 9:39) implies calling on Christ's name. 'They will cast out devils in my name' (Mark 16:17) must be understood as 'they will cast out devils through my power'. 'The prophets who spoke in the Lord's name'

(Prot., *Das Neue Testament Deutsch*, 1958), and by T. H. Robinson (Prot., *The Moffatt New Testament Commentary*, 1951); see also H. Bietenhard (Prot.), art *Onoma* in *Theologisches Wörterbuch . . .*, vol. 5.

1. *Abot.*, 3, 2 of Rabbi Hananiah Ben Teradyon, second century A.D.

2. Possible inquiry: should we see a connection between the 'two or three' of v. 19 and those of v. 16, in the light of Deut. 19:15?

(James 5:10) means those who come on behalf of the Lord. The most frequent sense of the formula is: by authority of, while calling on. The man who does something in the name of another calls on his help or claims his authority. A number of secondary shades of meaning go along with this principal sense.[1] In the background is the Aramaic form *beschem* (or *mischum*), found in rabbinical literature.

Behind the accusative, we find another Aramaic form, *leschem*. This form has a pronounced final sense. It means: *in view of,* in order to. This may be in order to do something, with a view to a state into which we want to enter or of an end to be attained. A thing is offered in (*leschem*) sacrifice to Jahveh. This means that it is not offered with a view to a sacrifice to idols. The slave allows himself to be plunged in a bath *in the name of* a free man (in order to become a free man). Circumcision is performed *in the name of* the covenant (in order to enter into the covenant). When it is a question of a thing that already exists, the formula indicates the intention or the reason. 'All those who busy themselves with the community should do it with a view to (*in the name of*) God.' 'Every act should be performed with a view to (*in the name of*) God.'[2]

This feature of the accusative is to be found in the formula *eis to onoma.* Faith in the name of Christ, of which St John speaks, implies an impulse towards the person of Christ considered as an end.[3] The same is true of the texts which deal with baptism.[4] To baptize in the name of the Father and of the Son and of the Holy Spirit is to baptize *for* the Father, *for* the Son and *for* the Holy Spirit. The accusative expresses real adherence.[5] It points to dedication to the persons of the Trinity.[6] Everywhere we find the idea of end and of intention. This is obviously what is meant by Heb. 6:10: charity shown in the name of Christ is charity shown towards Christ. The same is true of the three uses of the formula in Matt. 10:41-42: to receive a prophet in the name of prophet is to receive him *qua*

1. Cf. Bietenhard, p. 270, 27.
2. References to these various texts will be found in Bietenhard, p. 267, 28.
3. John 1:12, 2:23, 3:18; I John 5:13. This may be compared with St Thomas's commentary on the 'credere in Deum'. Cf. II-II, q. 2, a. 2,
4. Matt. 28:19; Acts 8:16, 19:5; I Cor. 1:13, 15.
5. Lagrange; 'Zueignung', says Bietenhard, p. 275, 21: 274, 39.
6. 'To baptize into a name was to baptize into the possession of the person who owned the name.' H. Robinson, *The Moffatt New Testament Commentary*, p. 237.

prophet, for that very reason.[1] (Cf. R.S.V. translation : 'He who receives a prophet *because he is* a prophet'.)

After these severe technical preliminaries, we are in a position to say that 'gathereed together in my name' means : gathered together *for* me, for Jesus. The *eis* indicates an impulsion *towards* Christ. Jesus exercises a sort of final causality on the meeting, whether the end is already there—the Lordship which Christ exercises here and now—or whether it must be waited for—the Lord on his eschatological return. On the philological plane, there is nothing more we can say. The meeting is *for* Christ.

But is it not possible to find parallels in the New Testament, in other meetings in connection with Christ?[2] One that comes to mind is I Cor. 11 :23-31, particularly verse 26 : 'until he comes'. The liturgical meeting lives in the expectation of the Lord, and it passes this waiting period in recollection, in anamnesis. The formula 'until he comes' gives a very pregnant sense to the passage we are studying : 'gathered together *for* Christ'. If this interpretation were correct, the meaning of the verse would thus be : When you are gathered together to await me, I am already there among you; your hope is already rewarded. Eschatology is already partly fulfilled.[3]

I am in the midst of them is simply the reply to the question : where? St Matthew uses the expression in the very simple sense of locality in the same chapter (18 :2). But the text that is a real parallel is the last verse of the gospel (28 :20) : 'I am with you all through the days that are coming, until the consummation of the world.' Of course, this does not refer to a visible presence. The significance of the passage is clear : it is a farewell meeting, and hence the end of a presence. The end of the world, which is spoken of, will be nothing less than the return of the Son of man in power and glory (Matt. 24 :30). The presence referred to here is thus an *invisible* presence

1. One final remark before we go on to comment on our own text (Matt. 18:20). In reality, the formula *eis to onoma* is equivalent to the simple preposition *eis*. When in I Cor. 1 :13 (see also 1 :15) Paul asks: 'Was it *in Paul's name* that you were baptized?' it is as if he were saying: 'Was it *for Paul as an individual* that you were baptized?' For Israel, as with other peoples of antiquity, there was a close link between the name and the personality of the man who bore it.

2. I should like to emphasize that this is no more than a suggestion.

3. There is a possible parallel here with the theology of anamnesis in the framework of the eucharist.

which the context should explain. On the basis of his omnipotence, Jesus has just entrusted the Eleven with a universal mission: to make disciples and to baptize. The presence which Jesus promises is obviously of the order of *assistance,* whose purpose is to guarantee this mission the conditions of success which its author desires. In other words, Jesus is saying: 'Be without fear, go ahead, my omnipotence is behind you.'[1] The presence is dynamic, even though it is not corporal.

Likewise, in the passage on the assembly, we are concerned with an invisible presence of the order of assistance. The remark has a general bearing: Jesus is in the assembly gathered together for him. But in this particular case, a precise effect is expected from this assistance; that the Father should grant the prayer of those who agree over their request (18:19). Christ assists us; to that end he is among us. In the final analysis it is his own prayer that is granted. 'When we do not know how to pray as we ought, the Spirit himself intercedes for us' (Rom. 8:26).[2]

This concludes our exegetical study. Christ promises his invisible presence and his assistance to the assembly gathered together for him—that is to say probably to the assembly gathered together in expectation of his return. *One of the effects* of this assistance is to ensure the efficacity of our prayer.[3]

IV. Complexity and Richness of the Presence of Christ in the Assembly and in the Church

Matt. 18:20 is a striking text which has been widely used in the Church.[4] An entire ecclesiology could not be built on the concept

1. Promises of the same kind are to be found in the Old Testament. See Gen. 28:15; Josue 1:5, 3:7.

2. Note: In order to avoid any confusion between this invisible presence and that of the sacrament of the eucharist, it is possibly wiser to speak in terms of action rather than in terms of presence. Action is moreover a form of presence. Remember Mgr Journet's phrase: *The mass, active presence of the Cross*. See chapter IV of *La Messe. Présence du sacrifice de la Croix*, Bruges and Paris 1957.

3. 'Ex quo fit oratio magis exaudibilis', says St Thomas with regard to this text in II-II, q. 84, a. 3, ad 2.

4. The assembly for the Lord comprises a presence of the Lord. That is the teaching of Matt. 18:20. The Fathers sometimes apply this text to the liturgical

of assembly, but it is fitting to allow the idea its rightful place in a theology of the Church.

The study of the presence of Christ in the assembly leads us to stress meticulously how many-sided the notion of presence is and its great variety of meanings. The use which *Mediator Dei* makes of it is extremely enlightening. In the text that follows we have numbered the different usages of the word :

'In the whole conduct of the liturgy the Church has her divine Founder present with her (1). Christ is present in the holy sacrifice of the altar, in the person of his minister (2) and especially under the eucharistic species (3); he is present in the

assembly. Martimort, in *La Maison-Dieu*, 57, p. 63, quotes in this connection a fine text of St John Chrysostom.

But it is not always realized that this verse is also one of the scriptural justifications for the meeting of councils and synods. It is quoted to this end in the bull *Aeterni Patris* of 29 June 1868 which convoked the Fathers to the First Vatican Council: 'The Lord Christ comforts us, revives us and consoles us wonderfully by these words: "Where two or thee are gathered together in my name, I am there in the midst of them." Thus we cannot doubt that he will be pleased to assist us himself in this council, in order that we may do all that which, from various points of view, concerns the greater good of his holy Church' (Mansi, vol. 50, col. 196).

The usage is an old one. St Gregory the Great (540-604) in a letter to three bishops of the Gauls, recalls the obligation to hold synods regularly: the law called for a twice-yearly meeting, but the pope agreed that they should confine themselves to an annual synod. After quoting the passage from Matthew, Gregory continues: 'If the Lord deigns to be present to two or three, how much more will he be present to an assembly of many priests?' (*Epist. lib.* 9, *ep.* 106; *PL*, vol. 77, col. 1032).

Working notes on this point:

(a) In the *Ordo ad synodum* of the present Pontifical, see the prayer 'Omnipotens sempiterne Deus, qui sacro verbi tui oraculo promisisti . . .' This prayer is to be found as far back as the Germanic Roman Pontifical of the mid-tenth century. *Cf. Maxima bibliotheca Veterum Patrum*, vol. 13, p. 740 ff.

(b) In the same *Ordo ad synodum*, see the prayer 'Adsumus, Domine Sancte Spiritus . . . in nomine tuo specialiter aggregati'. This is the same theme in connection with the Holy Spirit: there is an identity of functions between the Spirit and the glorified Christ in the work of redemption and in the Church. For the use of this text in the first Vatican Council, see Mansi, vol. 50, col. 232.

(c) It is somewhat strange to note that Calvin, who uses our verse three times in *Institutes of the Christian Religion* does so once to justify 'manifest prayers', that is to say common public and liturgical prayers (Liv. III, chap. XX, 30) and a second time with regard to councils: 'If it is asked what is the authority of councils according to the word of God, there is no promise fuller and clearer on which to base it than this sentence of Jesus Christ' (Liv. IV, chap. IX, 1). On this point, Calvin still echoes tradition. On the authority of councils, his entire discussion turns on the value of 'in the name of Christ'.

sacraments by his power which he infuses into them as instruments of salvation (4); he is present finally in the prayer and praise that are offered to God, in accordance with his promise : "Where two or three are gathered together in my name, I am there in the midst of them" (5).'[1]

At the mass, Christ is present in the person of his minister (2) This means that the priest is acting 'in persona Christi'. In this capacity he *occupies the place of Christ*, both as figure of the Lord and through the power he has received from him. Christ is present under the eucharistic species (3). This presence has been clearly defined by the council of Trent and developed by theology.[2] The whole of Christ, divinity and humanity, soul and body, is contained in the sacrament. Christ is present in the different sacraments, through his action which brings about the effect of each of them (4). His humanity, which is acting instrumentally (*instrumentum conjunctum*), brings about the sacramental effect through the instrumentality of the sign. This presence belongs to the order of action. Christ is present in the assembly, in the prayer and praise, through the assistance he renders those who are gathered together for Christ (5).[3] All these modes of presence constitute the total presence of Christ and of the Church in the whole conduct of the liturgy (1).

Presence is a philosophical notion which is not easy to pin down. Presence suggests the idea of contact. Absence and distance are both its opposites.[4] The main instances which we have been discussing

1. *AAS*, 1947, p. 528; C.T.S. translation p. 14. The word *praesens* occurs every time in the Latin text.

2. Denz., 883: 'Vere, realiter et substantialiter' . . . These three adverbs occurred earlier at the beginning of chap. 1 (Denz., 874).

3. In fact the encyclical deals only with the presence of Christ as object of the assembly's prayers.

4. This indeed is how it is understood by an author like John of St Thomas in a characteristic phrase: 'Quae dicitur praesens rebus, easque immediate et intime *tangere*' (*Vivès*, vol. II, p. 17). Or again 'De ratione formali, qua ista substantia divina *tangit* res, quibus redditur praesens' (ibid.).

This contact may be twofold, according as it concerns corporal or spiritual realities. In the first case it is based on quantity: a thing is present which is in the place where we are or of which we are speaking.

In the second case, there is a *contactus virtutis*, based on an action: the most striking is the presence of an object to the act of knowledge. The various presences will thus be judged of according to the two great categories of contacts, and in the

are different forms of the presence of Christ. To these, which all concern liturgical activity, we would add others, such as Christ's presence with those to whom he has entrusted an apostolic mission (Matt. 28:20) and above all the presence of Christ in the Church as such. Though we may have to judge of the specific nature of the presence of Christ—leaving aside his bodily presence in the eucharist—by the variety of its workings and hence of its results, the fact that Christ is head of the Church makes him present to the whole Church. He is indeed the cause of charity, and consequently of the unity of the Church which is wrought by charity.

V. The Assembly, an Act of Communion

Finally, the place of assembly in the Church leads us to the question of the relationship between the two forms of Christ's presence. This involves the relationship between the physical gathering of Christians in the Church and the unity of the Church itself, which brings us back to the basic considerations dealt with earlier. In analysing Cajetan's text, we distinguished between the *esse relativum* of each believer to the Church—his relationship as a part to a numerically single whole—on the one hand and, on the other, the behaviour consonant with this ontological position.[1] In everything he does, the believer should act as a part of the whole. The impetus of the Spirit affects not only the substance of our faith, but also its manner of working. Every act of the believer should be performed in, for and in accordance with the Church. His every act is an act of communion.

Among these acts of communion, the actual gathering of the assembly takes pride of place. The assembly by its very structure, is the group called on to show forth and to carry out in the most unambiguous way the '*agere ut pars*'. It is with good reason that certain theologians talk of the assembly as the 'Epiphany of the

case of the 'virtual contact', according to the varying modalities of the action in question.

This corresponds to the sense of the Latin word *praesentia*, from *praeesse*, to be before or in front of. On the plane of sensible experience, presence suggests proximity. On the notion of presence in contemporary philosophical literature, see the writings of L. Lavelle, *La dialectique de l'éternel présent*, four vols., Paris 1928-1952, and *La présence totale*, Paris 1934.

1. See chapter X.

Church'.[1] In I. H. Dalmais' phrase, the assembly is the 'act which expresses the Church'.[2]

Such is the theology of the assembly on the basis of *what it ought to be*. But the profound agreement which the assembly presupposes, the sort of harmony of which the gospel speaks (Matt. 18:19), is not automatically present in every gathering of believers. The assembly, as our text depicts it, is not an anonymous 'crowd' nor even a special human group such as an audience.[3] The members of the group must be aware of each other, must come face to face with each other.

The eucharistic assembly effects the presence of Christ of which our text speaks. But it effects other forms of Christ's presence also, as *Mediator Dei* very properly noted. Moreover, I do not for a moment think that we must restrict to the eucharistic assembly alone our general remarks about assembly in the Church in the sight of Christ. In one way or another, any legitimate meeting *in* the Church, held for Christ, is assured of a certain presence of Jesus, whether it be for not strictly liturgical devotions, or a group of families or a Catholic Action gathering.

What we have said of the assembly as a temporary group is true even more, and in a special way, of the religious community, the permanent group, whose object is to effect in symbolic fashion the *agere ut pars*. The religious society should be an intensification of this action. Hence the frequent reference to the first community in Jerusalem.[4] In this connection, readers can refer to the fine text known under the name of *Oratio sancti Augustini*, which the prelate uses as his allocution at the profession of certain regular canons.[5]

1. See Martimort, quoting Dom Hild in *La Maison-Dieu*, 40, p. 9.
2. *La Maison-Dieu*, 19, p. 15.
3. A crowd may be defined as the gathering of a considerable number of people round a common centre of attraction. With slight modifications, this definition will hold good of the audience, though numbers do not play the same role here. The common criterion is polarization. This is what distinguishes the crowd or the audience from intimate groups where the insertion of the part into the whole is effected by manifold relationships to the various elements of the whole.
4. See the *Rule of St Augustine*, for example.
5. 'Omnes, quamvis per gratiam baptismi, fratres simus in episcopo et unum Patrem habeamus in caelo, si ejus praeceptis prout possumus obsequimur; procul dubio *tunc maxime unimur* quando orationibus et beneficiis invicem nosmet copulamus quemadmodum in primitiva Ecclesia quibus cor unum erat et anima' (A. Carrier, *Coutumier du XIe siècle de l'Ordre de Saint Ruf en usage à la cathédrale de Maguelone*, Sherbrooke, 1950, p. 60).

As to the method we have followed, it should be noted that our concern has not been to explain by way of the idea of communion the necessity for Christ's special presence in the assembly, for the assembly is a privileged means of manifesting this presence. This special presence has been *revealed* by Christ. On the basis of this fact, which God has freely revealed to us, we are merely trying to 'account for' the scriptural assertion. To this end we have resorted to the basic principles of ecclesiology, and in particular to the theme of communion. If confirmation be needed, it is worth while remembering the twofold sense of the word *ekklesia*. In the New Testament this term designates simultaneously the community actually gathered together (the assembly) and the community itself as it permanently exists.[1] Today, when natural communities, the village for example, are in the course of inner dissolution under pressure of urbanization, it is of prime importance to develop the theology of assembly.

It is essential closely to collate Matt. 18:20 and Heb. 10:24-25. The author of the epistle recalls the injunction faithfully to attend the meetings of the assembly. He shows how the assembly gives mutual encouragement to those who take part in it: he is referring to that stimulation of charity of which St John Chrysostom speaks: 'As iron sharpens iron, so the meeting increases charity' (*In Ep. ad Heb., Cap X*: hom XIX). He also emphasizes its eschatological dimension. 'One of the gravest temptations—a deadly one—is that of isolation, of withdrawing oneself from the solidarity of the group.'[2] This text shows us clearly the active role of the assembly in relation to the permanent community of the Church. In the assembly are maintained and developed the brotherly links of communion which constitute the unity of the Church. But that implies that the assembly should allow this mutual stimulation and reciprocity. On this point, it would be a good thing to compare notes with the findings of social psychology on the role of primary groups in relation to secondary groups, the primary groups being characterized by intimate, personal association.[3]

1. On this point see Martimort in *La Maison-Dieu*, 60, p. 20.
2. C. Spicq, *L'épître aux Hébreux*, vol. I, p. 276; see also vol. II, pp. 318-320.
3. Cf. W. J. H. Sprott, *Human Groups*, Penguin books, A346, Harmondsworth, 1958, pp. 15-22. See also J. H. Fichter, *La sociologie, Notions de base*, Brussels and Paris 1960.

St Augustine, in his *Confessions* (VIII 2 :4), provides an indirect illustration of all this. In order to resolve his perplexities on the eve of his conversion, Augustine went to see the old man Simplicianus, who quoted to his visitor an objection which the rhetorician Victorinus had made to him before making up his mind to 'profess his salvation in the presence of the holy multitude' (ibid. 5). Because he used to read Scripture, Victorinus looked on himself as a Christian. Simplicianus told him : 'I shan't count you among the Christians till I've seen you in the Church of Christ.' Victorinus retorted ironically : 'So it's the walls that make the Christian, then?' No, the walls merely enclose the place of the assembly. What counts is the assembly.

VI. The Assembly in the Context of Eucharistic Symbolism[1]

In discussing the presence of Christ in the assembly, just as in considering the relationship between the unity brought about by the temporary gathering of Christians and that which constitutes the Church as such, *our survey was not confined to the liturgical assembly in the strict sense of the word.* The primitive Church accorded the assembly functions other than purely liturgical ones. According to the Acts of the Apostles, the community was more than once convened to deal with Church problems : to elect the successor to Judas (1 :15), to deal with the complaints of the Greek-speakers (6 :2) and to settle a dispute about the observation of the Law of Moses (15 :6). In these different passages there are distinct

1. Bibliography: L. Bouyer, *La vie de la liturgie*, Paris 1956, pp. 39-55, chap. III, Du Qahal juif à l'Ecclesia chrétienne' (English translation, *Life and Liturgy*, London 1956, pp. 23-37, chapter 3 'From the Jewish Qahal to the Christian Ecclesia'.); H. Chirat, *L'assemblée chrétienne à l'âge apostolique* (*Lex Orandi*, 10), Paris 1949; I. H. Dalmais, 'La liturgie, acte de l'Eglise', in *La Maison-Dieu*, 19, pp. 7-25, *Initiation à la liturgie*, Paris 1958, pp. 41-70; (English translation, *Introduction to the Liturgy*, London 1961, pp. 38-55); G. Dix (Anglican), *The Shape of the Liturgy*, second ed., London 1952, chap. II, pp. 12-35; A. G. Martimort, 'L'assemblée liturgique,' in *La Maison-Dieu*, 20, pp. 153-175', 'L'assemblée liturgique, mystère du Christ', in *La Maison-Dieu*, 40, pp. 5-29, 'Dimanche, assemblée et paroisse', in *La Maison-Dieu*, 57, pp. 56-84 and 'Précisions sur l'assemblée,' in *La Maison-Dieu*, 60, pp. 7-34; R. Paquier (Prot.), *Traité de Liturgique*, Neuchâtel, 1954, pp. 17-33; A. Rose, 'La présence du Seigneur dans l'assemblée liturgique', in *La vie Spirituelle*, 1951, vol. 85, pp. 78-85.

signs of a discussion (1:23, 6:3, 15:7). Furthermore, we took as our starting point for a consideration of the assembly the gift which was bestowed upon it, the presence of Christ, in other words the special assistance which Christ grants to each of the members actually present. It remains for us to describe the assembly in its external aspect, in close relationship with the eucharistic celebration. In what follows, we shall be dealing exclusively with the liturgical assembly.

The facts of the problem have been clearly noted by A. G. Martimort: 'The minimum required for (sacramental) validity was specified, and this marked a notable, indispensable and irreversible step forward; but the reverse of the medal is that this step only too often left a minister and a worshipper alone together, irrespective of any sort of community context.... So the assembly is not necessary for the mass and the sacraments to be not only valid, but also to be acts of the Church and the authentic expression of the prayer of the entire mystical body. But at the same time, we must insist most strongly that the mass and the sacraments summon the assembly and imperatively demand the real meeting of the Christian people.'[1]

The distinction Roguet suggests we draw between sign and symbol enables us to account for these facts.[2] The distinction is not absolute. 'It might be compared to that which exists between a pyramid and its point ... The sign, if we take it very strictly, is the extreme point of the symbol, the point at which the symbol is only a sign, its own nature being left out of account.'[3] The sign is a pure relation of meaning, the thing itself being disregarded. Its ideal is complete reference to the thing signified. The 'formal' sign is thus from a certain point of view sign in its purest form.[4] The symbol, on the contrary, is a nature which has its own consistency, 'to which there attaches itself a relation of meaning to a completely different object, a little as an accidental form attaches itself to a complete substance'.[5] Blushing is the *sign* of shame; the ship is the *symbol* of the city of Paris.

From the point of view of *exactness* of knowledge, the sign is superior to the symbol. The symbol has always a certain cloudiness, its symbolization remains indefinite; but from the point of view of

1. *La Maison-Dieu*, 60, p. 12.
2. A. M. Roguet, *Les Sacrements*, *Somme théologique*, pp. 314-324.
3. A. M. Roguet, *Les Sacrements* . . ., p. 314.
4. Roguet prefers the expression 'image-sign' to 'formal' sign.
5. A. M. Roguet, *Les Sacrements* . . ., p. 315.

richness of knowledge, the symbol is a long way ahead. The precision of the sign impoverishes it. The symbol, on the other hand, is potentially a plurality of signs. It provides a broad, mysterious knowledge of the object. There is the same difference between the sign and the symbol as there is between a commonplace photograph and an imaginative painting.

It is better to talk of symbolism than of signification to designate the sacramental phenomenon in all its fullness. The sign is constituted by the matter and the form of the sacrament. Symbolism 'orchestrates' the melodic theme which the sign determines exactly. In baptism, the matter and the form signify regeneration and admission into the divine family. But the rite as a whole, looked at through the eyes of faith, with its accompanying ceremonies : the salt, the breathings, the lighted candle, the wearing of the chrismal, the immersion and all the potential meaning of the water which is the matter of the sacrament summon up in concrete form a complete doctrine of baptismal life.

Let us apply this to the eucharistic celebration. The assembly does not form part of the sign. Given bread and wine and the words of consecration pronounced by a priest with the requisite intention, there is the sacrifice. But assembly is at the very heart of the symbolism. If eucharistic symbolism is to be *fully manifested* it presupposes this collegial dimension. To celebrate the eucharist is continually to found and renew the Church (*res eucharistiae*) as a communion. To celebrate is to unite, to assemble, to convene. It is desirable that all this should be present in the sacramental symbolism.

What the eucharistic celebration really effects is not the assembly or the local Church, but the Church as such. The *res eucharistiae* is the *unitas corporis mystici* in all its fullness, the universal communion.[1] What then is the role of the assembly? *Every* assembly of the Church 'for Christ' is a privileged exercise of the brotherly communion which gives the Church its structure, a stimulation of the mutual relations which make us parts of a single body. It is a particularly typical act of communion; it is an exceptional case of the *agere ut pars*. This stimulation of communion is at the same time a sign of it. These are our grounds for talking of an 'Epiphany of the Church'. At the symbolic level, the *eucharistic* assembly has a

1. One might demonstrate this from the captivity Epistles, but it is specially evident as early as I Cor. 10:16 and 12:12.

specific role and a special place in relation to all other assemblies. The symbol of the assembly, full manifestation of the sacramental sign, has its part to play in signifying better the effect of the eucharist in promoting communion.

Conclusion

COMMUNION, PERMANENT FORM OF THE UNITY OF THE CHURCH

THE Church's specific form of unity is communion. Every social group has its own particular form of unity. It is for the sociologist to determine what is responsible for the cohesion of the family, the team, the village, the school, the crowd, the board of directors, the workshop or the army. The theologian's business is to show, in the light of the faith—and naturally with the help of the sociologist—how the Church is one. 'Communion', as we have described it throughout this book, is the structural name for Catholic unity. It is the link binding the Church.

Communion is not a temporary dress for the Church. The people of God has passed and is passing through a succession of historical regimes of which God is the author. After the fall began the first state of the Church, an order of visible mediation dispensing grace and truth. But this first order, with its various achievements, was only a preparatory phrase for the entry of the Church into its final economy, with the visible mission of the Word in the incarnation and the visible mission of the Spirit in the Pentecostal assembly. This final economy comes into being in two successive orders : the earthly order and the heavenly order. We already possess the ultimate blessings : under veils, in obscurity, grasped by the hands of a still wounded nature. Later, the same blessings will be ours in all the strength and radiance of glory.

These three states of the Church are not merely juxtaposed. To be sure, neither are they purely and simply continuous. The oneness of a single design reveals itself both through hiatus and through progress. In the words of a striking simile which St Thomas borrowed from tradition, the new law is present in the old like the wheat in the growing ear.[1] There is a transition from the imperfect to the perfect but also a leap from the image to the reality. 'Just as the first state (that of the old law) is image and imperfection (*figuralis et imperfectus*) compared with the state of the gospel, so the present state is image and imperfection compared with the fatherland.'[2]

This abrupt transition from the image to the reality implies both deepening and deprivation. The law of sacramentality becomes more and more defined as the history of the people of God unrolls in the old economy. But grace still does not pass through the sacraments; they convey a meaning only, without producing the divine effects. In the present state of the Church, sacramentality is to be brought to perfection, both by the visible mediation of Christ incarnate and by the visible mediation of the apostolic and priestly body. But at the same time this sacramentality is purified. By being rooted in inwardness, the economy of the new law abandons a whole series of ceremonial precepts that belonged to an order that was finished and replaced.[3] The same applies to the transition to the heavenly city. The element central to perfect sacramentality remains for ever: i.e. the visible mediation of the human nature of Christ. It is in the Church triumphant that the bodily mediation of Christ will be plainly made manifest. Everything else will pass away. The visible hierarchy will no longer exercise mediation. The sacramental signs will be obsolete. 'When the consummation has come, the use of the sacraments will cease; for the blessed, in the glory of heaven, will have no further need of a sacramental remedy; for they will rejoice for ever in the presence of God, looking on his glory face to face and, transfigured from splendour to splendour in the abyss of the deity, they will taste the Word of God as he was in the beginning and as he will remain for all eternity.'[4]

After each of these metamorphoses, the Church becomes more nearly herself. Communion, which is inseparable from the nature of the Church, can only become deeper, purer and closer as it crosses these successive thresholds.

The complete manifestation of the mediation of the Incarnate

1. I-II, q. 107, a. 3.
2. I-II, q. 106, a. 4, ad 1.
3. I-II, q. 107, a. 4.
4. *Imitation of Christ*, book IV, chap. II.

Word will simultaneously and necessarily be the complete manifestation of the unity of communion. There is nothing surprising in the fact that Scripture depicts the Church triumphant by means of images and in a vocabulary that conjure up various aspects of the idea of communion. This Church is the messianic feast, the heavenly Jerusalem.

'As my Father has allotted a kingdom to you, so I allot you a place to eat and drink in my kingdom' (Luke 22 :29). The image of the meal is well calculated to suggest simultaneously the fellowship felt for him who has issued the invitations and presides over the table and that which unites the guests among themselves. 'There are many who will come from the east and from the west and will take their places in the kingdom of God with Abraham and Isaac and Jacob' Matt. 8 :11). Only the elect will partake of this meal (Luke 14 :24). It is thus quite natural that the theme of the eschatological meal should be combined with that of the wedding : 'Blessed are those who are bidden to the Lamb's wedding-feast' (Apoc. 19 :9). This feast celebrates the union of Christ with his elect, with the Church triumphant, and with the new Jerusalem 'all clothed in readiness, like a bride who has adorned herself to meet her husband' (Apoc. 21 :2). The illumination of the one theme by the other was already present in the parable of the wedding feast : 'Here is an image of the kingdom of heaven; there was once a king who held a marriage-feast for his son' (Matt. 22 :2).[1]

'Our mother is the heavenly Jerusalem, a city of freedom' (Gal. 4 :26). In this passage we find an antithesis drawn between the historical city, 'the Jerusalem which exists here and now; an enslaved city' (Gal. 4 :25), over which hangs the imminence of its destruction, and the new Jerusalem, the holy city, sent down by God from heaven (Apoc. 21 :2, 10).

The Vulgate usually translated *polis* in the New Testament by 'city'. With the exception of two cases, where it uses *urbs* (Acts 16 :12, 39), it always uses *civitas*. Now this has its disadvantages. 'City' suggests not only a compact body of dwellings, but also the organized society constituted by the inhabitants, the State. In secular

1. J. Daniélou, 'Les repas dans la Bible et leur signification', in *La Maison-Dieu*, no. 18, 1949, pp. 7-33. The whole group of the texts on the question is presented, in summarized form, in the article which the Protestant exegetist, J. Behm, devotes to *Deipnon* in Kittel, vol. II, pp. 33-35.

literature, *polis* has these two senses, and the reader frequently hesitates between the two. This is not the case in biblical Greek. *Polis* has no kind of political implications. For the Semite, the State was not *polis,* the city, but the kingdom. In the Bible, the word *polis* suggests above all a collection of buildings huddled close to each other, forming a whole, equipped to resist an enemy by the strength of its walls, which provided a guarantee of security for its inhabitants.[1] *Polis* designates a whole which has been *built,* solid and stable. The author of the epistle to the Hebrews tells us that Abraham already knew of the heavenly Jerusalem, for he was 'looking forward all the while to that city which has true foundations, which is God's design and God's fashioning' (Heb. 11 :10). In the Apocalypse, St John makes a point of describing this town and stronghold : 'a great wall was raised high all round it, with twelve gates' (Apoc. 21 :12). This wall 'had twelve foundation-stones; and these bore names, those of the Lamb's twelve apostles' (Apoc. 21 :14). The hymn for the dedication of a church makes happy use of this image : 'Jerusalem, happy city, well named "vision of peace", that is built in the heavens with living stones. . . . By their dressing and poising these well-polished stones are carefully fitted for their places by the craftsman's hand.'[2] Amid its wealth of symbolical suggestions, the theme of the heavenly Jerusalem incorporates also the idea of Church solidarity.

Communion is thus the happy and necessary condition of our pilgrimage, because it is part of the very structure of the city towards which we are journeying. It gives us a foretaste of these eschatological blessings. The city of the future is, as it were, already set in being by communion with and in Christ. 'The scene of your approach now is mount Sion, is the heavenly Jerusalem, city of the living God;

1. J. Comblin, 'La liturgie de la nouvelle Jérusalem', in *Eph. theol. lov.*, 1953, vol. 29, pp. 5-40; J. Huby, *Mystique paulinienne et johannique*, Paris 1946—on the 'heavenly Jerusalem', pp. 217-232; Y. Congar, *Le mystère du temple* (*Lectio divina*, 22), Paris, 1958, see particularly pp. 239-275. H. Strathmann, former professor of New Testament exegesis at the Protestant faculty of Erlangen, shows clearly the two senses in which the word *polis* is understood in profane and biblical literature: Kittel, vol. VI, pp. 523, 529 and 533.

2. I quote this hymn in its primitive version, which is preserved in the Dominican liturgy: 'Urbs Jerusalem beata/Dicta pacis visio/Quae construitur in caelis/Vivis ex lapidibus (. . .)./Tunsionibus, pressuris/Expoliti lapides/Suis coaptantur locis/Per manus Artificis'. This hymn was originally a Gallican chant for the pascal vigil to be sung in the baptistry.

here are gathered thousands upon thousands upon thousands of angels, here is the assembly of those first-born whose names are written in Heaven' (Heb. 12:22-23). This communion, which is entirely directed to the complete establishment of the kingdom, does not shut the Church in on itself. It stands open to the world. It is the form of unity willed by Christ for all mankind. So it is ready to welcome all the richness and variety set by God in his creation.

Appendix I

THE MAGISTERIUM WITHIN THE CHURCH[1]

THE believer performs his every act *as a member* of the Church, that is to say in, for and according to the Church (see Chapter X, pp. 179 ff). There are special grounds why this is true of the Church's apostolic functions entrusted to the hierarchy. The Church's three offices are performed with a view to the communion of the Church. But we should beware of an all too obvious error. We sometimes see some matter which belongs to the domain of the exercise of an office transformed into a juridical structure. At the First Vatican Council, the question arose whether the pope in himself enjoyed infallibility, without consulting either the Church or a general Council. Against the opinion of the minority, which was inspired by Gallican ideas, the Council defined that the infallible declarations of the Roman pontiff 'were irrevocable of themselves, and not *by virtue* of the consent of the Church'.[2] In expressing itself in this way, the Council intended simply to assert that the consent of the bishops is not the source or the *necessary juridical condition of the validity* of the pronouncements of the magisterium. The basis of the infallible definition is the assistance of the Spirit, and nothing else. But this being said, the Council was in no way opposed to such consultation. In the same constitution, *Pastor aeternus,* and in the same Chapter IV which defined infallibility, the Fathers of the Council introduced a passage in which it is explicitly stated that the popes, in their definitions of the faith, have always previously had recourse either to the calling of an Œcumenical Council, or to a sounding of the feeling of the Church spread over the whole world, or to special synods, or to

1. For how this appendix fits into the whole, see above, p. 190.
2. Denz., 1839.

other means furnished by divine Providence.[1] These different means —which can be very varied—concern the way of exercising infallibility, its actual historical practice. Infallibility is not, of course, omniscience. Before expressing a definitive decision, the pope must form a prudent opinion by means of research and assiduous care. Among these preparations, consultation with the episcopacy is assuredly one of the most obvious. Thus it was to the episcopacy that the popes appealed before proceeding to define the dogmas of the Immaculate Conception (1854) and the Assumption (1950). In the bull defining the Assumption, Pius XII recalled that he had directly requested all his brothers in the episcopate to be good enough to let him have their opinions. In the letter *Deiparae Virginis Mariae* (1 May 1946) he asked each of them the question : 'Do you . . . think that the bodily assumption of the Blessed Virgin can be proposed and defined as a dogma of the faith, and do you, your clergy and your faithful desire this?'. But this kind of preliminary consultation belongs to the manner of exercising infallibility and cannot be transformed into a juridical necessity. The Gallicans were right to recall that throughout the course of history popes had frequently asked for the opinion of the episcopate; they were wrong to make this a condition of validity.

The tendency to see everything *exclusively* from the juridical angle is a deplorable one; the great jurists have never been guilty of it. In an organized society, the juridical element is essential but it does not exhaust reality. If we try to reduce everything to the categories of the valid and the invalid, or merely the obligatory and the

1. Denz., 1837. See on this subject the whole of Chapter IV, particularly pp. 179-189, of J. P. Torrell's book, *La Théologie de l'Episcopat au premier concile du Vatican* (*Unam Sanctum*, 37), Paris 1961. In his conclusion, the author distinguishes very opportunely between the *sensus ecclesiae*, from which no organ of tradition can ever become independent, and the *consensus ecclesiae*, a juridical act of assent by the bishops which, for its part, is not necessary. The magisterium is in no way separate from the Church. Mgr Gasser, speaking in the name of the Deputation on the faith, for which he was reporter, recalled this very opportunely when he addressed the Fathers of the Council: 'Finally, we do not set the pope apart, and above all we do not separate him from the assent of the Church, provided that this assent is not laid down either as a previous or a subsequent condition. We cannot separate the pope from the assent of the Church, for this assent can never fail him. Since we believe that the pope is infallible through a divine assistance, we believe for that very reason that the assent of the Church can never fail him, because it is impossible that the body of the bishops should be separated from its head and because the universal Church cannot default' (Mansi, vol. 52, col. 1214 A).

permissible, we shall find ourselves neglecting other values in the Church which extend far beyond the compass of law. Let us take an example from a limited field. A liturgical celebration requires compliance with a certain number of rules and rubrics. But that is not all there is to it. If a liturgical act is really to meet the profound aspirations of religious life, we must also avail ourselves of a whole series of values on which it is impossible or inopportune to legislate. I will say nothing of the human values of taste, education and artistic sense, which will find expression in the vestments, the arrangement of the altar, the management of the place of worship and the way of singing. For all this, a certain compensation can sometimes be found. But what is most important is that we ourselves should be profoundly in harmony with the realities of liturgical worship and possess a genuine spiritual quality. Mere compliance with the rubrics, however scrupulous it may be, is here transcended.

We have referred briefly to the question of the *consent of the bishops,* as it was raised by the Gallicans at the First Vatican Council. We might draw a parallel with another subject, to which we alluded in connection with the definition of the Assumption : that of the *consultation of the faithful* through the organs of the magisterium. Here again we are in the domain of the *practical order* and of a possible manner of exercising hierarchical responsibility in the Church. Juridical necessity does not enter the question.

We must first remember that the body of the faithful are called on to play a role in the preservation and development of the faith. Through their baptism and confirmation, they have received the Spirit, and he does not lie idle. In each of them faith, through which they attain the truth of God, is a light, a personal principle of judgment, which assumes a social dimension through the *homologia,* the confession of faith. It is thus that all believers, especially parents and teachers (godparents also, but more in law than in fact), have a share in the propagation of the revealed deposit when they instruct children in the faith. But this sense of the faith in no way replaces the magisterium. On the contrary : the magisterium alone is competent as a guide to the meaning of the faith. It alone is the interpreter and judge of it. It is the Church's preaching that is echoed in faith : *fides ex auditu.* As a theologian who has written with great perspicacity on this question rightly remarks : 'If we want to find an equitable solution to the problem of the relations between the magisterium and the sense of the faith as it takes shape in the universal Christian awareness of the Church, we must beware of two extremes. We must neither simply subordinate the magisterium to the belief of the faithful in such a way as to give the latter precedence over the former, nor dissociate the magisterium from the contributions of the living tradition of the Church in such a way as to represent it as arbitrary in its edicts.'[1] When authority seeks the opinion of the faithful, it is not in order to set them up as judges of the faith. 'For the magisterium Christian opinion is not a norm to be followed, but an objective datum to be known.'[2] All the same, the attention devoted to the understanding of the faith is not a matter of simple curiosity. The actions of the magisterium are not dictated from outside. They are homogeneous with a faith which is already ours. 'The magisterium will take care to make certain, *by the appropriate means of investigation* (of which it is the sole judge) of the existence of this common faith.'[3]

Newman wrote an illuminating passage on this point. He was replying to severe critics who reproached him with having asserted that 'in the preparation of a dogmatic definition, the faithful are consulted', and who understood this in the strong sense of the word, as if the bishops determined their actions according to the opinions of their faithful. Newman answered them: 'The English word "consult", in its popular and ordinary use, is not so precise and narrow in its meaning; it is doubtless a word expressive of trust and deference, but not of submission. It includes the idea of inquiring into a matter of *fact,* as well as asking a judgment. Thus we talk of "consulting our barometer" about the weather:—the barometer only attests the *fact* of the state of the atmosphere. In like manner, we may consult a watch or a sun-dial about the time of day. A physician consults the pulse of his patient: but not in the same sense in which his patient consults *him.* It is but an index of the state of his health.' Then, reverting to the phrase in question, 'consulting the faithful', Newman went on to say: 'Doubtless their advice, their opinion, their judgment on the question of definition is not asked; but the matter of fact, viz. their belief, *is* sought for, as a testimony

1. C. Dillenschneider, *Le sens de la foi et la progrès dogmatique du mystère marial,* Rome, 1954, p. 348.
2. C. Dillenschneider, *Le sens de la foi* . . ., p. 349.
3. Ibid.

to that apostolic tradition, on which alone any doctrine whatsoever can be defined.'[1]

The magisterium bears the responsibility for the meaning of the faith. In the context which we have outlined, and which Newman phrased so well, it alone can take the initiative of consulting opinion, and it does so in complete freedom. But such consultation is in itself consonant with the nature of the Church, which is communion.

1. *On Consulting the Faithful in Matters of Doctrine*, an article first published in *The Rambler*, July, 1859. Critical edition, edited with an introduction by John Coulson, London, 1961. The passage quoted is on pp. 54-55 of this edition.

On the point covered in this appendix, reference may advantageously be made to the collective pastoral letter of the Dutch episcopate on *Le sens du Concile*; this appeared in French translation both in the *Documentation catholique* of 18 June 1961, vol. 58, and in book form in the series 'Présence chrétienne', Bruges and Paris 1961.

Appendix II

THE EPISCOPAL BODY UNITED WITH THE POPE[1]

COMMUNION has a special application at the level of the leadership of the universal Church. In this additional note, we will study the authority in the Church of the episcopal body united with the pope according to the proceedings of the First Vatican Council. On Tuesday 5 July 1870, Mgr Frederic Zinelli, bishop of Treviso, came forward to make a report 'in the name of the Deputation on the Faith' on the amendments proposed by the Fathers to Chapter III of the first Constitution *de Ecclesia* (*Pastor Aeternus*). There were many amendments, and the speaker devoted greater or less attention to them according to their relative importance. He dwelt particularly on two, number 35, proposed by Mgr Joseph Papp-Szilágyi of Illesfalva, bishop of Grosswardein in Hungary of the Greco-Rumanian rite, and number 36, proposed by Mgr Aimé Guilbert, bishop of Gap. Here is how Mgr Zinelli summed up these proposals: 'The Right Reverend authors of the two amendments would like the Vatican Council to approve the principle that the entire supreme ecclesiastical power is lodged, not in the Roman pontiff, but solely in the Roman pontiff with the bishops.'

One single, but composite, subject of supreme power in the Church?

This is a precise summary. It exactly corresponds to the proposals put forward in the amendments. Their authors came, however, from two very different backgrounds. The first, a bishop of the Oriental rite, was concerned not to shut the door on the Eastern churches separated from Rome. The second favoured, though with

1. The place of the present topic in the general scheme of this book is indicated at the beginning of Chapter XI.

moderation, the Gallican views of the minority. He gave more than one proof of this during the Council. He was one of the eighty-eight who on 13 July 1870 rejected the Constitution *Pastor aeternus* by a *non placet*. These two men were agreed on the question which interests us here. Papp-Szilágyi stated: 'The whole power of government in the Church resides in the episcopate together with its primate, the Roman pontiff, in other terms the government of the Church is Petro-apostolic.' For Guilbert, the pontifical primacy 'is not that absolute and complete power which Christ gave to the Church'. There can thus be no question of opposing the power of the Supreme Pontiff to 'this power of the bishops, which they exercise all together with the successor of Peter as legislators and judges of the faith'.[1]

Before and during the Vatican Council, this thesis found its theologian in Mgr Henri Maret, titular bishop of Sura and dean of the faculty of theology at the Sorbonne. He deals with this subject in the preface to his great work: 'The Church, we believe, is a monarchy effectively tempered by an aristocracy.... The Pope is by divine right the supreme head of the Church; the bishops by divine right participate, under his authority, in the general direction of the religious community. Spiritual sovereignty is thus composed of two elements—one the principal: the papacy, and the other subordinate: the bishops. Infallibility, which forms the highest attribute of spiritual sovereignty, is necessarily composed of the essential elements of sovereignty. It is only to be found, with absolute certainty, in the cooperation and agreement of the pope with the bishops and the bishop with the pope; and the absolutely obligatory rule of the Catholic faith, under sanction of the penalties imposed on heresy, is thus entrusted to this cooperation and agreement between the two elements of spiritual sovereignty. Such is the essential basis of the constitution of the Church.[2]

As it is formulated by the authors of the amendments, summarized by Mgr Zinelli and clearly expressed in this quotation from Mgr

1. Our quotations are taken from Mansi. Mgr Zinelli speaks 'nomine ipsius Deputationis', vol. 52, col. 1100; he summarizes the two amendments, col. 1108; their complete text is in cols. 1091/1092. The speech of Mgr Papp-Szilágyi, proposing and pleading for his amendment, cols. 601-605; Mgr Guilbert proposes his amendment in public session without any comments, col. 620.

2. H. L. C. Maret, *Du concile général et de la paix religieuse*, vol. I, Paris, 1869, pp. xx-xxi.

Maret, the position comes down to acknowledging in the Church only *one sole and single subject* of supreme power, a *composite subject* in which the pope and the bishops each have their respective place.

The reply of the Deputation on the Faith.

Mgr Zinelli simply rejected the two amendments. These texts were absolutely contrary 'to the position of the Deputation on the Faith, which bases itself on Scripture, tradition and the definitions of Councils. When these sources of revelation are considered, it becomes quite clear that a plenary and sovereign power (*plenam eamque supremam in Ecclesia potestatem*) has been given to Peter and his successors, so that this plenitude cannot be limited by any human power superior to it, its sole limitation consisting in natural law and divine law.'

But Mgr Zinelli could not call on the Fathers to reject these amendments without simultaneously offering a positive explanation of the role which falls to the episcopate in the government of the Church. 'Certain right reverend Fathers will perhaps say: does not this plenary and sovereign power reside equally in the Ecumenical Council? Was it not to all the apostles that Christ promised his presence? Was it not to the apostles that he said: "All that you bind on earth shall be bound in heaven. . . . ?" This we willingly concede.'

There follows an extremely important explanation which can be summarized as follows:

1. Sovereign and plenary ecclesiastical authority over all the faithful (*in fideles omnes*) is vested in the body of bishops united with their head. 'The bishops, whether gathered together with their head in an Ecumenical Council, in which case they represent the whole Church, or scattered but united with their head, in which case they constitute the Church (*quo in casu sunt ipsa Ecclesia*) really possess the plenitude of power.'

2. The faithfulness to the scriptural data which leads us to acknowledge the *plena et suprema potestas* of the Church united with its head must lead us also to assert that the *plena et suprema potestas* has been given to Peter and his successors, even independently of common action with the other bishops.

3. Since these two powers are not distinct and separate, all danger

of dualism and confusion is ruled out. 'To separate the head from the members is peculiar to those who would subject the pope to the bishops considered as a collective body, or represented by the General Council; then indeed we might have on one side the pontiff, even in his character as supreme pontiff, and on the other the bishops.' Our view is quite different. 'If the supreme pontiff together with the bishops, either scattered or gathered together, really makes use in a *joint and several manner* (*in solidum*) of the plenary and sovereign authority, no conflict is possible. Since the *plena et suprema potestas* cannot really exist in the body apart from the head, individual bishops, however many they may be, cannot in the absence of the pope in any way exercise the *plena et suprema potestas* without their head; on the other hand, as we have said, the pope as head can exercise his supreme authority even independently of the cooperation of the bishop.'

What is the authority of this text, the content of which seems so very important? It is not the opinion of just any theologian, or even of a Father of the Council picked at random from the others, but a declaration from the spokesman of the Deputation on the Faith and made in the name of this Deputation. Mgr Zinelli concludes his exposition on the two amendments by saying: 'This was absolutely necessary to show the serious reasons which led the Deputation on the Faith to exclude the proposed amendments, which contained some rather dangerous ideas, contrary to the intention of their authors.' It should be added that this declaration was made to explain and justify the sense of a vote put to the Fathers. The report of the sitting shows us that the Fathers did follow the Deputation's lead. The amendments were rejected almost unanimously by the assembly (*fere omnes rejecerunt*). It is for the theologian to judge of the value of this document, without exaggerating it. To be sure, this text is not binding on our faith. It does not even settle the theological controversy. But it remains that over this question and on this occasion, Mgr Zinelli can be regarded as a privileged and particularly authoritative witness to the thinking of the Deputation on the Faith and also, though in a lesser degree, to that of the Council.[1]

1. Mansi, vol. 52, cols. 1108-1110, gives that part of Mgr Zinelli's statement devoted to the two amendments; the result of the vote, col. 1118.

Father Kleutgen's schema.

The assent which this position commanded among the Fathers of the Council was again shown by Father Kleutgen's Schema. We know that the Constitution *Pastor aeternus* which bears the title of *First dogmatic constitution on the Church of Christ* was to have been followed by a second, the drafting of which was entrusted to Father Joseph Kleutgen, of the Society of Jesus, who had already collaborated successfully in the recasting of the schema *de Fide*.[1] Although a talented theologian, Father Kleutgen had not been asked to participate in the preparation for the work of the Council. For the purpose of the task assigned to him he had at his disposal, however, not only the original schema *de Ecclesia Christi,* which had been distributed in general congregation on 21 January 1870, but also the comments of the Council Fathers on the first eleven chapters and on the supplementary chapter.[2] This last text, the supplementary chapter on infallibility, was not handed out till 6 March. For the drafting of the Constitution *Pastor aeternus,* chapter XI and the supplementary chapter were detached from this original Schema.

These remarks seem to me to be of value for an understanding of the method of work which Father Kleutgen following in the framing of his draft entitled *Schema of the second constitution on the Church of Christ recast* (*reformatum*) *in accordance with the comments of the Right Reverend Fathers,* which was not published till 1927.[3] The title is a programme in itself. Father Kleutgen was at constant pains to reap the maximum benefit from the statements made by the members of the Council throughout its proceedings. The *relatio*[4] which went with the Schema, and which was a commentary on it, is studded with phrases like these: many Fathers think ... some Fathers assert ... some Fathers would like ... a number of Fathers proposed ... many Fathers disliked ... some took offence at the assertion ... and so on. The author was obviously engaged in

1. I am relying here on the statements of T. Granderath, *Histoire du concile du Vatican,* French translation, vol. II, second part, Brussels, 1911, pp. 12 and 13. (Original edition, *Geschichte des vatikanischen Konzils,* 3 vols, Freiburg 1903-1906.)
2. See these commentaries in Mansi, vol. 51, cols. 731-1072.
3. In Mansi, vol. 53, cols. 308-317. This text is followed by *Josephi Kleutgen relatio de schemate reformato,* cols. 317-332.
4. In one passage of the *relatio* (col. 322), Father Kleutgen shows himself anxious to take advantage of an amendment proposed to Chapter III of *Pastor Aeternus.* He thus in no way confines himself to the comments on the original schema. The whole Council is his concern.

a constant give and take with the bishops, in the hope of producing a document which would obtain widespread approval, and also of convincing those who felt reservations by shedding light on the underlying reasons for the proposed texts. The Council was interrupted. What would have been the document's fate had it been presented to the Deputation on the Faith and to the Council as a whole? It is of little use to raise that question. We can never guess what might have been. What seems to me incontestable is that Father Kleutgen's Schema was based as a whole on an excellent summary of the views of the great majority of the Fathers, and was drafted by a man of considerable shrewdness, who had participated from the inside in the work of the Council and who had previously given evidence of his talents in the elaboration of the *Constitution on the Catholic Faith*. I have no hesitation in saying that Father Kleutgen's document is the least distorted picture we possess of the common convictions of a very large part of the Council at the time it broke up. Neither the historian nor the theologian can say more. None of this was defined, nothing was discussed *ex professo* at the First Vatican Council. But this does nothing to diminish the exceptional value, at its own level, of Father Kleutgen's testimony.

In his chapter devoted to the hierarchy—Chapter IV—Kleutgen was at pains to set the doctrine forth in clear and precise language, well within the comprehension of the faithful, and without any recourse to technical terminology. Here are a few passages: 'They alone (the bishops), each in his diocese, or assembled in synods, decide (*decernunt*) doctrine and discipline, declare laws and exercise justice.... Doubtless the bishops participate likewise (*expertes non sunt*) in the supreme responsibility of teaching and governing the universal Church. This power of binding and loosing, which was given to Peter on his own, was bestowed likewise on the college of the apostles, though united with its head, as is testified by the words of the Lord: "I promise you, all that you bind on earth shall be bound in heaven, and all that you loose in earth shall be loosed in heaven." For this reason, from the first beginnings of the Church, the decrees and laws of Ecumenical Councils have very properly been accepted by the faithful with as supreme respect and equal submissiveness as the judgments of God and the wishes of the Holy Spirit. But since the primacy was given to Peter, in order to manifest at once the unity of the Church and the singleness of the Chair, the other bishops are subject to the Roman pontiff, each of them in the administration of his own Church and all together in the conduct of affairs common to the (universal) Church.... They cannot regulate or decide anything as concerns the universal Church without having been summoned by the reigning Pope to share in his solicitude (*in partem sollicitudinis vocati*), and although when convened by him they enact decrees on faith and disciplinary laws as veritable judges, it nevertheless appertains to the Roman pontiff not only to summon and to dissolve General Councils of bishops, but also to direct and confirm them.'[1]

It will be noted that Father Kleutgen sees in the text of Matt. 18:18 the scriptural basis for the role of the bishops in the teaching and administration of the universal Church. In the *relatio*, the author gives us the theological foundations of Chapter IV, in exact line with Mgr Zinelli's position.[2] It is doubtless unnecessary to return here to what the two have in common. We will confine ourselves to the points where Kleutgen elucidates the position either by more precise formulation or by new proofs or by answers to possible objections. After having emphasized on the one hand that the bishops called on to share in the solicitude of the supreme pontiff are not mere advisers but judges and definers, and on the other hand that the whole plenitude of the supreme power is lodged in the Roman pontiff, Father Kleutgen concludes: 'Consequently this power exists in a twofold subject, in the body of bishops united with the pope, and in the pope alone.'

The introduction of the term subject (*subjectum*) provides an invaluable clarification of Mgr Zinelli's thinking: the *plenitudo supremae potestatis* is just one thing; its presence in two subjects does not multiply it.[3] The doctrine is not new, Father Kleutgen adds. 'It was generally admitted also by those who defended the positions of the Roman pontiff in the controversy that followed the Councils of Constance and of Basel. Let it suffice us here to quote the testimony of Bellarmine, who wrote: "Those who teach that the pope is superior to a Council held without him also teach that there is

1. Mansi, vol. 53, col. 310.
2. For the comments on Chapter IV, see Mansi, vol. 53, cols. 320-322.
3. Mgr Zinelli, however, had already used the word *subjectum* in the general congregation of 11 July 1870: 'Plenitudo enim essentialiter significat qualitatem inesse subjecto in toto suo ambitu' (Mansi, vol. 52, col. 1201).

intensively the same authority in the pope alone and in the Council with the pope, though extensively this authority is greater in the Council (*intensive licet extensive major sit in concilio*); and consequently such a Council cannot judge or condemn the pope . . . because an equal has now power over his equal." '[1] In Kleutgen's view, the thesis of the twofold subject is simply another formulation of the teaching of St Robert Bellarmine.

Between these two subjects, distinct without being separate, discord is impossible. The episcopal body does not exist as a subject except in its union with the pope. If the bishops in a Council draw up a decree which the Supreme pontiff does not approve, this act cannot be considered as an act of the supreme power (*non est sententia summae potestatis*). 'It must furthermore be remarked,' Father Kleutgen adds, 'that if by *the episcopal body* we understand, not the bishops assembled in council, but the bishops scattered over the whole surface of the world, it is impossible that the episcopal body should be of an opinion contrary to that of the pope, in those things in which the Church cannot err or fall from the truth.'

The author of the *relatio* gives three proofs of this: the promise made to the Church that it should endure for ever; the divine assistance promised not only to Peter, but also to the apostles as a body in the words: 'Behold I am with you . . .' (Matt. 28:20); and finally the text of Matt. 18:18 already quoted by Mgr Zinelli. Father Kleutgen ends his account of this part of Chapter IV by saying: 'In itself, the decree enunciates an absolutely certain dogma of the faith.' He was referring to the decree on the role of the bishops proposed in the letter of Chapter IV.

The explanations given in the *relatio* certainly do not all enjoy the same authority in the eyes of their author. Nevertheless, we should note that while dependent simply on theology, they were put forward here to account for an incontestable fact of the faith, and to protect it against Gallican positions, on the basis of a weighty biblical foundation, in full harmony with the authorized declaration of Mgr Zinelli, in continuance of Bellarmine's teaching and in the absence of rival explanations of similar weight. These are some of the elements which should make it possible to get a clearer view

1. The passage of Bellarmine which Kleutgen quotes here is in *De conc.*, lib. 2, c. 13.

of the theological status of the two inadequately distinct subjects at the time of the First Vatican Council.

Certain difficulties.

Certain objections have been raised to the theology of the twofold subject as it has been presented above. Chief among them are the two following: 1. This theology is incompatible with primacy as it was defined at the Vatican; 2. It is equally incompatible with the immediate communication by the supreme pontiff of the power of jurisdiction, as this is taught by the *communior sententia* of the theologians. This twofold objection was vigorously stated by Father Domenico Palmieri,[1] in a book whose first edition appeared in 1877. We are convinced that this author would have seen things differently had he had at his disposal all the documents of the Vatican Council. Now the seventh volume of the *Collectio lacensis,* which contains the decisions and discussion of the Council, including Mgr

1. 'Ex Christi institutione non est duplex suprema potestas in Ecclesia seu non est duplex subjectum praeditum suprema potestate . . . porro suprema potestas ipsa est potestas primatus atque unicum ejus subjectum, nempe Romanus Pontifex . . . Neque ipsis (episcopis) prout sunt unum corpus sive dispersi sive uniti in Synodum confertur immediate a Deo talis potestas . . . *Institutio enim Primatus excludit supremam potestatem ab universitate Pastorum*' (*Tractatus de Romano Pontifice,* editio 4a. emendatus a J. Filograssi, Rome, 1931, p. 491). We have italicized in this passage what seems to us the most characteristic phrase. It will be noted: 1. that Father Palmieri does not distinguish between the supreme power and the subject of the power; since the power is necessarily single, he deduces that the subject is too; 2. that he cannot envisage the doctrine of the episcopal body forming with the pope a second subject of supreme power except in the context of an immediate communication by God of this power of jurisdiction: it is this therefore that lies behind his categorical denial. Father Antonius Straub, who had the advantage of knowing the *Collectio lacensis,* which he quotes, shows clearly the weakness of some of the arguments advanced against the thesis of the inadequately distinct twofold subject. See his *De Ecclesia Christi,* Innsbruck, 1912, vol. II, no. 795-796, pp. 157-161.

The reason why Father Palmieri found it so difficult to entertain the thesis of the inadequately distinct twofold subject was that he was crossing swords with a single opponent, Father Jean Vincent Bolgeni, author of the book *L'episcopato, ossia la potesta di governare la Chiesa,* published in Rome in 1789. Broadly speaking, Father Bolgeni held two views: on one hand what we can call the theory of the inadequately distinct twofold subject, and on the other, the immediate origin from God, through episcopal consecration, of the universal jurisdiction of the body of bishops. As he saw it, these two views were not dissociated: the first depended on the second. Mgr Zinelli and Father Kleutgen, who do not, it must be added, mention Bolgeni, showed clearly that the first can be held quite independently of the second. Henceforth any discussion on the twofold subject should be conducted in company with the two latter authors.

Zinelli's report, did not appear till 1890. And as we have said, Father Kleutgen's Schema was not published for another thirty-seven years.

It was precisely in the context of the explanations he had to give on the primacy of the supreme pontiff that Mgr Zinelli formulated the doctrine of the *plena et suprema potestas* which is vested likewise in the episcopal body united with the pope. We saw this earlier in connection with the general congregation of 5 July. In order to dispel all misgivings, the reporter of the Deputation on the Faith reverted to the question in the following general congregation, that of Monday 11 July : 'As regards the plenitude of the power of jurisdiction in the pontiff, a plenitude to be accepted in all its fullness, there are no grounds for hesitation. By according the complete plenitude of the power of jurisdiction to the supreme pontiff, we should, it may be said, be in some degree injuring the dignity of the Ecumenical Council. Let nobody concern himself with this anxiety! Indeed, what I said in our last general congregation regarding the *potestas plena et suprema* of the Ecumenical Council still holds good. Rightly understood and in the context of the conditions and declarations of which I have spoken sufficiently, this plenary and supreme power is in particular agreement (*unice consistere potest*) with the doctrine of faith which acknowledges in the supreme pontiff the complete plenitude of supreme power.'[1] Father Kleutgen's position is absolutely in line with this.

The documents of the Vatican Council also give the lie to the second difficulty raised. The meeting intended not to settle the controversial question of the origin or the derivation of episcopal jurisdiction. In the congregation of 16 July, the last of the Council, after the voting on 13 July of the Constitution *Pastor aeternus* as a whole, Mgr Zinelli stated, in a report on the reservations expressed by certain Fathers on Chapter III : 'Theologians have been debating the question whether the bishops' power of jurisdiction derives immediately from God or immediately from the supreme pontiff. Those Catholic theologians who assert that the power of jurisdiction derives immediately from God declare, however, as is correct, that the jurisdiction is conferred by God in genuine and complete dependence on the supreme pontiff. This question aroused much excitement at the Council of Trent, but the supreme pontiff did not want to settle

1. Mansi, vol. 52, cols. 1201-1202.

it at that time. To be sure, we ourselves did not try to define it either, whether in our canon or in the interpolation in it'[1] (The reference is to the canon which follows Chapter III). Mgr Zinelli had already declared in substance that they were leaving this question open, in the course of the text in which he proposed the doctrine of the *plena et suprema potestas* conceded to the body of bishops united with the pope.[2] A similar statement appears in Father Kleutgen's Schema.[3] In the view of the Deputation on the faith, its reporter and its theologian, it is therefore clear that the doctrine of the twofold subject did not in any way imply, as a necessary basis, a choice of position concerning the question of the origin of jurisdiction. In themselves, the two theses discussed at Trent can both end up in a theology of the twofold subject. This already allows of an adequate answer to the objection which sees an incompatibility between one of the two contrasting theses and the doctrine of the *duplex subjectum*. But that is not all. Father Kleutgen points out that the thesis of the pontifical origin of jurisdiction is the *longe communior sententia*.[4] By this assertion, he makes it clear that it is also his own. Now none has urged more explicitly than he the theology of the inadequately distinct double subject.

Straying a little from historical research on which we have been engaged up to now, we should like to draw attention to one point. When it meets in Council, the episcopal body united with the pope exercises its *plena et suprema potestas* in a collective act, that is to say a *consensus*.

(a) To be sure, within this consensus the pope plays the determining role of head. It rests with him to convene, to direct and to dissolve the meeting of the Council, and to confirm its acts.

(b) But this does not in any way have the effect of setting the action of the Council in juxtaposition to that of the pope. What this is is, strictly speaking, a collective, interdependent act. In the Council, the pope does not merely ask the episcopate to associate itself with his personal decision. Though its internal structure is hierarchical, we have here a real *consensus,* in which the episcopate

1. Mansi, vol. 52, col. 1314.
2. Mansi, vol. 52, col. 1109.
3. Mansi, vol. 53, col. 321.
4. Ibid.

has its co-responsible part. Decisions are reached in 'concert', to use a term which is a little outmoded today but was in current political use in the last century.

(c) This co-responsibility exercises its proper authority only in the *act* of the collectivity, that is to say at the moment when the decision is taken by the body of bishops *in partem sollicitudinis vocati* and confirmed by the pope. But it is rooted in a capacity, in a basis of divine right, among those who are the 'successors of the apostles' in the Church.[1] A mind open to the universal needs of the Church and availability for the summons *in partem sollicitudinis* thus constitute an essential and necessary dimension of the episcopal office, because of the divine institution. This open mind and this availability naturally imply that mind and heart are constantly preoccupied with the problems of a Church the whole of which is engaged in a universal mission.

(d) All this seems to be excellently expressed and explained by the theology of the double subject. The *plena et suprema potestas* is exercised in the first place through a personal act, the act of the supreme pontiff, who is heir to the promises made to Peter alone.... To this personal act there corresponds a *personal subject,* the Roman pontiff. Such is the teaching of Chapter III of *Pastor aeternus* and of the corresponding canon. The same *plena et suprema potestas* is also expressed through a collective act, in line with the promise made collectively to the college of apostles headed by Peter. How can we explain this collective act, which was described above, without resorting to a *collective subject,* constituted by the episcopal body united with the pope? That is all Mgr Zinelli and Father Kleutgen wanted to say.

1. Though the context is different, we should like to recall here the words of Pius XII in his encyclical *Fidei donum*: 'Doubtless it was to the apostle Peter alone and to his successors, the Roman pontiffs, that Jesus entrusted the whole of his flock: *Pasce agnos meos, pasce oves meos* (John 21:16-18); but though each bishop may be the proper pastor only of the portion of the flock committed to his care, his position as legitimate successor of the apostles by divine institution makes him jointly responsible for the apostolic mission of the Church, according to the words of Christ to his apostles: *Sicut misit me Pater, et ego mitto vos* (John 20:21). This mission, which must extend to every nation and every age (cf Matt. 28:19-20), did not cease with the death of the apostles; it goes on in the person of all the bishops in communion with the Vicar of Jesus Christ' (*AAS,* 1957, vol. 49, pp. 236-237). There is a commentary on this text in the chapter devoted by Mgr A. M. Charue to the 'universal mission' of bishops, in his recent book *Le clergé diocésain tel qu'un évêque le voit et le souhaite*, Tournai and Paris, 1960.

The same analysis can be applied, with the necessary transpositions, to the episcopate scattered over the world and united with the pope. This body also possesses the *plena et suprema potestas*, but how does it exercise it? The ordinary and universal magisterium propounds the faith authoritatively. But, independently of other criteria, it is not easy to *recognize* with certainty the points on which a *consensus* has been obtained in general moral unanimity, with the express or tacit assent of the pope.

For the reasons which we have set forth throughout this note, the theology of the inadequately distinct twofold subject demands the serious attention of the theologian.[1] Those who put it forward

1. Let us sum up the position in the words of Father Kleutgen himself: 'Tota plenitudo supremae potestatis est in duplice subjecto, in episcoporum corpore papae conjuncto, et in papa solo' (Mansi, vol. 53, col. 321; we are quoting Father Kleutgen's text with purely grammatical modifications in order to turn a part of a sentence into a complete statement). We have not thought it necessary to give a bibliography here. G. Ruffino gives one in 'Gli Organi dell' Infallibilità della Chiesa', in *Salesianum*, 16 (1954), pp. 39-76: see the 35 titles cited on p. 40. In fact he is concerned with the twofold subject of *infallibility*. This is a different theme from ours: we are discussing *potestas*. But since the two themes are related, it is sometimes possible to go back from one to the other.

Recent works on the episcopate include M. R. Gagnebet, 'L'origine de la juridiction collégiale du Corps épiscopal au Concile, selon Bolgeni', in *Divinitas*, 1961, vol. 5, pp. 431-493; G. Dejaifve, *Pape et évêques au premier concile de Vatican* (Présence chrétienne), Bruges and Paris, 1961; G. Thils, 'Parlera-t-on des éveques au concile?' in *NRT*, 1961, vol. 83, pp. 785-804; K. Rahner and Joseph Ratzinger, *Episkopat und Primat* (*Quaestiones Disputatae*), Freiburg-im-Br., 1961. (English translation, *Episcopacy and the Primacy*, Edinburgh 1962). In the exercise of the infallible magisterium, K. Rahner does not admit two inadequately distinct subjects of the supreme power in the Church—the pope alone and the episcopal body united with the pope—but only one. He thinks in fact that the infallibility of the pope when he defines 'alone' is also that of the college of bishops (pp. 86-93). That at least is how I understand the pages he devotes to this subject. The author undoubtedly wants to recall that the pope, even when he is speaking *ex cathedra* in the conditions defined in *Pastor aeturnus*, is still the voice of the body of bishops. There is no contesting the truth of that. The infallible definitions of a pope are always the expression of the faith of the Church; by virtue of this they express in a clear and formal manner the revealed truth entrusted to the episcopal body as a whole, united with the pope. But I do not see how this reminder of one of the great foundations of ecclesiology is calculated to challenge the thesis of the inadequately distinct double subject, at least in the way in which it was put forward at the First Vatican Council by Mgr Zinelli and by Father Joseph Kleutgen. This thesis is, indeed, the clear expression *of the juridical conditions* of the exercise of the supreme power in the Church. Father Rahner does not distinguish *here* between the domain of law and that of everyday practice, an essential distinction to which nevertheless he often has recourse elsewhere. On this distinction, see Appendix I.

have more than one claim on our hearing. But there is nothing absolute about it. There is still room for research. Another theology could be valid, but only if it accounted completely not only for the dogmatic teaching of the Constitution *Pastor aeternus* on the primacy of the successor of Peter and also for the particular testimony of Scripture and tradition on the episcopal office understood in all its fullness, which the First Vatican Council was intending to define at the moment when it was broken off.

Appendix III

THE WORD 'COMMUNION' AND ITS USES IN PHILOSOPHY AND IN THEOLOGY

If we are to understand each other we must specify the meaning of the words we use. It is possibly worth while recalling here that philosophers and theologians do not employ the term which has been the principal subject of discussion in the present work in the same way.

René Le Senne deals with communion at the end of a philosophical description of the mind, in an analysis of the form of human plurality represented by the *We*.[1] Communion is the deepest kind of union of souls. 'It proves the wonderful power of love, which consists in causing the other to be accepted *qua* other' (p. 416). But since love in man is rare and fragile, 'communion must be complemented and clarified by communication between intelligences and collaboration in actions, as it must be expressed and strengthened by concord, where it attains its own fruition, the ultimate if not the definitive form of consciousness' (p. 416). Nevertheless, Le Senne does not make an absolute of this communion which he so exalts. It is in solitude that metaphysical union is realized. 'It is in this solitary quest, meditation or premeditation, musing or prayer, that we establish what is now a *metaphysical* union with Value' (p. 417).

1. R. Le Senne, *Introduction à la philosophie* (*Logos* series) third ed., Paris 1949; the first ed. appeared in 1927.

M. Nédoncelle's book, *La réciprocité des consciences*, Paris, 1942, deals in its way with the theme of communion. In a recent study on *Le personnalisme* (*Encyclopédie francaise*, vol. 19, first part, section A, Chap. III, 4), M. Nédoncelle sets out synthetically his views on the reciprocity of human consciousnesses and human-divine reciprocity.

In an analysis of moral action, G. Bastide does not hesitate to talk of the 'ambiguities of communion'.[1] A certain irrational immediacy is the characteristic of communion, a questionable transposition to the plane of human relationships of a 'rare and privileged form of the theandric relation in a few exceptional souls'. The author is very reserved on this theme. Here is the definition he gives of it: 'The idea of *communion* in and through *love* is presented as that of a privileged form of union between the *I* and the *You* in which, without any rational mediation, verbal or discursive, the persons not only enter into immediate contact, but experience a reciprocal penetration of existences, through a participation or fusion which creates a sort of *community* (a *We*) which is ontologically deeper and axiologically stronger than the association usually resulting from the intercourse of thinking subjects through intelligence and reason' (p. 54). Communion is represented as being consummated beyond language. There is a demand for 'silence and even obscurity, which are the atmosphere necessary for authentic communion' (p. 55).

There is no question of contesting the reality of certain of the states appealed to (the human couple, the ties of blood), but it is important to know 'on what axiological plane we should place them; it is from this point of view that we are constantly plunged into ambiguity' (p. 55). Analysis alone can foil 'certain of the deceptions that lurk under the alibis of the irrational' (p. 56). The exposition ends with a quotation from Pascal, who was not unacquainted either with mystical experience or the human soul: 'Let us endeavour to think clearly, that is the principle of moral science' (Pensées, quoted in p. 60).

The notion of communion has also found a place in contemporary

1. G. Bastide, *Traité de l'action morale* (*Logos* series), two vols., Paris 1961. In chapter II, *L'exaltation mystique*, the author tackles 'the ambiguities of communion' (pp. 54-60). M. Bastide wants to clear up the ambiguities of a certain vocabulary. What does the 'fusion of consciousnesses' mean? 'There are moments when the philosopher must know how to choose, even in simple language (. . .) Either love is fusion, in which case it is an alienation of liberties in the unconscious depths of passion, or it respects and favours autonomies, and it can only do this by taking into consideration the intellectual value of the truth (. . .). Any exhortation extolling love outside the light of the intelligence will never produce anything but obscurity with the contaminating impregnation of the spiritual by the biological, of disinterestedness by passion' (p. 57).

sociology.[1] According to G. Gurvitch, it is one of the forms of sociability, that is to say one of the 'many manners of being linked up by the whole and in the whole' (p. 172). These forms are represented as being three in number: the crowd, the community and the communion.[2] As Gurvitch sees it, this new division should replace the classification into community and society (*Gemeinschaft* and *Gesellschaft*) adopted by Tonnies and Scheler. These three forms of sociability are 'degrees of intensity of sociability through partial fusion'.[3] The criterion that distinguishes them is thus more quantitative than qualitative. Furthermore, the common element, *fusion*, should be understood as unity psychologically lived by a *We*. Here is how Gurvitch sums up his ideas: '*Crowd* conveys the minimum degree of intensity in participation in the *We*, accompanied by the strongest pressure and the weakest attraction exerted on the whole by the participants ... By *community* is meant the medium degree of intensity in participation in the *We*, accompanied by a medium pressure and also a medium attraction exerted by the whole on the participants.... In *communion* we see the maximum degree of intensity in participation in the *We* accompanied by the weakest pressure and the strongest attraction exerted by the whole on the participants' (p. 176).

We can end our inquiry here. Incomplete though it may have been, it has allowed us to grasp the broad lines of the contemporary philosophical employment of the word communion. We share the views of G. Bastide in rejecting ambiguous analogies, such as that of fusion. We are also with him when he says: 'If we want to give a moral value to the idea of communion, we should not say that people live in communion *in one another* (a way of speaking be-

1. See G. Gurvitch, 'Problèmes de sociologie générale' in *Traité de sociologie* (published under the editorship of G. Gurvitch), vol. I, Paris 1958, pp. 155-251. M. Gurvitch had already tackled the problem in his *Essai d'une classification pluraliste des formes de la sociabilité*, Paris, 1938. This was an extract from the *Annales sociologiques*, 1938, Series A, section 3, pp. 1-48.

2. The category of 'form of sociability', as it is put forward by G. Gurvitch, deserves close study, but it also calls for vigorous criticism. On this subject, see our notice, 'Ecclesiology and sociology' in *Social Compass. Review of socio-religious studies*, 1960, vol. 7, pp. 325-339. Whenever we have used the expression 'forms of sociability' in the present work, it is in its generally accepted sense, not in the context of a particular system.

3. G. Gurvitch, *La vocation actuelle de la sociologie*, Paris, 1950, p. 153.

longing more to psycho-analysis than to philosophy), but that they live in communion *with one another in a common value*' (p. 56).

But it is no business of ours to criticize the philosophical *idea* of communion. We are confining ourselves here to comparing two uses of the *word*, the use of the philosophers, of which we have just given a few characteristic examples, and the use we have put forward in this book, after pursuing an inquiry into Scripture, the history of ecclesiastical institutions and theology.

Let us first of all say that we did not remain on the level of psychology, but tackled the problem in its ontological reality. It is in the *being* of the Christian that we discover the communion. The believer *is* part of a whole which is numerically one. Communion behaviour, in its various forms, is simply a consequence of the ontological communion which is rooted in baptism and grace, the work of Christ and of the Spirit. To be sure, in any study of the total reality of the communion, as it appears in concrete form, the psychological aspects are important, but they remain secondary in regard to the fundamental elements present in the being.

This ontological rootedness is that of relation, which can alone succeed in accounting at once for the independence peculiar to the human personality and its real implantation in the whole formed by the mystical Body. The other categories compromise this first element. We must take care not to let ourselves be deluded by imagination.[1]

For us too, communion indicates a way of being and a form of sociability, but not only that. The form of sociability has given its name to the ecclesiastical institution, the social body, from which it is inseparable, which supports it on the one hand and on the other expresses it. It is the whole of the Church that is a communion.

With qualifications varying from author to author, contemporary philosophy generally speaking locates communion in the actual experience of love, in an intimacy which is being lived through. In theology also, love and communion are closely connected. We should nevertheless note that the love we have been considering is not merely the rational love which is based on the objectivity of the intelligence, but also and at the same time the love that issues from the purified gaze of faith. Moreover, the communion which

1. Since G. Gurvitch has adopted the idea of fusion, it is not surprising that he rejects that of relation. See *La vocation actuelle de la sociologie*, p. 220.

results from it does not exhaust itself in a momentary experience of closeness; it has its stable and permanent forms. In the souls of the faithful, it has foundations which can withstand many a storm.

LIST OF ABBREVIATIONS

AAS: *Acta Apostolicae Sedis. Commentarium officiale,* Rome.

BT: *Bulletin thomiste,* Le Saulchoir, Etiolles (Seine-et-Oise).

CSEL: *Corpus scriptorum ecclesiastorum latinorum,* Vienna and Leipzig.

DC: *La documentation catholique,* Paris.

DDC: *Dictionnaire de droit canonique,* Paris.

DTC: *Dictionnaire de théologie catholique,* Paris.

ETL: *Ephemerides theologicae Lovanienses,* Louvain.

LTK: *Lexikon für Theologie und Kirche,* second ed., Freiburg-im Breisgau (first volume, 1957).

NRT: *Nouvelle revue théologique,* Louvain.

PG: *Patrologiae cursus completus, Patres, doctores scriptoresque Ecclesiae graecae,* ed by J. P. Migne, Paris.

PL: *Patrologiae cursus completus, Patres, doctores scriptoresque Ecclesiae latinae,* ed. by J. P. Migne, Paris.

RGG: *Die Religion in Geschichte und Gegenwart. Handwörterbuch für Theologie und Religionswissenschaft,* third ed., Tübingen (first vol. 1957).

RHPR: *Revue d'histoire et de philosophie religieuses,* Strasbourg and Paris.

RSPT: *Revue des sciences philosophiques et theologiques,* Paris.

RSR: *Recherches de science religieuse,* Paris.

RT: *Revue thomiste,* Toulouse and Paris.

RSPT: *Revue des sciences philosophiques et théologiques,* Paris

ZKT: *Zeitschrift für katholische Theologie,* Vienna.

DENZINGER: *Henrici Denzinger Enchiridion Symbolorum, definitionum et declarationum de rebus fidei et morum,* thirty-first ed., ed. by K. Rahner, Freiburg-im-Breisgau, 1957.

FRIEDBERG: *Corpus juris canonici,* ed. by E. A. Friedberg, second ed., Leipzig, two vols. 1879-1881.

KITTEL: *Theologisches Wörterbuch zum Neuen Testament,* ed. by G. Kittel, Stuttgart (first volume, 1937).

MANSI: *Sacrorum conciliorum nova et amplissima collectio,* vols 49-53, ed. by L. Petit and J. B. Martin, Arnhem and Leipzig, 1922-1927.